RESTAURANT

CHINA
Volume 1
Identification & Value Guide for
Restaurant, Airline, Ship
& Railroad Dinnerware

by
Barbara J. Conroy

COLLECTOR BOOKS
A Division of Schroeder Publishing Co., Inc.

The current values in this book should be used only as a guide. They are not intended to set prices, which vary from one section of the country to another. Auction prices as well as dealer prices vary greatly and are affected by condition as well as demand. Neither the Author nor the Publisher assumes responsibility for any losses that might be incurred as a result of consulting this guide.

Cover design by Beth Summers with foreground photographs by Joe Conroy and background photograph of A. Sabella's restaurant (San Francisco, California) courtesy of Gasser Chair Company of Youngstown, Ohio. Book design by Barbara Conroy.

Searching for a Publisher?

We are always looking for knowledgeable people considered to be experts within their fields. If you feel that there is a real need for a book on your collectible subject and have a large comprehensive collection, contact Collector Books.

Collector Books
P.O. Box 3009
Paducah, KY 42002-3009
www.collectorbooks.com

Copyright 1998 by Barbara J. Conroy
Values Updated, 2000

This book is dedicated to our Father in heaven, through whom all things are possible, and to my late father, Frank Bussmann, who was in the foodservice industry from 1935 through 1962.

Dad opened his first ice cream store in 1935, at the age of nineteen. Several stores in the Minneapolis/St. Paul, Minnesota, and the Redwood City/San Carlos, California, areas followed.

Acknowledgments

The assistance of following people was instrumental. Each contributed without reservation on numerous occasions.

Joe Conroy, Larry Paul, Dick Luckin, and Robert Delman

The following people also supplied invaluable information and generous support:

Dave Conley, Dave Detwiler, Steve Giurlani, Everson Hall, Mary Moorcroft, Roger Pitts, Bob Ritchie, Angela Stanisci, Dave Turner, and Dr. Pat Tway

In addition each of the following is responsible in some way for the contents of this work:

Al Alberts	A.F. Kalberer	Darlene Rapalien
Donald Bryson	Mary Kelley	August Riccono
Bill Burden	Marc Kohlman	Nicole R. Roblyer
O.L. Cannon	Hans-Chr. Kontni	David Roger
Kathleen Carlisle	Gary Krimmel	Chris Sato
Roy Carpenter	Daniel Krummes	John G. Sayle
Pedro Caupers	Jane LaSure	Jennifer Saxton-Mace
Martin Chaplin	Moe Lastfogel	Norbert Schmieglitz
Mike Chapman	Lois Lehner	Birgit Schoenig
Frank Choirazzi	Nancy Lewis	Schönwald's Marketing Director
Tony Choirazzi	Bertil Lundgren	Andrea Schwarzl
Paul Collins	Mr.Lunscher	Lila and Fred Shrader
Allan H. Conseur	Sandi Maack	Maureen Sessions
Eileen Daily	Charles McAvoy	Hoi Shum
Aleen Dammann	Erin L. Markey	Brenda Smith
Will Davis	Lynne, Ron and Nathan Martin	Larry D. Smith
Perry Delman	Ed Massey	Chris Soenksen
Josephine Dillon	Michael McGrogan	Paul Trosko
Dave Dowding	Margaret Michell	Dick Wallin
Audrey Dudson	Patrick Murray	Stephanie Watts
Max Dudson	Ohio Historical Society	Mr. Weiherer
Chris Dwyer	Neil Orzeck	R. Gene Williamson
Susanne Eisen	Claude Peiffer	Susan Williamson
Eschenbach's Export Manager	R. L. Phipps	Andrej Wisniewski
Dee Frankish	F. Scott Pierce	Stefan Wisniewski
Bob Gasbarro	Emma Popolow	Topper Woelfer
Barbara Hansen	Jim Pratt	Barbara Wolf
Don C. Hoffmann Sr.	Don F. Price	Dennis Zontini
Vern Jones	Mike Ralph	Jean Zuckerman

Pages and extracts from pages of publications are reproduced in this volume with the kind permission of the companies listed below. If permission was granted by an associated company, its name is also listed. Neither the Author nor the Publisher has any connection whatsoever with these companies. Any opinions expressed are those of the Author and not necessarily endorsed by any of these companies.

ABCO International
by Delco Tableware International, Inc.

Arabia of Finland
by Hackman Rörstrand AB

Bauscher Porsellanfabrik

H. F. Coors China Company

The Dudson Group

Eschenbach Porcelain GmbH

Hall China

Jackson China
by Delco Tableware International, Inc.

The Homer Laughlin China Company

Noritake Co., Limited

Öspag Österreichische Sanitär,
Keramik und Porzellan Industrie AG

Pickard Incorporated

Porsgrunds Porselænsfabrik A/S

Rego Corporation

Royal Doulton plc

Schönwald Porzellanfabrik

Christian Seltmann GmbH

Sterling China

Syracuse China

Tognana Porcellane

Villeroy & Boch Tableware Ltd.

WorldCrisa Corporation

Wedgwood Hotel and
Restaurant Division

Wessco International

Contents

Contents (cont'd)

Introduction

Scope

These volumes cover dinnerware, oven-to-table serving pieces, and accessories specifically designed for use in commercial food service, as opposed to household tableware. Referred to as restaurant ware, cafe ware, diner china, or institutional china, it is almost always called hotelware or commercial china in the industry. In addition to restaurants, it is used on board airplanes, ships, and trains, as well as in the dining areas of hotels, railroad stations, airports, government offices, military facilities, corporations, schools, hospitals, department and drug stores, amusement and sports parks, churches, clubs, and the like.

Commercial china includes some of the finest quality ware ever produced, far surpassing that of non-vitrified household china. A break and chip resistant rolled or welted edge is characteristic of American ware produced from the 1920s through the 1970s and is still frequently used, though no longer a concern on the extremely durable high alumina content bodies. To reduce loss from wear, most decoration is applied to bisque, then glazed and glaze fired (i.e., underglaze) or to glaze-fired ware, then fired into the glaze (i.e., in-glaze). Glazes are formulated to resist utensil scratching, food staining, detergent abrasion, and thermal shock. With the exception of early non-vitrified hotelware, glaze crazes only when applied too heavily.

To date only books on transportation commercial china have been published. The railroad, ship, and airline china sections in Volume 1 supplement those works with lengthy alphabetical china topmark lists, transportation logo drawings, and illustrated piece value ranges. In addition there are chapters on military, government, western theme, Oriental theme, sports related, casino, amusement park, department and drug store, and company cafeteria dinnerware, as well as manufacturer samples and commemoratives, and in-depth sections on item identification, body material, and manufacturing and decoration techniques.

Volume 2 is organized alphabetically by manufacturer, offering brief histories, commercial china information, date codes, backstamps, photographs of ware with value ranges, and numerous catalog pages. American and foreign china companies are covered, because both have played a significant role in the United States and worldwide foodservice industry. While the history of several was altogether undocumented until now, certain manufacturers are covered extensively in other works, though data on their commercial china products is generally limited or neglected completely.

Commercial China History

Most commercial tableware produced in America before and at the turn of the century has a non-vitrified body. This ware is heavy gauge, sometimes called "double-thick," is  more porous, less durable, and was fired at a lower temperature than porcelain or vitrified china. However, Union Porcelain Works of New York made hard paste porcelain as early as 1866 and Syracuse China (then known as Onondaga Pottery), as well as Maddock Pottery Company made fully vitrified china beginning in the 1890s. Before 1900 American dining concerns primarily used the products of these companies, non-vitrified ware, or European porcelain.

By the 1920s, and through the 1960s, the majority of commercial china used in America was heavy or medium-heavy gauge American vitrified china made primarily of kaolin (a pure form of natural clay; also called china clay), feldspar, and quartz. Vitrified china is fired at a higher temperature and vitrified during the first (bisque) firing, then fired at a lower temperature in the second (glaze or gloss) firing. During vitrification the body components fuse together, making the china: (1) non-porous, thus resisting penetration of liquids even when glaze is worn or chipped and (2) more durable, resisting breakage caused by heat and handling.

Modern commercial bodies such as *Syralite*™ by Syracuse China, *Jac-alume*™ by Jackson China, and *Alox*® by H. F. Coors were introduced in the 1960s. Each is a dense and durable medium gauge ware with high alumina (aluminum oxide) content. In addition, commercial ware is also made of glass-ceramic (e.g., Corning's *Pyroceram*), glass laminate (e.g., Corning's *Comcor*), glass (e.g., Anchor Hocking's *Fire-King*), melamine (e.g., National Plastics' *Prolon*), pewter-like metal (e.g., Wilton's *Armetale*), and silverplate. Topmarked plates made of the latter materials are a challenge to find.

With the exception of a few companies that specialize in hotelware (e.g., Dudson Brothers after 1891, Grindley Hotel Ware, and Bauscher Brothers), there was little differentiation between domestic and commercial china outside America before the 1960s. Most dining facilities purchased medium to heavy gauge porcelain or heavy gauge ironstone tableware, while high-end concerns used fine gauge porcelain or bone china.

British and Continental European china manufacturers began operating commercial china divisions during the 1960s and 1970s.

Airlines use fine gauge china in first and business class, due to space and weight factors. And beginning in the late 1970s, fine gauge porcelain and bone china became a popular choice of upscale American restaurants, hotels, and country clubs. Companies such as Woodmere China began operating in the United States to take advantage of this niche in the market.

The following is quoted from information sent by Syracuse China: "The 1980s brought explosive growth to the foodservice industry. Syracuse China benefited during this period. It was an age of extravagance and spending. People had disposable income to spend. Upscale restaurants were serving French Nouvelle cuisine. Family style restaurants like Ponderosa, Bonanza, and Pizza Hut benefited from two-income households who didn't have time to cook. Theme restaurants like TGI Friday's and Bennigan's took off. Foodservice growth came to a halt in late 1989. Jobs were being phased out and corporate downsizing was putting executives out of work in record numbers; all being done to increase productivity in an ever increasing competitive world economy. Disposable income shrunk and restaurant growth stopped. Towards the end of the 1980s, foreign competition mushroomed from what it was in the 1970s. For example, in the late 1970s there were eight china manufacturers exhibiting at the NRA (National Restaurant Association) show; in 1990 there were 57. The 1990s will go down in history books as the age of value. With limited disposable dollars to spend, consumers will look for the best value for their hard earned dollars. Although the restaurant business is flat, there are pockets of opportunity."

It is estimated that 80 percent of today's commercial ware is plain or embossed white. In comparison to the 1930s

through 1960s, custom designs are seldom ordered. Long gone are the days of deep tan, blue, pink, and yellow bodies. On the other hand, when the beautiful and creative designs of today's decorated hotelware (as illustrated on the manufacturer catalog pages) reach the secondary market, the attractive patterns and custom crested pieces will undoubtedly be sought by collectors.

China Patterns

Custom patterns

(1) Any pattern topmarked with a name, initials, or logo. Additional decoration, such as lines or borders may be of custom or stock design. The word "Pullman," for example, was added to the "Indian Tree" stock pattern. While the original stock pattern remained part of a standard product line, the addition of the word "Pullman" created a custom pattern.

(2) Exclusive patterns do not have a logo, name, or initial topmark. After a design is submitted to and accepted by a customer, it is produced exclusively for that customer. Many exclusive designs are fairly distinctive. Several have overall decorations, for example, Great Northern's "Glory of the West" pattern. Others are adaptations of stock patterns with altered colors or the addition or elimination of a decorative element such as a band or flower; for example, Amtrak's "National" pattern which has only a custom colored band and line.

Stock patterns

These are part of a standard product line and available to any customer. Therefore, stock patterns used by railroads and ship lines were most likely used in many restaurants and hotels as well. Unless stock ware is customer backstamped, proof of usage by a specific foodservice concern is impossible to establish.

You may notice that a single pattern is made by several china companies. This often happened when the original manufacturer went out of business. Customers had to reorder from other companies that copied the patterns as closely as possible. Secondly, when a manufacturer was purchased by another company, pattern and shape rights were included in the purchase. Manufacturers also copied each others non-copyrighted patterns.

Collecting Preferences

For decades collectors have searched for railroad and ship china. Interest in airline china is on the rise and pieces are becoming more difficult to find. Attractive standard (stock) patterns are now also sought by many. Western motifs and stencil airbrushed designs are especially treasured. The popularity of high quality American-made Oriental designs has increased. Many prefer traditional medium-heavy gauge American vitrified china, though fine china collectors no doubt favor translucent foreign porcelain or the commercial china products of Pickard or Woodmere. While some find it difficult to pass up any dining concern or transportation system topmarked piece, others seek ware that's specifically topmarked with a military logo or department store, casino, or amusement park name. Some collect only creamers, others butters or teapots. Some look for ware made by a particular manufacturer (e.g., Tepco), others specific patterns, such as "Willow" or "Indian Tree," or pink, blue, yellow, or tan body colors.

Desirability is a matter of personal preference and the field of commercial china offers a broad spectrum.

Home Use of Commercial China

It is currently considered fashionable to serve meals on mismatched topmarked hotelware. Some people enjoy the nostalgia that ware produced during the 1920s through the 1960s seems to provide. Reminiscent of days gone by, a piece of restaurant or railroad china brings to mind prefreeway cross-country vacations by car or rail. Dining out was an event in the 1950s, unlike the quick stops at today's fast food and family style restaurants. Others simply like the sturdy look and smooth feel of American commercial china produced during that period.

Availability

There was a time when many (perhaps most) diners and small restaurants regularly ordered custom china. But today the chance of finding a piece topmarked with the name of one of the old diners continues to dim. Amid the vast array of collectibles, even stock patterns are seen less frequently. Only plain white and tan, as well as green lined white pieces and a few patterns that were manufactured for several decades, are plentiful. Most transfer printed and decaled patterns are becoming scarce. Stencil airbrushed designs are on the endangered species list. Ware with a western theme seems to be available in most antique stores, but high price tags reflect its desirability. High quality Oriental scenes, other than "Willow" which is sought in any type of ware, are seldom seen. Even plain pink, blue, and particularly yellow bodies have become difficult to locate. The decrease in supply and increase in demand, simply makes the search more exciting.

On the secondary market, commercial china can be purchased at antique shops and shows, auctions and flea markets, as well as railroad, airline, and transportation shows. Annual transportation shows are listed in the airline, ship, and railroad sections. Mail-order lists are advertised in many collector publications.

Unless a foodservice concern chooses to make its china available for sale, for the sake of the business and fellow collectors, please don't consider it a source for an attractive pattern. China is a major investment and replacement costs are prohibitive. Due to high costs and customer pilfering, many establishments can no longer justify the purchase of custom-crested china, thus limiting the number of patterns that will some day reach the secondary market and our collections.

The Word *China*

The words *china* and *tableware* are used interchangeably in this book. That is, all commercial tableware, be it vitrified china, true or hard porcelain, bone china, ironstone, or any non-vitrified ceramic body, as well as glass-ceramic, glass, and plastic, is referred to as *china* in the generic sense.

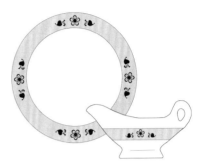

Manufacturers and Distributors

Manufacturers in Volume 2 include companies that either produce or subcontract the manufacture of commercial tableware that is backstamped with their own mark. However, if a company is primarily a distributor or importer whose name or trade name has only occasionally been marked on commercial china, or the actual manufacturer's name is also backstamped on its ware, the company appears in the Distributors section in Volume 2.

Ware produced by each manufacturer seems to have a combination of distinctive characteristics, such as body material and colors, shapes, gauge (thickness), type of edge, style of decoration, and degree of quality. Because of this, many experienced collectors can identify the manufacturer before looking at the backstamp.

Product Information

Though most of the manufacturers covered in these volumes produced both household and commercial china, generally only commercial china information is included. However, occasionally an exception is made if relevant or of particular interest.

Thickness and Weight of Ware

Body thickness is described in gauge rather than weight. This is partially because the foodservice industry uses the word *gauge*. But more important, a heavy gauge (i.e. very thick) porous body (i.e., earthenware) may be fairly light in weight, while a medium gauge vitrified body is relatively heavy in weight. Gauges are designated as fine, fine-medium, medium, medium-heavy, or heavy in this volume.

Backstamps

A backstamp or mark is found on the bottom of ware. It identifies one or more of the following: the manufacturer, subcontractor, distributor, importer, decorator, customer, trade name, or pattern name. Many marks are stamped on bisque (that is, after the ware has been fired once) with ink (pigmented liquid; ceramic color) either by hand or more recently with a mechanical stamping device. Other marks are embossed (in-mold; raised or recessed on ware) or impressed in greenware by hand. Transfer print and decal marks are applied to bisque before glazing or decal marks may be applied to glaze-fired ware prior to a decoration firing. Therefore, *backstamp* does not necessarily indicate that a mark is stamped. Due to surface area limitations, small base items such as butters, creamers, double egg cups, A. D. cups, and sauceboats frequently remain unmarked.

While the author has made every effort to include all known standard commercial china backstamps for each manufacturer in Volume 2, custom marks (e.g., "Made Especially For") and marks with both manufacturer and distributor or importer are rarely illustrated. Household china backstamps are shown only if also marked on commercial china. Most marks were not drawn at actual size; some in fact appear on ware in various sizes.

Date Codes and Usage Dates of Tableware

A date code signifies the date (usually month and year) in which the china body was manufactured, if it is impressed in greenware or marked on bisque immediately after firing. Sometimes, particularly in earlier years, bisque was stockpiled for a long period before being glazed. Consequently the code pre-dates usage by one or even a number of years. Similarly, glazed ware may have been stored before overglaze decoration was applied. In addition, a distributor may stock ware for some time before it is sold, and finally a customer, such as a major hotel chain, might store it before it is put to use.

Topmarks

Customer logos, initials, and full names that appear on the top of flatware pieces (e.g., plates) and on the side, inside, or the top of hollow ware pieces (e.g., cups and teapots) are simply called topmarks herein. There is no differentiation made between a sidemark and a topmark.

Photographs

Joe Conroy photographed over 1,300 pieces of china. Great care was taken to color match each piece. Many prints were processed repeatedly by Ritz Camera. However, processing chemicals vary consistently, consequently some of the white and ivory pieces have a green, blue, yellow, or gray tint. Colored bodies and glazes may also vary slightly. Cobalt blue and deep forest green decorations sometimes look black, and metallic gold often appears to be brown.

More than 300 photographs were taken by Larry Paul (commercial china historian and author of *Sparkling Crystal*, a Collectors Guide to Railroad Glassware). Others were submitted by Richard Luckin (author of *Dining on Rails* and other transportation china books), August Riccono, and Dick Wallin (author of *Commercial Aviation Collectibles*).

Dimensions in photograph captions: diameter of plates, length of platters, and all other dimensions are given to the nearest quarter inch.

If you have photographed your collection and would like one or more of your pieces to appear in the next edition, please send photographs along with manufacturer backstamp information (particularly date code), size (diameter of plates, length of oblong pieces, and height of pitchers), and any background notes to Barbara Conroy, P.O. Box 2369, Santa Clara, California 95055.

Error Notification, Relevant Information, Comments, and China Catalogs

Notification of errors of any kind, information regarding commercial china manufacturers, restaurants, or hotels (particularly chains), ship line history, airline logo usage dates, and comments on value ranges are sought for the next edition. Please send information you wish to share to Barbara Conroy at the address listed above. A self-addressed stamped envelope would be very helpful, should you desire a reply. Those on the internet can e-mail the author at *restaurantchina@earthlink.net* and vist her web site at:
http://home.earthlink.net/~restaurantchina/index.html which contains an overview and details of both Volume 1 and Volume 2, along with links to many restaurant china sites.

If anyone has access to recent or out-of-date manufacturer or distributor catalogs, any copy or photocopy would be most beneficial and appreciated by the author. In addition, historical information and stories from former or present commercial china company employees are eagerly sought.

Factors in Determining Value

Type of piece

Large pitchers, cake covers, beverage pots (coffee, tea, and cocoa), match stands, compotes, sherbets, ice cream shells, double egg cups, pickles, service plates, compartment plates, vases, and candle holders are more difficult to find than plates or platters. So are sugars with matching covers, since many were supplied without covers, and cups and saucer sets, because they are so frequently separated.

Some collectors specialize in specific pieces regardless of the type of china, thus increasing demand. These include creamers, butters, double egg cups, large and small pitchers, teapots, and heavy gauge mugs.

Size: in general, larger pieces of the same type have a higher value. This is not true in the case of cups and saucers, because the smaller A.D. (after dinner) size is considerably more popular.

Service plates often have a higher value, but this is due to the attractive or elaborate decoration typical of such pieces, rather than type of piece.

Subject of decoration

The following is a general list of subjects in order of greatest to least in value, though arguably so; exceptional pieces of any subject listed can easily change the order:

• scarce railroad topmarked and other particularly desirable railroad pieces
• scarce older ship and airline topmarked
• older topmarked and elaborately decorated restaurant and hotel service plates
• automobile company topmarked
• major league sports team restaurant topmarked
• popular western theme patterns
• common railroad topmarked or exclusive patterns
• casino and amusement park topmarked
• unusual or quite desirable topmarked airline, restaurant, hotel, military, government, club, executive dining room, hospital, school, church, and so forth
• child's theme and common western patterns
• common ship topmarked
• high quality Oriental theme patterns
• common or less desirable topmarked airline, restaurant, hotel, government, club, executive dining room, hospital, school, church, and so forth, as well as ware with an unidentifiable topmark
• common military topmarked

Type of decoration

Types of decoration in order of greatest to least in value: hand-painted designs, stencil airbrushed patterns, acid-etched gold designs, colored slip incised decorations, decaled designs, multiple lines of varied colors, airbrushed bands or accents, colored glaze, gold or platinum lines and bands, and finally single color lines. Attractive, interesting, intricate, colorful, or unusual designs, as well as multiple decoration types increase value.

An undecorated white or tan piece has little value to a commercial china collector, unless it was manufactured before 1900 (white only) or is a particularly desirable piece, such as a large pitcher.

Body color

Body colors include white, ivory, tan, blue, pink, and yellow. Blue, pink, and yellow are becoming difficult to find, because these colors have not been manufactured for decades. Tan is much more common, because it was produced in tremendous quantities until circa 1970.

Quality of body, decoration, and glaze

A well made piece of commercial china is smooth to the touch. Body should be free of nicks with mold lines completely removed.

Decoration should be clear with lines applied evenly. Transfer prints and decals should have no splits or voids. Bits of prints, decals, paint, or gold should not appear in areas where they do not belong.

Glaze should be smooth. Pits, void spots, glaze bubbles, or local crazing indicate uneven glaze application. With the exception of very early or non-vitrified pieces, commercial china glaze very rarely crazes due to thermal shock.

Such imperfections decrease the value of ware manufactured by Syracuse China, Shenango China, or any company that generally produced hotelware without the above flaws. However, these defects are typical of Tepco and Wallace china, having little effect on value.

Condition

Check for chips, cracks (especially hairline cracks that may be difficult to see in poor light), scratches, worn glaze, and wear on overglaze decoration, such as gold banding and decals. A chip or "crow's foot" on the bottom may be acceptable to some collectors, if the piece is desirable and the price reduced accordingly; even a hairline crack or top chip, if the piece is truly difficult to find.

Many collectors prefer and are willing to pay more for pieces that are or appear to be unused; i.e., so-called "mint." However, others find a piece showing slight wear more desirable, because it seems more authentic — to have a history of its own.

Age

Pre-1920 ware is the most valuable, followed by 1920s through 1940s, 1950s through 1960s, and finally 1970s to present. Age is less important on topmarked ware, because the quantity being produced continues to decline.

Stamped dates and date codes are, of course, the easiest way to determine the age of a piece. But not all china manufacturers have date codes and some codes remain indecipherable. Various companies did not maintain date code records and others lost files in fires or floods.

Volume 2 contains many date codes. Known or estimated usage dates are shown under nearly all manufacturer backstamp illustrations.

Rarity

Most custom patterns were produced in a considerably smaller quantity than stock patterns. A pattern with the name or logo of a single restaurant or hotel is of course less common than those made for a chain.

Stock pattern rarity on the secondary market is impossible to determine and varies in geographical areas. Most patterns were not copyrighted and some were produced by several manufacturers. It's always possible that a hoard of any pattern could be located in the seldom used basement of an old building that once served as a restaurant. In fact, an old warehouse filled with Tepco china was found in 1994. On the other hand, the majority of any pattern may have been depleted by eventual wear and breakage or simply discarded due to lack of use.

In summary, the type of piece, subject and type of decoration, and condition are the primary factors in determining value. Body color, quality, age, and rarity are also considerations. If a piece has all the plus factors, it may very well command a premium price.

Value Ranges

Generally a 20 to 25 percent range is given for each item. All of the factors listed above were considered, with the exception of condition. Pieces are assumed to be in good condition without cracks, chips, or excessive wear. As with all collectibles, values vary widely from one area of the country to the other. Please keep in mind that the value ranges listed are meant as a guide only. In actuality, a selling price is ultimately determined by the requirements of the seller and the desire and willingness of the buyer.

Closing

May the volumes of this book fill a void, and the information contained herein help you identify the manufacturer and production period of most of your commercial china. Unfortunately, even after extensive research some backstamps remain unidentified, particularly Asian and South American. Hopefully they will be covered in the next edition.

May you always enjoy the thrill of the hunt — the challenge to find a piece of your favorite commercial china hidden in a junk box at a flea market or the nook of an "antique" shop.

To quote Ed Carson of Homer Laughlin, "There's something about dinnerware, once you become interested in it. They take a little bit of clay and mix it up with water and fire it and make something out of it. There's a romance to that. It just gets in your blood."

Dining in the Sky.....

United Airlines School and College Service, 1956

Airline Foodservice History

As the turn of the century draws near, we can look back on 70 years of inflight food service. Imperial Airways began serving boxed lunches in 1927, followed by Lufthansa and Western Air Express in 1928. Pan American Airways, American Airlines, and others started serving pre-heated meals on china in the 1930s.

Originally there was no differentiation in flight class. Braniff International and Pan American, among others, began offering first class along with tourist class in the 1940s. By the late 1950s and early 1960s, when flying became very common and larger planes were ordered, nearly all airlines had first class, as well as coach or economy service. During the 1980s many of the larger airlines added business class and now have three classes on international and certain domestic flights — first (in the front of the plane), business (slightly less spacious, located just behind first class), and coach (at the rear of the plane). International first class (IFC) is the most prestigious, followed by international business class (IBC) and domestic first class (DFC), then domestic business class, and finally coach or economy class.

Collecting Airline China

Airline china has not yet reached its peak as a collectible and the hobby is clearly growing. Now is an optimum time to enter the field. Some collectors specialize in one or two specific airlines, others in the airlines of a particular country (frequently not the United States), while many have worldwide collections.

Availability

When an airline goes out of business or changes its name or china pattern, a great deal of china floods the secondary market if it is discarded or sold to airline employees or directly to the public. The pattern's value remains low with the supply exceeding the demand until the majority reaches collectors. Occasionally an airline uses china bearing a discontinued logo until their inventory becomes inadequate due to wear or breakage, thus limiting the number of pieces that will one day reside in the home of a collector.

A number of patterns will be common for a while, but attempting to locate older china or examples of tableware from long-defunct or short-lived carriers or those that operate on a limited scale presents an exciting challenge.

Airline China Characteristics

Though those who are not familiar with airline china may assume all meals are served on plain white casseroles, in actuality well over 200 decorated fine china patterns are in use today and at least as many have been discontinued over the years.

Rectangular or square casseroles (also called entree dishes or "doggie-dishes" in the industry), are used in all classes. They were designed to accommodate airline galley space limitations. First and business class casseroles are often decorated with the airline's logo and perhaps a gold or platinum line. Coach casseroles are usually undecorated ceramic or plastic with the airline's name recessed or stamped on the bottom.

Many airlines serve first and business class meals on plates made of fine gauge porcelain or bone china; usually coupe, less frequently narrow-rim, and seldom wide rim. Due to space limitations, cups are sometimes supplied without saucers and large plates (ten inches plus in diameter) are uncommon. A small number of international airlines use special patterns for Oriental or other specific service flights and some use different patterns in first class and business class. Meals are seldom, if ever, served on fine china in coach class.

Airline china is almost always topmarked or backstamped with the airline name or logo and sometimes both top and bottom marked. This identification is necessary because most meals are prepared by catering operations that serve many carriers.

If china is topmarked with a logo that has no initials or words and is not backstamped with an airline name, identification can be difficult. The Airline Logos and China Topmarks table on pages 83–105 illustrates 355 of these artistic devices, along with airline name, country, dates of operation, logo usage period, and occasionally china topmark variation notes.

Airline China Manufacturers

Noritake, Royal Doulton, and ABCO International have produced china for the greatest number of airlines, and Wedgwood has made quite a few patterns. TQ Tradex of Canada and Wessco of Los Angeles, though small companies, specialize in airline china. Pfaltzgraff and Corning have manufactured coach-class casseroles for a multitude of airlines. A limited number of patterns were produced by the Bauscher, Coors Porcelain, H.F. Coors, Dudson, Hall, Hutschenreuther, Jackson, Homer Laughlin, Mayer, Rego, Ridgway, Rosenthal, Schönwald, Shenango, Sterling, and Syracuse china companies. Even Alvarez, Arklow, Bernardaud, Crown Lynn, Eschenbach, Heinrich, Langenthal, Royal Copenhagen, Royal Grafton, Royal Stafford, Sango, Spode, and Vista Alegre have made ware for one or more airlines.

Airline Collectible Shows

Currently there are annual (or semi-annual, if noted) shows in the following cities, usually held at a hotel near the airport:
- Irvine, California, in January or February and August
- Dallas, Texas (Arlington or Irving, Texas), in March or April (transportation show)
- South San Francisco, California, in March or April and October or November
- Rosemont, Illinois ("Chicagoland"), in April or May
- Washington D.C. (Arlington, Virginia) in May
- Baltimore, Maryland (Timonium, Maryland), in May (transportation show)
- Kansas City, Missouri, in May
- Denver, Colorado, in June or July
- St. Charles, Illinois, in June (transportation show)
- Long Beach, California, in August
- St. Louis, Missouri, in September
- Miami, Florida, in October
- Seattle, Washington, in October
- Gaithersburg, Maryland, in November (transportation show)
- Houston, Texas, in November

Dates and specifics are advertised in the World Airline Historical Society's *Captain's Log*, along with additional shows. Advertising flyers, some with admission discount coupons, may be available at your local antique shows and shops a month or two prior to a show.

Airline Historical Society

The World Airline Historical Society or WAHS, boasting a current membership of 1,350+, produces the *Captain's Log*, a 48 to 60 page quarterly journal which includes a two to five-page article on airline china by Richard Luckin. For membership information, write to:

Airline China References

ButterPat World, 1st edition, © 1995, 256 pages, by Richard W. Luckin, includes photographs and background information on 217 airline, 127 ship, 230 railroad, and other transportation china patterns, as well as coverage of reproduction, fake, and bogus patterns.

To obtain information write to:
RK Publishing
621 Cascade Court
Golden, CO 80403-1581

Commercial Aviation Collectibles, 1st edition, © 1990, 161 pages, by Richard R. Wallin, covers china, glassware, silverplated and stainless steel flatware and hollow ware, uniforms, wings, service pins, patches, timetables, brochures, advertising items, playing cards, and miscellaneous.

To obtain availability and other information write to:
Richard Wallin
P.O. Box 1784
Springfield, IL 62705

Also see the bibliography on page 107 for additional airline references.

Courtesy of United Airlines

UNITED AIRLINES
Food Service Through the Years

Early airline food service included bouillon, coffee, and juice carried on board by stewardesses in thermos bottles and box lunches of chicken, rolls, and cake. Here a nurse, serving as an early stewardess, pours coffee in floral stock pattern china.

United Air Lines began preparing meals in its own flight kitchens in 1936. Hot food stayed warm in heavily wrapped individual casseroles. In 1946 United added warming equipment to its aircraft galleys.

Photograph at right:
Breakfast in bed on a DC-3 sleeper aircraft, circa late 1930s – 1940s. When not in use upper berths folded up into the ceiling and lower berths converted to seats.

Courtesy of United Airlines

FLY UNITED

At 10:30 in the morning, you take off from San Francisco on the fastest, most luxurious flight to Honolulu, United's DC-6 Mainliner 300 flight, "the Hawaii."

Aboard you find travel features which are unexcelled anywhere. For example, at noon a delicious Mainliner meal.

The hours fly by all too fast in the quiet, pressurized DC-6 cabin, shared with holiday-bound traveling companions.

Another festive feature, exclusive on "the Hawaii" —delicacies from the buffet for a tempting afternoon snack.

United Air Lines 1949 advertisement

1950s foodservice. Notice the casserole. Hall china produced medium and darker blue versions from 1946 through 1954, topmarked "UNITED AIR LINES." Coors Porcelain made a medium blue version without a topmark in 1951 and 1952.

United Air Lines School and College Service, 1956

"Meals and beverages are included in the cost of a first class ticket and are served by the stewardesses on specially built lightweight trays at individual seat tables. Almost all meals served by United Air Lines are prepared in company-owned flight kitchens located at strategic points along the route. On the plane, foods are kept hot in electrically heated casseroles and boxes. Cold foods are kept at proper temperature through the use of dry ice. Two stewardesses can prepare the trays and serve 50 or more passengers in about one hour."

United Air Lines School and College Service, 1956

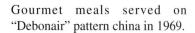

Gourmet meals served on "Debonair" pattern china in 1969.

Courtesy of United Airlines

Two level Boeing 747s were introduced in 1969. Photographs illustrate United's Royal Hawaiian service. Meals were partially prepared in flight service kitchens on the ground with the balance cooked in the aircraft galley.

United's Trader Vic's Service, 1971

Courtesy of United Airlines

1973 Deli Service served on "Chicago" pattern china

Courtesy of United Airlines

Photographs above and below:
United Airlines international first class meal served on "Intertwined Platinum" pattern (UAL-14), 1990 – present (1996)

Airline Advertisements

Pan American World Airways advertisement, 1951

Japan Airlines advertisement, 1970;
"JAL Crane Logo" pattern

Japan Airlines advertisement, 1968

Trans World Airlines advertisement, 1983; "Ambassador" pattern

Delta Air Lines advertisement, 1989; official airline of Disneyland and Disney World; "Signature - White" pattern

1984 advertisement featuring British Airways "Concorde" pattern

TAP - Air Portugal Navigator Class brochure, 1986; "Navigator" pattern

Northwest Airlines advertisement, 1971; "Minneapolis" pattern

Qantas Airways first class brochure, late 1980s; "Melbourne" pattern

1980s KLM international business class brochure; "Amsterdam" pattern

1987 KLM Royal Class brochure; "Orange Tulip" pattern

1990s Air France Economy Class brochure

1987 Air France brochure; "Première" pattern

1993 advertisement featuring Delta Air Lines international first class china
by ABCO International; "Blue-Gold Rope-IFC" pattern (DAL-7); pattern discontinued in 1999.

Airline China Manufacturer Catalog Pages

South African Airways
First Class

Royal Jordanian Airlines

South African Airways
Business Class

Guyana Airways

Carnival Air Lines   Lloyd Aereo Boliviano

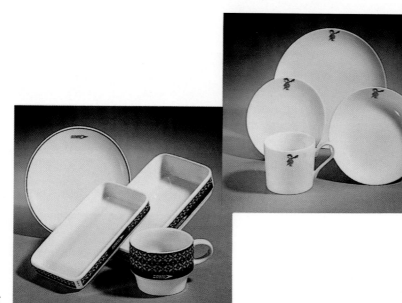

Cayman Airways

SAETA—Ecuador

Trans World Airlines

Delta Air Lines
International First Class

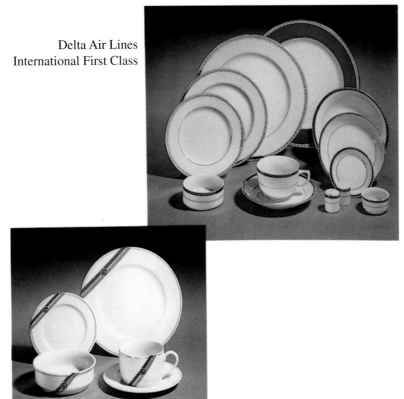

Air Jamaica

Aeromexico

Delta Air Lines
International Business Class

Delta Air lines
Domestic First Class

Midwest Express Airlines

ACES—Columbia

Tower Air

World Airways

America West Airlines

Hawaiian Airlines

Mexicana Airlines

CHINAWARE
PORCELAINWARE
by
abco
TRADING CORP.

United Airlines

Gulf Air

Cathay Pacific Airways

Japan Airlines

Mandarin Airlines

Malaysian Airline System

Asiana Airlines

Eva Airways

Qantas Airways

American Airlines

Avensa

China Airlines

Varig

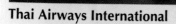

Thai Airways International

Saudi Arabian Airlines

Japanese Style Dinnerware

Kaiseki

A uniquely Japanese dining custom, *Kaiseki* is a traditional, prestigious meal, originally created for shoguns. Like a fine French dinner, each course is presented individually as a work of art, in its own ceramic or lacquerware work of art. In addition to fresh seasonal foods, great care is taken to prepare dishes that include delicate flavors reminiscent of the mountains or the sea. Each *Kaiseki* dinner is presented to reflect the season of the year during which it is served. Therefore, it is essential to have available a selection of dinnerware designs symbolizing or complementing the four seasons in order to serve in the most authentic *Kaiseki* style.

British Airways

All Nippon Airways

Northwest Airlines

Shokado

Similar to *Kaiseki* in that it features the individual presentation of each dish, *Shokado* is unique in that it utilizes a lacquerware *bento box* to serve all of the dishes at once, and yet keep them separate so the integrity of each flavor can be maintained. *Shokado* evolved as a convenient way to serve meals at outdoor gatherings such as flower and maple tree viewings. Because of this convenience, because of the obvious advantage of all food and dishes being securely held in the *bento box*, and because of its compactness, the *Shokado* style is rapidly becoming a standard of inflight meal service. Noritake is in a unique position to supply the most authentic and most beautiful *Shokado* systems to the airline industry.

United Airlines

Virgin Atlantic Airways

Air New Zealand

Sake Service

Sake is traditional Japanese rice wine. It is served with the meal in a distinctive ceramic bottle (*choshi* or *tokkuri*) and poured into a special cup (*sakazuki* or *choko*) designed for sipping and savoring the subtle flavors.

Air France

Tea Service

Green tea for the Japanese has almost the same role as tea for the English. It is served throughout the day at home, at work and with meals. Japanese green tea is served in a cup called a *chawan*, usually made of china.

Cathay Pacific Airways

Noritake airline china. Airlines and patterns are identified on the following page.

Noritake airline china, page 39 —
    Row 1: left - unknown
        center - Air Caledonia International "Caledonie Hibiscus" pattern (ACI-1)
        right - Canadian Airlines "Gray Arrow" pattern (CDN-1)

    Row 2: left - Avianca Columbia "Scadta" pattern (ALE-4)
        right - Ecuatoriana Airline "Quito" pattern (EEA-1)

    Row 3: left - Air Pacific "Pacific" pattern (FJI-2)
        center - Dragonair "Kowloon" pattern (HDA-1)
        right - Air-India "Executive Class" pattern (AIC-1)

    Row 4: left - Garuda Indonesian Airways "Indonesia" pattern (GIA-3)
        right - Iran Air "Simorgh" pattern (IRA-1)

    Row 5: left - Royal Jordanian "Jordan" pattern (RJA-3)
        center - Korean Air "Taeguk-Silver" pattern (KAL-4)
        right - Middle East Airlines "Beirut" pattern (MEA-3)

Noritake airline china, page 41 —
    Row 1: left - Aeromexico "Cabarga" pattern (AMX-2)
        right - unknown

    Row 2: left - Royal Nepal Airlines "Nepal" pattern (RNA-1)
        center - Air Niugini "Port Moresby" pattern (ANG-1)
        right - Pakistan International Airlines "Karachi" pattern (PIA-1)

    Row 3: left - Philippines Air Lines "Manila" pattern (PAL-1)
        right - SilkAir "Tradewinds" pattern (SLK-1)

    Row 4: left - China Airlines "Chiang Kai-shek" pattern (CAL-1)
        center - Thai Airways International "Royal Orchard" pattern (THA-2)
        right - Emirates "Emirates Business" pattern (UAE-2)

    Row 5: left - unknown
        right - Air Lanka "Columbo" pattern (ALK-2)

Noritake airline china. Airlines and patterns are identified on the previous page.

AIRLINES

Travelling in style

In the world of civil aviation every detail counts in helping an airline maintain a prestigious and impeccable reputation for quality and service. Royal Doulton is the world's largest supplier of bone china to international airlines and as competition increases the use of our exclusive brand identity in upgrading inflight service is becoming a significant strategic weapon for many carriers.

Royal Doulton now has an exclusive partnership agreement with the Dutch company De Ster, market leader in the design, development, production and distribution of disposable and rotable food service items for some 300 airlines.

The addition of Royal Doulton fine bone china, stronger and lighter in weight than alternative ceramic bodies, to the established De Ster ranges will provide each client with functional integrated concepts in Economy, Business and First class – a powerful competitive advantage.

Royal Doulton and De Ster – Serving your image.

BRITISH AIRWAYS

Courtesy of Royal Doulton

British Airways "Heathrow" pattern (BAW-5); 1989 – present (1995) first class

AEROFLOT · AIR CANADA · AIR MAURITIUS · AIR NEW ZEALAND · AIR OUTRE MER

ALL NIPPON AIRWAYS · AVIANCA · BRITISH AIRWAYS · CANADIAN AIRLINES INTERNATIONAL · CYPRUS AIRWAYS

VIVA AIR · AND MANY MORE

TURKISH AIRLINES · ROYAL BRUNEI AIRLINES

NATIONAL AIR · NIGERIA AIRWAYS · QATAR AMIRI FLIGHT

PORTUGALIA

ALL NIPPON

VIVA AIR

AIR OUTRE MERE

MIDDLE EAST AIRLINES · FLITESTAR · ETHIOPIAN AIRLINES · EMIRATES AIRLINES · DUBAI AIRWING

Eschenbach und Airlines wünschen Bon Voyage

Lufthansa "Deutschland Dots" pattern (DLH-1); late 1980s – present (1995)

At any time of day or night across the six continents of the world there will be an airliner equipped with Wedgwood 'in-flight' bone china. It could be Air Canada, British Airways, British Caledonian, Qantas or Trans Australia Airways.

Clockwise from top right: Alaska Airlines "Seattle-Tacoma" pattern (ASA-2) used in first class china since 1991, American Airlines international business class, 1989 – 1995, American Airlines international first class, 1989 – present, and United Airlines "Intertwined Platinum" pattern (UAL-14) used in international first class since 1990.

International Flagship Service for
American Airlines

Jackson 1983 catalog

American Airlines "Cobalt and Platinum" pattern, circa 1983 – 1989

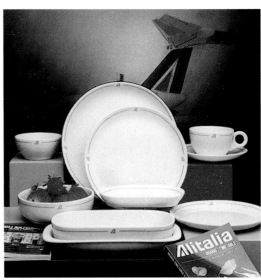

Courtesy of Tognana Porcellane

Alitalia "Italiane" pattern (AZA-2);
current (1995) usage

Courtesy of Wedgwood

Virgin Atlantic Airways "Upper Class" pattern, 1985 – 1994

Courtesy of Royal Doulton

Viva Air "Vuelos" pattern (VIV-1);
current (1995) usage

SKY CHEFS, HARTFORD UNIT

Skychef restaurant, 1945

Skychef, an American Airlines subsidiary, began operating airport restaurants in 1941.

Airline China and Value Ranges

Pattern Names and Codes

To promote continuity in the hobby, pattern names and codes (airline code and dash number) as designated in *ButterPat World* by Richard W. Luckin are listed in photograph captions. Additional patterns were named by others. Patterns were assigned an existing or new airline code, as necessary, and a sequential dash number.

Manufacturers

Although many patterns were produced by several manufacturers, in some cases only the maker of the photographed piece is noted.

China Backstamps

The manufacturer's name (usually shortened to one word) and manufacturer's trade name (if included on backstamp; e.g., *Airlite*) are listed preceding the acronym "b/s" for backstamp. If the piece is also bottom marked with the airline name, initials, or logo, this information precedes the manufacturer's name. "No b/s" indicates that the illustrated piece has neither a manufacturer nor an airline backstamp.

Airline Usage of Stock Patterns

While a number of stock patterns are known to have seen airline usage, proof of such usage can only be established with an airline name, initials, or logo backstamp. If a stock pattern piece does not bear such a backstamp, it was most likely sold on the retail market for household use or may have been produced for an upscale restaurant, hotel, or similar foodservice concern. Consider any lined or banded pattern without additional decoration a stock pattern. Other stock patterns are noted in photograph captions. *See definition of stock and custom patterns in the Introduction.*

Dates

Decades and date ranges refer to the period in which the pattern was used by the airline, unless otherwise indicated. Date codes are those marked on illustrated pieces.

Value Ranges

Each value range reflects the *illustrated piece only:* pattern, item, and size, as well as airline backstamp or lack of same on stock patterns. Any variance can change the value considerably. Pieces are assumed to be in good condition without cracks, chips, or excessive wear.

Because the asking price of airline china varies greatly from source to source and region to region, it is difficult to offer accurate values. However, in an attempt to be as realistic as possible, prices gathered from collector shops, transportation shows, and mail order lists, along with estimates offered by experts from various regions of the United States were combined and averaged. Final figures were reverified by additional airline china specialists. Again, please keep in mind that prices vary a great deal and that actual selling prices are ultimately determined by the requirements of the seller, along with the desire and willingness of the buyer. *Also see Factors in Determining Values in the Introduction.*

Comments on individual values would be welcomed for value range listings in future editions.

Photograph Order

Photographs are in alphabetical order by airline, then in most cases date of usage order. For alphabetical purposes, abbreviations and acronyms are treated as full words with spaces or hyphens in names disregarded, as is common practice in airline references. Airline souvenirs, advertising pieces, and airport restaurant china appear at the end of the airline china photograph segment.

Endnotes

Superscript numbers in photograph captions represent endnotes containing supplemental information. Endnotes immediately follow airline souvenir and advertising piece photograph pages.

Larry Paul Collection

Aer Lingus "Ireland" pattern cup & saucer (EIN-6); Aer Lingus and Noritake b/s; circa 1980s; $24.00 – 30.00.

Richard Wallin Collection

Aer Lingus "Green Shamrock" pattern 8" plate (EIN-5); b/s information unknown; 1990s; $18.00 – 22.00.

Aeroflot "Moscow" pattern pitcher (AFL-2); cobalt blue and gold decoration; no b/s; circa 1970s; $45.00 – 60.00.

Aeroflot "Democracy" pattern (AFL-4); Florencia b/s; l990s. A.D. cup & saucer; $28.00 – 35.00. Cup & saucer; $25.00 – 30.00.

Aeromexico "Aztec" pattern ramekin (AMX-1); Noritake b/s; circa early 1990s – present; $7.00 – 10.00.

Aeroflot "Semeneu" pattern 7" plate (AFL-3); no b/s; circa 1970s; $30.00 – 40.00.

Aerolineas Argentinas "Limoges" pattern 5¼" long amenity tray (ARG-7); Aerolineas Argentinas and Valade Limoges b/s; circa 1970s; $10.00 – 15.00.

Air Canada "Gold Scallops" pattern 6" plate (ACA-3); stock pattern; Air Canada and Royal Stafford b/s; 1964 – 1970s; also used by predecessor, Trans-Canada, and b/s accordingly; $14.00 – 18.00 airline b/s; $2.00 – 3.00 no airline b/s.

Air France 2¾" butters; recessed Air France b/s; left, "Hippocampe-Blue" pattern (AFR-2); right, "Hippocampe-Encircled-Blue" pattern (AFR-6)[1]; $8.00 – 12.00 each.

Air France "Première" pattern butter (AFR-4); Air France and Bernardaud b/s; 1970s – current (1996) Première Class; $15.00 – 20.00.

Larry Paul Collection

Air-India "Bombay" pattern 5¼" long casserole (AIC-3); Air India and Langenthal b/s; 1967 date code; $15.00 – 20.00.

Air-India "Bombay" pattern 6¾" long casserole (AIC-3a); Noritake b/s; circa 1970s; $14.00 – 18.00.

Richard W. Luckin Collection

Air-India "Floral Air-India" pattern butter (AIC-2); Royal Doulton b/s; 1994 – current (1996); $15.00 – 20.00.

Air New Zealand "Mari" pattern 3" butter (ANZ-2); Air New Zealand and Crown Lynn Potteries b/s; circa 1970s – early 1980s; $14.00 – 18.00.

Air New Zealand "Tasman Empire" pattern 5¾" plate (ANZ-3); Air New Zealand and Noritake b/s; 1980s; $10.00 – 15.00.

Air New Zealand "Tropical" pattern tumbler (ANZ-4); made in New Zealand b/s; reportedly used in flight for special drinks; $12.00 – 15.00.

Richard W. Luckin Collection

Air Outre Mer "Outre Mer" pattern ramekin (AOM-1); Royal Doulton b/s; mid-1990s – current (1996); $9.00 – 12.00.

Richard W. Luckin Collection

Air Vietnam "Saigon" pattern cup & saucer (AVM-1); gold and cobalt blue decoration; Noritake b/s; early 1970s; $75.00 – 100.00.

Alaska Airlines "Gold Coast" pattern cup & saucer (ASA-1); Alaska Airlines and Racket b/s; 1980s Gold Coast Service; $18.00 – 22.00.

Alaska Airlines "Gold Coast" pattern 8" plate (ASA-1); Alaska Airlines b/s; 1980s Gold Coast Service; $14.00 – 18.00.

Richard W. Luckin Collection

Alia Royal Jordanian Airline "Amman" pattern cup & saucer (RJA-2); cobalt blue decoration; Cloudland b/s; 1980 – 1986; $27.00 – 35.00.

Richard W. Luckin Collection

Alia Royal Jordanian Airline "Alia" pattern butter (RJA-1); rust color decoration; b/s unknown; circa 1970s; $24.00 – 30.00.

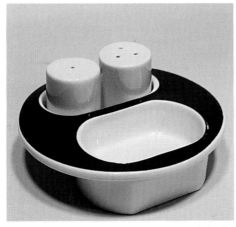

America West Airlines "Tribal Dance" pattern (AWE-3); gold appears black in photo; America West and TQ Tradex b/s; 1980s Hawaiian service (used with AWE-3a). Creamer, $18.00 – 24.00; cup, $14.00 – 18.00.

Larry Paul Collection

Alitalia "Colombo" pattern salt, pepper & sugar packet tray (AZA-1); chocolate brown and white; Alitalia and Richard Ginori b/s; circa 1970s; $30.00 – 40.00.

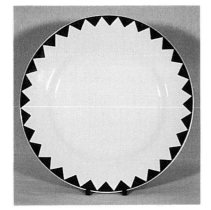

Richard Wallin Collection

America West Airlines "Tribal Dance" pattern 8" plate (AWE-3a); gold appears black in photo; America West and TQ Tradex b/s; 1980s Hawaiian service (used with AWE-3); $12.00 – 15.00.

America West Airlines "Desert Cactus" pattern bowl (AWE-2); Rego b/s; late 1980s – current (1995); $8.00 – 12.00.

August Riccono Collection

American Airlines "American Eagle I" pattern 9" plate (AAL-4); Scammell's Trenton b/s; 1930s; $650.00 – 750.00.

August Riccono Collection

American Airlines "American Shelledge" pattern 8" plate (AAL-5); American Airlines and Syracuse Shelledge[2] b/s; circa late 1930s – early 1940s; $300.00 – 400.00.

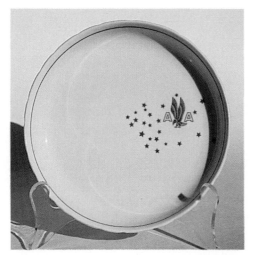

August Riccono Collection

American Airlines "American Eagle II" pattern 6" plate (AAL-6); American Airlines and Syracuse Airlite[3] b/s; produced in 1946; $100.00 – 150.00.

American Airlines "American Eagle II" pattern cup (AAL-6); American Airlines and Syracuse Airlite[3] b/s; produced in 1946; $35.00 – 50.00.

Richard W. Luckin Collection

American Airlines "Admiral Club" pattern cup & saucer (AAL-7); Syracuse China b/s; 1958 date code; used in American's Admiral Club airport lounges; $50.00 – 65.00.

American Airlines "Royal Blue" pattern soup (AAL-8); American Airlines and Mayer/Interpace b/s; 1968 – 1970; $6.00 – 8.00.

American Airlines "American Traveler" pattern (AAL-1); American Airlines and Sango, Michaud or Abco b/s; late 1970s – current (1996) domestic first class, as well as 1995+ international business class[4]. 6" plate; $5.00 – 7.00. 5" plate; $4.00 – 6.00.

American Airlines "Baumgardner" pattern 8" plate (AAL-2); platinum line and white on white design; American Airlines and Mayer/Minners b/s; 1970 date code; $12.00 – 15.00.

American Airlines "American Eagle III-IBC" cup & saucer (handle behind cup; AAL-10); American Airlines and Wessco b/s; ordered 1989 – 1995 international business class; $20.00 – 25.00.

American Airlines "Cobalt and Platinum" pattern[5] 7½" plate (AAL-3); American Airlines and Jackson, Sterling or Syracuse b/s; circa 1983 – 1989 international first class; $8.00 – 11.00.

American Airlines "American Eagle III-IFC" pattern cup & saucer (handle behind cup; AAL-9); American Airlines and Wessco b/s; 1989 – current (1996) international first class, as well as current (1996) Admiral's Club lounge; $15.00 – 20.00.

American Airlines "American Eagle III-IBC" pattern ramekin[6] (AAL-10a); navy blue American logo on ramekin only; American Airlines and Wessco b/s; early 1990s IBC; $20.00 – 25.00.

American Airlines "American Eagle III-IFC" salt and pepper (AAL-9); no b/s; 1989 – current (1996) international first class, as well as current (1996) Admiral's Club lounge; $12.00 – 16.00.

Richard Wallin Collection

Avianca Columbia "Cali" pattern cup & saucer (ALE-3); Noritake b/s; circa 1960s – mid-1970s; $50.00 – 60.00.

Larry Paul Collection

Braniff International Airways "Braniff Black" pattern mug[7] (BNX-2); Braniff and Hall, Real or IAC b/s; 1970s; $7.00 – 12.00 (high end, Hall b/s).

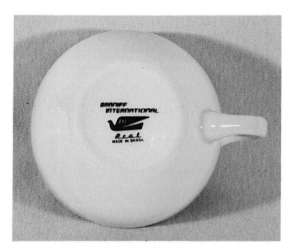

Braniff International "Braniff White" pattern plain white cup (BNX-3); Braniff International and Real b/s; 1970s; $4.00 – 6.00.

British Airways "Coat of Arms" pattern butter (BAW-2); British Airways and Royal Doulton b/s; 1972 – 1989 first class; $12.00 – 16.00.

Larry Paul Collection

British Airways "Concorde" pattern 7" casserole (BAW-3); British Airways and Royal Doulton b/s; 1976 – circa 1985 on Concorde only; $18.00 – 22.00.

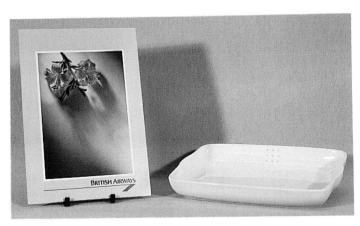

British Airways "Club" pattern 6½" long casserole (BAW-1); British Airways and Royal Doulton b/s; 1989 – current (1996) Club Class; $8.00 – 12.00.

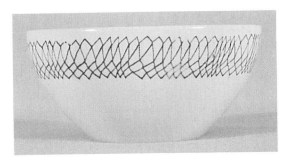

British Overseas Airways "Black Net" pattern bouillon (BAX-4); B. O. A. C. and Ridgway b/s; 1960s; $22.00 – 27.00.

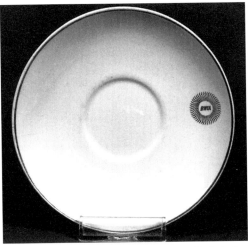

Richard W. Luckin Collection

British West Indian Airways "Sunburst" pattern saucer (BWA-2); Spode b/s; circa 1960s. Saucer, $10.00 – 12.00; cup & saucer, $30.00 – 40.00.

Richard W. Luckin Collection

BWIA International Airways "Golden Ibis" pattern casserole (BWA-1a); metallic gold logo; BWIA and Pfaltzgraff b/s; 1980s; $7.00 – 10.00.

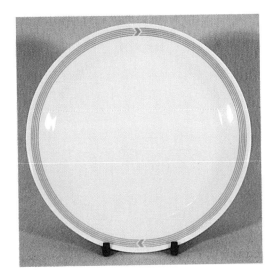

Canadian Airlines "Gray Arrow" pattern 5½" plate (CDN-1); Canadian and Noritake Inflight Top b/s; 1988 – current (1996); $6.00 – 8.00.

China Airlines "Cobalt Flowers" 4½" plate (CAL-4); China Airlines and Chinese manufacturer's logo b/s; 1980s; $9.00 – 12.00.

Continental Airlines "Golden Eagle" pattern sake (COA-8); Noritake b/s; 1959 – 1964; $22.00 – 27.00.

China Airlines "Nanking" pattern sauce (CAL-3); no b/s; circa 1980s; $9.00 – 12.00.

Continental Airlines "Woodgrain" pattern 5" handled soup[8] (COA-9); Continental Airlines and THC b/s; 1971 – 1979; $5.00 – 7.00.

Continental Airlines "Contrails-Gold" pattern 6¼" long casserole (COA-4); Continental Airlines and Corning b/s; 1966 – 1970; $12.00 – 15.00.

Continental Airlines "Contrails-Red" 5¾" square casseroles (COA-3); Continental Airlines and Abco, Rego, THC or TQ Tradex b/s; early 1980s – 1992; $5.00 – 6.00 each.

Continental Airlines "Contrails-Red" 6" long casserole (COA-3); Continental Airlines and Rego b/s; early 1980s – 1992; $6.00 – 8.00.

CP Air "Multi-Mark" pattern; C. P. Air and Japan b/s; logo used 1968 – 1986. 6½" long casserole (metallic gold logo, CPC-1a), $9.00 – 12.00; Oriental cup (mustard logo, CPC-1), $6.00 – 8.00.

CP Air "Multi-Mark" pattern (CPC-1); mustard logo; C. P. Air and Japan b/s; logo used 1968 – 1986. 6" plate, $6.00 – 8.00; cup & saucer, $15.00 – 20.00.

CP Air "Multi-Mark" pattern 4½" high teapot (CPC-1a); metallic gold logo; Noritake b/s; logo used 1968 – 1986; $60.00 – 80.00.

Delta Air Lines "Delta White" pattern plain white 7" long casserole (DAL-5); Delta Air Lines and THC (1970s; shown), Pfaltzgraff (1990s), Hall or Corning b/s; $1.50 – 2.50.

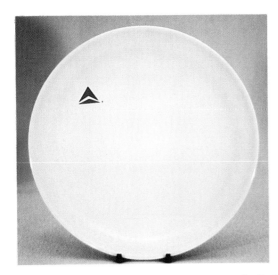

Delta Air Lines "Widget" pattern 8" plate (DAL-6); Delta Air Lines and Mayer or Abco b/s; 1973 – 1983 Mayer date codes; Abco, mid-to-late 1980s; $5.00 – 7.00.

Delta Air Lines "Widget" pattern footed cup (DAL-6); Delta Air Lines and Mayer or Abco b/s; Mayer 1970s – mid-1980s; Abco, mid-to-late 1980s; $5.00 – 7.00.

Delta Air Lines "Delta Dogwood" pattern 6" plate (DAL-2); gray decoration; Delta Air Lines and Mayer b/s; late 1970s – early 1980s international first class (1980 date code); $9.00 – 12.00.

Delta Air Lines "Signature-Ivory" pattern (DAL-3b); ivory body; Delta Air Lines and Mayer b/s; 1984 – 1991 date codes; international first class. Fruit, $6.00 – 8.00; grapefruit, $8.00 – 10.00; 6" plate, $7.00 – 9.00; 7½" plate, $10.00 – 12.50; 9¾" plate, $15.00 – 20.00.

Ethiopian Airlines "Addis Ababa" pattern A.D. cup & saucer (ETH-1); Noritake b/s; circa 1970s; $35.00 – 45.00.

Delta Air Lines "Signature-White" pattern (DAL-3a); white body; Delta Air Lines and Abco b/s; 1985 – circa 1991 domestic first class. Bowl, $5.00 – 7.00; cup, $6.00 – 8.00.

Eastern Air Lines "Eastern Platinum Line" pattern cup & saucer (EAL-1); Eastern and Rego b/s; circa 1980s – circa 1991; $15.00 – 18.00.

Eva Air "Eva Leaves" pattern cup & saucer (EVA-2); Eva Air and Narumi b/s; early 1990s; $24.00 – 30.00.

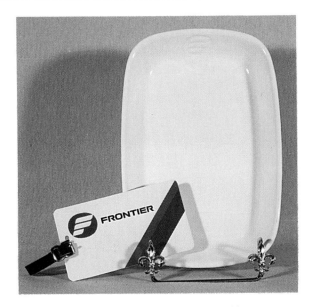

Frontier Airlines "Frontier Embossed Logo" 7½" long casserole (FLX-2); topmarked with embossed Frontier logo; Frontier Airlines and Abco or Wessco b/s; logo used late 1970s – 1986; $7.00 – 9.00.

Richard W. Luckin Collection

Garuda Indonesian Airways "Garuda-Blue" pattern 6" plate (GIA-1); cobalt blue decoration; Wedgwood b/s; early 1990s – current (1995); $10.00 – 12.50.

Richard W. Luckin Collection

Ghana Airways "West African" pattern salt & pepper (GHA-2); bronze logo; made by Royal Doulton; current pattern (1996); $24.00 – 30.00.

Richard Wallin Collection

Gulf Air "Sultanate of Oman" pattern cup (GFA-4); Gulf Air and Noritake b/s; circa 1980s. Cup, 12.00 – 15.00; cup & saucer, $28.00 – 35.00; salt & pepper, $25.00 – 32.00; sauce or butter pot, $12.00 – 16.00.

Richard Wallin Collection

Gulf Air "Golden Falcon" pattern cup & saucer (GFA-1); Gulf Air and Noritake b/s; circa early 1990s – current (1996); $24.00 – 30.00.

Hawaiian Airlines "Honolulu" pattern (HAR-1); Hawaiian and Abco b/s; 1980s – current (1996). 5" plate; $10.00 – 12.00. Cup; $12.00 – 15.00.

Highland Express "Scotland" pattern cup & saucer (HEX-1);
Royal Doulton b/s; late 1980s; $35.00 – 42.00.

Iberia "Spanish Globe" pattern butter (IBE-4); Alvarez b/s;
1970s; $30.00 – 40.00.

Japan Air Lines "Initials" pattern (JAL-3); JAL logo and Noritake b/s; dated 1962 and 1969. Cup, $24.00 – 30.00; 9" plate,
$30.00 – 40.00.

Japan Air Lines "JAL Crane Logo" pattern 4¼" bowl (JAL-4);
Noritake b/s; dated 1966; $24.00 – 30.00.

Japan Air Lines "JAL Crane Logo" pattern 3" ashtray (JAL-4a);
BITO b/s; circa 1970s; $12.00 – 15.00.

Japan Air Lines "JAL Crane" Oriental cup (JAL-5); JAL b/s;
1970s first class and 1980s Executive Class; one, two, or three
birds appear individually or in clusters on various pieces;
$12.00 – 15.00.

Japan Airlines "Tokyo" pattern cup (JAL-6); JAL logo and Noritake b/s; early 1990s – current (1996); $8.00 – 11.00.

JAT - Yugoslav Airlines "Beograd" pattern cup & saucer (JAT-1); Titov Veles b/s; 1980s; $32.00 – 40.00.

KLM "Amsterdam" pattern 6¾" long casserole (KLM-4); KLM and Hutschenreuther b/s; 1980s international business class; pattern also used in airport lounges; $8.00 – 10.00. Shown with postcard of a 1960s KLM Super Constellation L 1049G.

KLM "Orange Tulip" pattern 3" high teapot (KLM-1); KLM and Hutschenreuther b/s; to late 1980s Royal Class; larger matching pieces (KLM-1a) incorporate tulips in decoration; $28.00 – 35.00.

KLM "Royal Class" pattern (KLM-2a)[9]; KLM and Hutschenreuther b/s; late 1980s – current (1995) Royal Class. Napkin holder, $8.00 – 10.00; cup & saucer, $18.00 – 22.00.

KLM "Royal Class" pattern 9¾" plate (KLM-2b)[10]; pale blue plate center; KLM and Hutschenreuther b/s; late 1980s – current (1995) Royal Class; $12.00 – 15.00.

Korean Air Lines "Prestige" pattern cup & saucer (KAL-2); cobalt blue decoration; Korean Airlines b/s; 1970s – 1984; $32.00 – 40.00.

Korean Air "Taeguk-Aqua/Platinum" pattern 6½" casserole (KAL-5); Korean Air b/s; current (1995); $8.00 – 10.00.

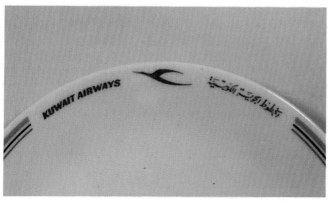

Kuwait Airways "East-West" pattern 7½" plate (KAC-1); Kuwait Airways and Hutschenreuther b/s; 1980s – current (1996); $12.00 – 16.00.

Loftleidir "Icelandic" pattern cream pitcher (LOF-1); Rosenthal b/s; pre 1974; $50.00 – 65.00.

Lufthansa "Lufthansa White" pattern plain white cup (DLH-8); Lufthansa logo and Rosenthal b/s; 1950s; $10.00 – 12.50.

Lufthansa "Wagenfeld Cobalt" pattern 3½" square ramekin (DLH-7); Lufthansa logo and Hutschenreuther b/s; late 1970s – circa late 1980s; $5.00 – 7.00.

Lufthansa "Deutschland Dots" pattern 3¼" square ramekin (DLH-1); Lufthansa and Hutschenreuther b/s; late 1980s – current (1996); $5.00 – 7.00.

Richard W. Luckin Collection

Malaysian Airline System "Golden Club" pattern salt & pepper (MAS-1); multicolored with red logo; Noritake b/s; 1980s business class; $28.00 – 35.00.

Richard W. Luckin Collection

Malaysian Airline System/Malaysia Airlines "Hibiscus" pattern salt & pepper (MAS-2b)[11]; Noritake b/s; 1980s – current (1996) first class; $24.00 – 30.00.

Richard W. Luckin Collection

Malaysian Airline System "Hibiscus" pattern[12] cup & saucer, (MAS-2a); Noritake b/s; 1980s first class; used with MAS-2b (*see photograph at left*); $30.00 – 40.00.

Richard Wallin Collection

Malaysian Airline System "Hibiscus" pattern 8" plate (MAS-2a); Noritake b/s; 1980s first class; replaced by identical china with current logo (MAS-2, not shown); $18.00 – 22.00.

McClain Airlines "McClain" pattern (MCL-1); McClain Airlines and Rego b/s; 1986 – 1988. 6" plate, $7.00 – 9.00; cup & saucer, $24.00 – 30.00.

MGM Grand Air "Lion I" pattern (MGM-1); Royal Worcester b/s; late 1980s. Cup & saucer, $40.00 – 50.00; smaller plate, $22.00 – 28.00; larger plate, $28.00 – 35.00.

MGM Grand Air "Lion II" pattern 7¾" plate (MGM-2); Langenthal b/s; late 1980s – early 1990s; $28.00 – 35.00.

MGM Grand Air "Lion III" pattern cup & saucer (MGM-3); gold decoration; Dudson b/s; circa 1992 – 1994; $40.00 – 50.00.

Middle East Airline "Cedar Tree" pattern cup (MEA-1); MEA and Royal Doulton b/s; 1980s; $12.00 – 15.00.

Midwest Express "Milwaukee" pattern casserole (MEP-3); Midwest Express and Abco b/s; mid-to-late 1980s; $9.00 – 12.00.

Midwest Express "Appleton" pattern 6¾" long casserole, (MEP-1); airline name repeated below line; Midwest Express and Abco b/s; 1992 – 1996; $12.00 – 15.00.

National Airlines "Sun King" pattern 7" long casserole (NAT-1); Sterling China b/s; 1974 date code; $24.00 – 30.00.

Nigeria Airways "Lagos" pattern 8" plate (NGA-3); Nigeria Airways and Royal Doulton b/s; circa 1980s; $30.00 – 40.00.

Richard Wallin Collection

Northeast Airlines "Yellowbird-NE" pattern (NEX-1); Northeast Airlines and Hall b/s; late 1960s – 1972. Footed cup, $28.00 – 35.00; plate, $35.00 – 45.00; bowl, $28.00 – 35.00.

Northwest Airlines "Minneapolis" pattern 6½" casserole (NWA-3); Northwest and Racket b/s; early 1970s – 1980s domestic first class; $9.00 – 12.00.

Northwest Airlines "Minneapolis" pattern (NWA-3); early 1970s – 1980s domestic first class; Noritake b/s on plate; cup not b/s. 5¾" plate or cup, $9.00 – 12.00 each.

Northwest Airlines "Regal Imperial" pattern salt, pepper & tray (NWA-2); Northwest Airlines and Royal Porcelain (made by Rego) b/s on tray; 1983 – circa 1994 international first class; $24.00 – 30.00.

Northwest Airlines "Regal Imperial" pattern bowl (NWA-2a); Royal Doulton b/s; 1983 – circa 1987 international first class; used with NWA-2; $18.00 – 24.00.

Northwest Airlines "Regal Imperial" pattern 6¾" plate (NWA-2a); Royal Doulton b/s; 1983 – circa 1987 international first class; $20.00 – 25.00.

Northwest Airlines "Detroit" pattern bowl (NWA-4); Northwest and Abco Trading, Racket or Wessco b/s; late 1980s; $12.00 – 15.00.

Northwest Airlines "Brown & Beige Lines" pattern bowl (NWA-5); Northwest and TQ Tradex b/s; early 1990s; $7.00 – 9.00.

Northwest Airlines "Brittin" pattern (NWA-1)[13]; circa 1994 – current (1996); international first class. Sauce or butter pot (Northwest and Rego b/s), $10.00 – 12.00; salt & pepper (no b/s), $15.00 – 20.00.

Richard W. Luckin collection

Pan American Airways "Flying Boat" pattern cup & saucer (PAA-2); cobalt blue decoration; Homer Laughlin or Buffalo b/s; 1935 – 1942; $600.00+.

Pan American World Airways "President" pattern A.D. cup, (PAA-3); Noritake b/s; late 1950s – early 1960s. A.D. cup, $24.00 – 30.00; A.D. cup & saucer, $50.00 – 65.00.

Pan American World Airways "Pan Am Mustard Line" pattern 9½" long handled casserole (PAA-4); Pan Am and Cloudland b/s; 1980s; $10.00 – 12.50.

Pan American World Airways "President" pattern 7½" plate, (PAA-3); Noritake China b/s; late 1950s – early 1960s; $30.00 – 40.00.

Pan American World Airways "Pan Am Gold Line" pattern handled bouillon (PAA-5); Pan Am and Bauscher b/s; circa late 1970s – early 1980s; $12.00 – 15.00.

Pan American World Airways "White Wave" pattern 6" plate, (PAA-6); embossed white on white design; Pan Am and Bauscher b/s; circa mid-to-late 1980s – 1991; $8.00 – 10.00.

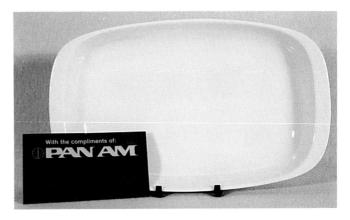

Pan American World Airways "White Wave" pattern 8" long handled casserole (PAA-6); embossed white on white design as on plate at left; recessed Pan Am and TQT b/s; circa mid-to-late 1980s – 1991; $12.00 – 15.00.

Philippine Air Lines "Philippines" pattern 6¾" long casserole (PAL-2); Philippine Airlines and Nikko b/s; early to mid-1980s; $15.00 – 20.00.

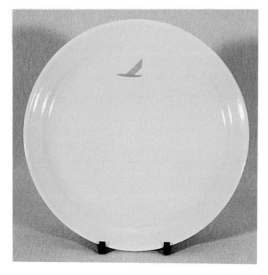

Piedmont Airlines "Piedmont Blue Bird" pattern 6" plate (PAI-1); Piedmont and Mayer b/s; circa 1987 – 1989 first class; $8.00 – 10.00.

Richard W. Luckin Collection

Regent Air "Royal Regent" pattern cup & saucer (RGT-1); cobalt blue and gold decoration; Spode b/s; 1983 – 1986; $90.00 – 120.00.

Philippine Air Lines "PAL Logo Repetition" pattern cup (PAL-3); Noritake b/s; circa early to mid-1980s. Cup, $12.00 – 15.00; cup & saucer, $25.00 – 35.00.

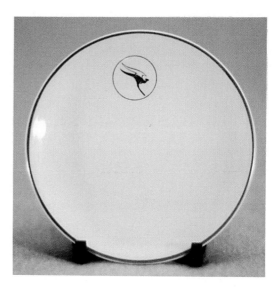

Qantas Airways "Alice Springs" pattern butter (QFA-1); Qantas and Wedgwood or Royal Grafton b/s; circa 1970s – 1985; $18.00 – 22.00.

Larry Paul Collection

Royal Air Maroc "Morocco" pattern butter (RAM-1); Royal Air Maroc and Bernardaud b/s; 1980s; $24.00 – 30.00.

Richard W. Luckin Collection

Royal Brunei Airlines "Brunei Blue" pattern cup & saucer (RBA-2); cobalt blue decoration; Royal Doulton b/s; circa 1990 – current (1995); $20.00 – 25.00.

Richard Wallin Collection

Saudia (Saudi Arabian Airlines) "Arabian" pattern (SDI-2); actual colors are gold trim on white body; Rosenthal b/s. Cup & saucer, $45.00 – 60.00; plate, $30.00 – 40.00; salt & pepper, $40.00 – 50.00.

Richard Wallin Collection

Scandinavian Airlines System "SAS" pattern cup (SAS-2); SAS and Gustavsberg b/s; 1980s; $10.00 – 12.50.

Singapore Airlines "Singapore Gold" pattern bowl (SIA-4); Singapore and Narumi or Royal Doulton b/s; 1980s business class; $12.00 – 15.00.

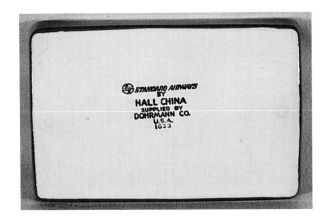

Singapore Airlines "Jurong" pattern 6½" plate (SIA-1); Singapore and Narumi b/s; 1990s business class; $15.00 – 20.00.

Standard Airways "Charter" pattern 6½" long casserole (STN-1); Standard Airways and Hall b/s; 1960s on worldwide charter flights; $16.00 – 20.00.

Larry Paul Collection

Thai Airways International "Thainter" pattern 4" high vase (THA-3); unknown manufacturer b/s; 1980s; $12.00 – 16.00.

Transamerica Airlines "Oakland" pattern cup (TIA-1); Transamerica and TQ Tradex b/s; 1979 – 1986. Cup; $12.00 – 16.00. Cup & saucer; $28.00 – 35.00.

Richard Wallin Collection

Trans-Australia Airlines "Hobart" pattern cup (TAA-1); Wedgwood b/s; circa 1970s – 1986; $14.00 – 18.00.

Richard W. Luckin Collection

Trans-Canada Air Lines "TCA Maple Leaf" pattern handled bouillon (TCX-2); cobalt blue and gold decoration; TCA and Royal Stafford b/s; 1950s; $75.00 – 95.00.

Trans World Airlines "TWA Platinum Line" pattern 4½" bowl (TWA-5); platinum line on edge; TWA logo and Sterling China b/s; 1960s – circa 1974 domestic first class; $10.00 – 12.00.

Trans World Airlines "Royal Ambassador" pattern cup & saucer (TWA-6); TWA and Rosenthal b/s; 1960s – circa 1975 Royal Ambassador international first class; $24.00 – 30.00.

Trans World Airlines "Ambassador" pattern[14] (TWA-1); TWA and Michaud, Abco, Rackett, or Rego b/s; 1981 – present (1996) Ambassador international business class and circa 1975 – present Royal Ambassador international first class; 6" plate, $8.00 – 10.00; cup, $9.00 – 12.00.

Trans World Airlines "Ambassador" pattern (TWA-1); TWA and Michaud, Abco, Rackett, or Rego b/s. 3¾" bowl, $8.00 – 10.00; sauce or butter, $9.00 – 12.00. Shown with pre-1975 swizzle stick.

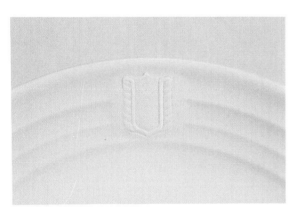

United Air Lines "United Embossed" pattern 5" pale blue plastic plate (UAL-1); raised United Air Lines b/s (also Plastics Inc. b/s on later pieces); 1930s – early 1950s; $9.00 – 12.00.

Richard W. Luckin Collection

United Air Lines "Mainliner" pattern plate (UAL-2); cobalt blue decoration on fine gauge white body; Shenango b/s; circa 1946 – 1950s; $300.00 – 400.00.

United Air Lines "United Blue TM" pattern 6" long casserole[15] (UAL-3); Hall b/s; 1946 – 1954; $28.00 – 35.00.

United Air Lines "Debonair" pattern 6½" plate (UAL-4); Syracuse Silhouette[16] Debonair b/s; early 1960s – 1970 first class; $28.00 – 35.00.

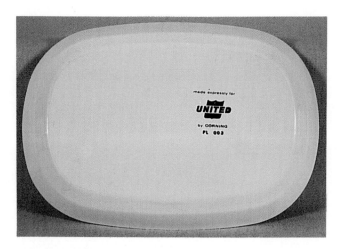

United Air Lines "United White" pattern 6¾" long plain white casserole (UAL-5); United logo and Corning b/s; 1960s – early 1970s coach class; $7.00 – 9.00.

United Airlines "Red Carpet Club II" pattern cup & saucer (UAL-6); Sterling or Thomas b/s; 1970s Red Carpet Club airport lounges; $20.00 – 25.00.

United Airlines "Brown Crockery" pattern handled soup (UAL-7)[17]; United Airlines and Eastrock Int'l. b/s; circa 1970s; $5.00 – 7.00.

United Airlines "Chicago – Border Line" pattern[18] 6½" plate (UAL-8); no b/s; 1970 – 1974 first class; $18.00 – 22.00.

United Airlines "Soup's On" pattern cups produced in a variety of colors; brown lettered ceramic cup (UAL-10) produced by Sterling or unknown manufacturer in late 1970s – 1980s; red lettered milk glass cup (UAL-10a) with Pyrex by Corning b/s, used mid-1980s – 1991; $3.00 – 8.00 each (high end: Sterling b/s).

United Airlines "U Platinum" pattern curve-sided cup[19] & saucer (UAL-11); United or UAL and THC, Michaud, Rego, Abco, or Wessco b/s; circa 1977 – late 1980s first class cup shape; $15.00 – 20.00.

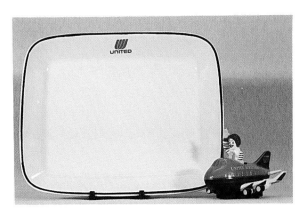

United Airlines "U Platinum" pattern 7" long casserole[20] (UAL-11); United and Wessco b/s; late 1980s – 1992 first class; $10.00 – 12.00.

United Airlines "U Platinum" pattern 8" plate (UAL-11); United or UAL and THC, Rego, Abco, or Wessco b/s; circa 1977 – 1992 first class; $12.00 – 15.00.

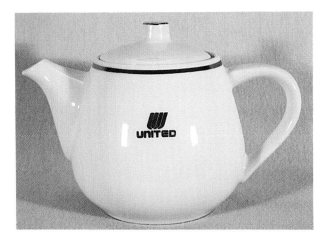

United Airlines "U Platinum" pattern straight-sided cup[22] (UAL-11); United Airlines and Wessco b/s; late 1980s – 1992 first class; $7.00 – 9.00.

United Airlines "U Platinum" pattern teapot[21] (UAL-11); UAL and Rego b/s; circa 1977 – 1992 first class; $40.00 – 50.00.

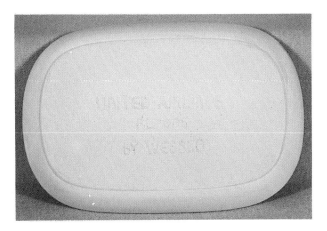

Richard Wallin Collection

United Airlines "United White" pattern 6¾" long plain white casserole (UAL-5a); United and Wessco recessed b/s highlighted with blue for visibility in photograph; 1980s – present coach class; $1.50 – 2.00.

United Airlines "Red Carpet Club III" pattern cup & saucer (UAL-12); UAL b/s; 1980s – present (1996) Red Carpet Club airport lounges; $15.00 – 20.00.

United Airlines "Red Line Crockery" pattern handled soup (UAL-13); United Airlines and Wessco b/s; circa early 1990s; $4.00 – 6.00.

United Airlines "Connoisseur" pattern (UAL-15); United (name & logo) and Noritake b/s; 1992 – present (1996) Connoisseur business class and domestic first class. 5½" plate, $7.00 – 9.00; 7¼" casserole, $12.00 – 15.00.

United Airlines "Shokado" pattern 3¼" square (UAL-16); United (name & logo) and Noritake b/s; currently (1996) used for Japanese Shokado service; $15.00 – 20.00.

US Air "Pont" pattern 5" plate (USA-2); US Air and Mayer b/s; 1979 – 1989 first class; $12.00 – 15.00.

US Air "First Class-US Air" pattern 5" plate (USA-1); US Air and Mayer b/s; 1990 – 1996 first class; $8.00 – 10.00.

UTA (Union de Transports Aériens) "Compass" pattern 3" butter (UTA-1); UTA logo and Royale Limoges b/s; $15.00 – 20.00 with some wear on gold; $24.00 – 30.00 full gold.

Richard W. Luckin Collection

VARIG Brazilian Airlines "Rio de Janeiro" pattern handled bouillon and saucer (VRG-2); white and platinum decorated stock pattern; Noritake and Varig b/s; 1980s business class; $30.00 – 40.00 airline b/s; $7.00 – 9.00 no airline b/s.

VARIG Brazilian Airlines "Varig Platinum Line" pattern A.D. cup & saucer (VRG-3); VARIG, Steatita, and Schmidt b/s; $15.00 – 20.00.

Jim Pratt Collection

VASP "Braziliero" pattern A.D. cup (VSP-1); Real b/s; 1980s; $8.00 – 11.00.

VASP "São Paulo" A.D. cup & saucer (VSP-2); Porcellana Maua b/s; $18.00 – 22.00.

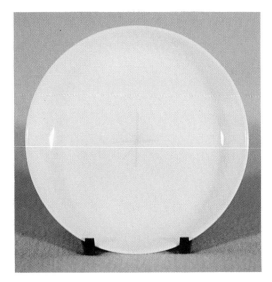

Virgin Atlantic Airways "Blue Star" pattern butter (VIR-3); Virgin and Royal Doulton b/s; circa early 1990s; $15.00 – 20.00.

Richard W. Luckin Collection

Wardair "Repton-Ward" pattern[23] cup & saucer (WDA-1); brown and tan decorated stock pattern; Royal Doulton and WD b/s; 1980s; $28.00 – 35.00 airline (WD) b/s; $7.00 – 9.00 no airline b/s.

Western Airlines "Fiesta" pattern 10¾" plate (WAL-1); stock pattern; Vista Alegre and WAL b/s; mid-to-late 1970s on DC-10 service to Mexico and Hawaii; $28.00 – 35.00 airline (WAL) b/s; $4.00 – 6.00 no airline b/s.

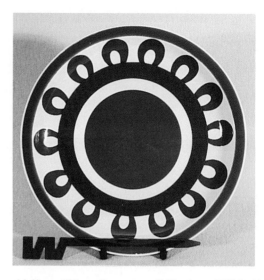

Western Airlines "Fiesta" pattern 6½" plate (WAL-1); stock pattern; Vista Alegre and WAL b/s; mid-to-late 1970s on DC-10 service to Mexico and Hawaii; $15.00 – 18.00 airline (WAL) b/s; $2.00 – 4.00 no airline b/s.

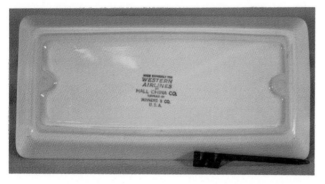

Western Airlines "Western White" pattern 12½" long plain white serving tray (WAL-3); Western Airlines and Hall b/s; circa 1960s; $9.00 – 12.00.

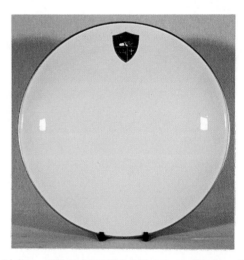

Western Airlines "Wallybird Shield" pattern 8" plate (WAL-4); Western Air Lines and Mayer b/s; 1966 – 1976 date codes; $28.00 – 35.00.

Western Airlines "Wallybird Shield" pattern cups & saucer (WAL-4); cups decorated with gold line only; Western Air Lines and Mayer b/s; 1966 – 1976 date codes; saucer & either cup; $30.00 – 40.00.

Western Airlines' "Wallybird Shield" topmark; 1966 – 1976.

Western Airlines "60th Anniversary Shield" pattern (WAL-5); Western Airlines and Abco b/s; 1986. 5½" plate, $12.00 – 15.00; creamer, $20.00 – 25.00.

Western Airlines "60th Anniversary Shield" pattern cup & saucer (WAL-5); Western Airlines and Abco b/s; 1986; $24.00 – 30.00.

Western Airlines' "60th Anniversary Shield" topmark; 1986.

World Airways "World Gold Line" pattern 5¾" plate (WOA-1); gold line on edge; World Airways and TQ Tradex b/s; circa 1970s – 1988; $12.00 – 15.00.

Zambia Airways "Lusaka" pattern cup & saucer (ZAC-1); green line with yellow-orange logo; Wedgwood or Richard Ginori b/s; circa 1980s; $35.00 – 45.00.

Souvenirs, Advertising Pieces, and Airport Restaurant China

Alitalia 3½" tray; may be souvenir; airline food service usage unknown; Alitalia and Richard Ginori b/s; $7.00 – 9.00.

American Airlines white glass mug; Anchor Hocking b/s; 1980s; $4.00 – 6.00.

Larry Paul Collection

Civil Aviation Administration of China pattern egg cup; given in pairs as a souvenir; airline food service usage unknown; no b/s; $4.00 – 7.00.

Iberia 3¾" tray; may be souvenir; airline food service usage unknown; Iberia and Bidasoa b/s; circa 1980s; $6.00 – 8.00.

Linee Aeree Italiane 6" ashtray; b/s unknown; 1950s; $40.00 –
50.00.

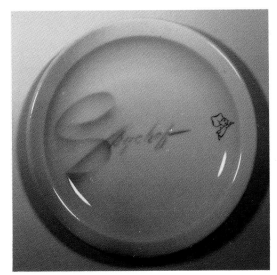

Pan American World Airways 6½" ashtray; Noritake b/s; 1970s;
$40.00 – 50.00.

Richard Wallin Collection

Scandinavian Airlines System souvenir; b/s unknown; late
1970s; $15.00 – 20.00.

Larry Paul Collection

Skychef airport restaurant "Skychef" pattern 6½" plate (SKY-1);
Syracuse b/s; 1956 date code; Skychef, an American Airlines
subsidiary, began operating airport restaurants in 1941; $35.00 –
45.00.

Swissair 6" souvenir plate; Swissair
and Langenthal b/s; $8.00 – 10.00.

Endnotes

[1] Variations decorated in maroon, mustard, green, or other colored glazes.

[2] *Shelledge* is a fine gauge body initially designed for household use.

[3] *Airlite* is an extremely fine gauge body designed for airline food service.

[4] Shown with pre-1970 swizzle stick.

[5] Largest plate only (not shown) has platinum American Airlines logo at 12 o'clock position on rim below band; $24.00 – 30.00.

[6] Shown with postcard of an American Airlines DC-7, circa 1950s.

[7] Identical mug made in plastic (BNX-2a); $1.50 – 2.50.

[8] Shown with postcard of a Continental Express Saab SF340A painted in standard Continental colors, circa 1989.

[9] Used with KLM-2b (*see next photograph*) and KLM-2 (not shown, but identical to Northwest's NWA-1 pattern, except b/s; *see Northwest photograph*).

[10] Used with KLM-2a (*see previous photograph*) and KLM-2.

[11] Used with MAS-2a (*see next photograph*) and MAS-2 (current "Hibiscus" pattern; *see the following endnote*).

[12] Current (1996) "Hibiscus" pattern (MAS-2) is identical except logo; new Malaysia Airlines logo replaces illustrated logo.

[13] Identical to KLM's "Royal Class" pattern (KLM-2), except backstamp.

[14] Saucer (not shown) has gold logo without diagonal stripes.

[15] An identical casserole in shape and color without United Airlines topmark was made by Coors Porcelain: United Air Lines "United Blue" pattern 6" long casserole (UAL-3a); UAL and Coors b/s; dated 1951 or 1952; $16.00 – 20.00.

Hall also made a darker blue version with double lines near inside edge; United Air Lines "United Blue TM Lined" pattern 6" long casserole (UAL-3b); UAL and Hall b/s; dated 1954; $28.00 – 35.00.

If any of these casseroles have a plastic cover that is topmarked "Mainliner," the value increases considerably.

[16] *Silhouette* is a fine gauge body designed for household use.

[17] Variations decorated with green ("Green Crockery," UAL-7a), white ("White Crockery," UAL-7b), or yellow ("Yellow Crockery," UAL-7c) glaze.

[18] "Chicago – Edge Line" pattern (platinum line on edge, rather than 1/8" from edge as shown in photograph; UAL-8a). United's 1974 – circa 1977 first class china, "San Francisco" pattern (UAL-9), has a platinum line, but no topmark.

[19] Shown with 1991 McDonald's Friendly Skies Happy Meal white plane: Ronald as pilot, $7.00 – 10.00; Grimace as pilot $9.00 – 12.00.

[20] Shown with 1994 McDonald's Friendly Skies Happy Meal gray plane: Ronald or Grimace as pilot, $7.00 – 10.00 each.

[21] Teapot reportedly continues to be used in combination with current international first class "Intertwined Platinum" pattern (UAL-14) which is shown on page 46.

[22] Also produced in a shallow (2" high) version without platinum line (UAL-11a); UAL and Wessco b/s; $7.00 – 9.00. Shown with 1994 McDonald's Friendly Skies Happy Meal hangar and plane: Ronald as pilot, $7.00 – 10.00.

[23] This pattern was also used by Wardair's successor and backstamped accordingly; Canadian Airlines "Repton" pattern (CDN-2); 1989+.

Airline Logos and China Topmarks

Use these logos to identify airline china and related collectibles, particularly glassware and silverplate or stainless steel hollow ware and flatware, as well as narrow down its period of manufacture.

An airline name followed by an asterisk signifies that the illustrated logo topmarks airline china. If the china topmark is not exactly as shown, modifications and variations are noted. Logos that solely backstamp china are not flagged.

For alphabetical purposes, abbreviations and acronyms are treated as full airline names and spaces or hyphens in names are disregarded, as is common practice in airline references.

Airline information

Airline date range denotes period of operation under the name shown. Many airlines originated years or decades earlier under another name. The end of the range is the latest verifiable date. A plus sign (+) signifies an unknown period beyond the year listed. "Current" and "Present" are 1995 unless otherwise stated. "Taken over by" indicates that the airline's name was discontinued and its aircraft and routes were taken over by the noted airline.

Logos

Occasionally an airline has chosen to topmark its china with an artistic device other than its standard logo, for example, a detailed crest (British Airways) or a shield (Braniff Airways). A number of these logos are illustrated with the notation "china topmark shown."

Logo date range indicates period of logo usage. Dates are based on extensive historical documentation, dated advertisements, airline schedules, and so forth (*see Airline Section Bibliography on page 107*). Years preceded by "circa" are estimates based on the same sources, however use of these logos may extend beyond the years listed.

Note: When an airline changes its logo, part or all of its fleet may be repainted immediately to reflect the change, or a number of years later. Therefore, while dated photographs are useful in documenting the beginning of a logo usage date range, they are an unreliable source for establishing the end of the range.

 ACES * (Aerolineas Centrales de Columbia SA) **Columbia** **1972 – present** china topmark shown: current logo: 1972 – present; "a" is centered in circle, rather than offset, on actual logo	 **Aer Lingus - Irish Air Lines** (Aer Lingus Teoranta) **Republic of Ireland** **1936 – 1959** (became Aer Lingus - Irish International Airlines) logo: 1950s – 1960	 **Aer Lingus - Irish International Airlines** (Aer Lingus Teoranta and Aerlinte Eireann Teoranta joint operation) **Republic of Ireland** **1960 – present** logo: 1960s – 1974	 **Aer Lingus - Irish International Airlines *** (Aer Lingus Teoranta and Aerlinte Eireann Teoranta joint operation) **Republic of Ireland** **1960 – present** logo: 1974 – present
 **Aer Lingus- Irish International Airlines *** (Aer Lingus Teoranta and Aerlinte Eireann Teoranta joint operation) **Republic of Ireland** **1960 – present** china topmark logo shown (*see similar logo on Aer Lingus photograph*) china topmark: with "*IRISH AER LINGUS*" below logo	 **Aer Lingus - Irish International Airlines *** (Aer Lingus Teoranta and Aerlinte Eireann Teoranta joint operation) **Republic of Ireland** **1960 – present** china topmark shown: current business class	 **Aeroflot *** **Russia** **1932 – present** logo: circa 1960s – present china topmark variations: as shown, winged logo without airline name, or airline name without winged logo	 **Aerolineas Argentinas *** **Argentina** **1949 – present** logo: circa 1960s – present china topmark variations: as shown or without circled "AA," each with or without "*AEROLINEAS ARGENTINAS*" below logo

Aeromexico
Mexico
1972 – present

logo: 1970s

Aeromexico
Mexico
1972 – present

logo: early 1980s – 1988

Aeromexico *
Mexico
1972 – present

logo: 1988 – present

china topmark:
inverted logo shown at right

Aeronaves de Mexico
Mexico
1934 – 1972
(became Aeromexico)

logo: circa early 1960s – 1972

Aero Peru *
Peru
1973 – present

logo: 1973 – circa 1991

Aero Peru *
Peru
1973 – present

logo: circa 1991 – present

Aeropostal
(Linea Aeropostal Venezolana)
Venezuela
1930 – 1994+

logo: current

Air Afrique *
Cote d'Ivoire
1961 – present

logo: 1961 – present

Air Algerie *
Algeria
1953 – present

logo: circa 1960s – present

Air Aruba *
Aruba, Dutch Antilles
1986 – 1994+

logo: 1988 – 1994+

Air Botswana *
Botswana
1972 – 1994+

logo: current

Air Caledonie International *
New Caledonia
1983 – present

logo: current

Air Canada
Canada
1964 – present

logo: 1964 – present

Air China International *
China
1988 – 1994+

logo: circa 1990 – 1994+

china topmark:
"AIR CHINA" opposite logo

Air Europa *
Spain
1986 – 1994+

Air Europe *
Great Britain
1979 – 1991

logo: used by both of these
associated airlines for entire duration

Air France *
France
1933 – present

logo: 1933 – present (originated with
predecessor, Air Orient, in 1932)

china topmark variations: circled logo
between "AIR" and "FRANCE" or
embossed or decal logo as shown

additional china topmarks:
modernized recessed or decal seahorse

Air Holland *
The Netherlands
1984 – 1994+

logo: 1984 – 1994+

Air-India *
India
1962 – present
(Air India International 1948 – 1962)

logo: circa late 1950s – present; used
concurrently with new logo (oval sun-
like device inside oval) since 1989

china topmark variations:
as shown or without circle

additional china topmark: "*AIR-INDIA*"

Air Inter
France
1958 – present

logo: circa 1960s – circa late 1980s

Air Inter
France
1959 – present

logo: late 1980s – present

Air Jamaica
Jamaica
1968 – present

logo: circa 1975 – present

Air Lanka *
Sri Lanka
1979 – present

logo: 1979 – present

Air Liberia
Liberia
1974 – 1975+

Air Malawi
Malawi
1964 – 1994+

logo: 1964 – 1994+

Air Mali
Mali
1960 – 1994+

logo: 1960 – circa 1970s

Air Malta *
Malta
1973 – 1995

logo: 1973 – 1990

china topmark:
"AIR MALTA" at left of logo

Air Malta *
Malta
1973 – present

logo: 1990 – presemt

china topmark:
"AIR MALTA" below logo

Air Mauritius *
Mauritius
1972 – 1994+

logo: 1977 – 1994+

china topmark variations:
"AIR" above and "MAURITUS"
below logo or solid logo, rather than
outlined as shown

Air New Zealand
New Zealand
1965 – present

logo: 1965 – 1974; also used by predecessor, Tasman Empire Airways
Ltd., for an unknown period

Air New Zealand *
New Zealand
1965 – present

logo: 1974 – present

Air Niugini *
Papua New Guinea
1973 – present

logo: 1973 – 1989

Air Niugini *
Papua New Guinea
1973 – present

logo: 1989 – present

Air Outre Mer
France
1988 – 1992
(merged with Minerve and became
AOM - French Airlines)

logo: 1988 – 1992
(new logo very similar: *see AOM -*
French Airlines)

Air Outre Mer *
France
1988 – 1992
(merged with Minerve and became
AOM - French Airlines)

china topmark shown

Air Pacific *
Fiji
1971 – present

logo: current

Air Seychelles
Seychelles
1979 – present

logo: 1985 – present

Air Siam *
Thailand
1965 – 1976

logo: 1965 – 1976

Air Tahiti
Tahiti
1987 – present

logo: 1987 – present

Air Tanzania *
Tanzania
1977 – present

logo (above): circa 1980s – present

china topmark (below): stylized "T"
extends further on older china

Air Transat
Canada
1986 – present

logo: 1986 – present

AIR 2000

Air 2000 *
Great Britain
1987 – present

logo: 1987 – present

Air Vietnam
Vietnam
1951 – 1976

china topmark: similar dragon with
"AIR VIETNAM" inside circle

Air Zaire
Zaire
1971 – present

logo: 1971 – present

Air Zimbabwe *
Zimbabwe
1980 – present

logo: early 1980s; slight variations
on later logo, e.g., wings are lower

Alaska Airlines
USA
1943 – present

logo: 1960s (also
without circle and star)

Alaska Airlines
USA
1943 – present

logo: 1980s – present (same logo with
varied facial expressions in the 1970s)

china topmark:
"Gold Coast SERVICE"

Alia Royal Jordanian Airline *
Jordan
1963 – 1986
(became Royal Jordanian)

logo: late 1960s – circa late 1970s

Alia Royal Jordanian Airline *
Jordan
1963 – 1986
(became Royal Jordanian)

logo: circa 1980 – 1986

Alitalia
(Aerolinee Italiane Internazionali)
Italy
1947 – present

logo: 1947 – 1969

Alitalia *
(Aerolinee Italiane Internazionali)
Italy
1957 – present

logo: 1970 – present

Allegheny Airlines
USA
1953 – 1979
(became US Air)

logo: circa 1960 – 1979

All Nippon Airways
Japan
1958 – present

logo: current

ALM Antillean Airlines *
(Antilliaanse Luchtvaart Maatschappij)
Netherlands Antilles
1964 – present

logo: 1964 – present;
position of stars vary

Aloha Airlines
USA
1959 – present

logo: circa 1980s – present

America West Airlines *
USA
1983 – present

logo: 1983 – present

American Airlines *
USA
1934 – present

logo: 1934 – 1945;
also used by predecessor,
American Airways, 1930 – 1934

china topmark variations:
as shown or with logo artwork
outlined (*see photographs*)

American Airlines *
USA
1934 – present

china topmark shown:
late 1930s DC-3 service

American Airlines *
USA
1934 – present

logo: 1945 – at least 1966;
eagle faced left in mid-1940s;
later faced right

additional china topmark:
early Admiral Club logo
(*see photograph on page 54*)

American Airlines *
USA
1934 – present

logo: at least 1971 – present

china topmark variations:
as shown or eagle only inside oval

additional china topmark:
Admiral Club logo with
5 stars inside circle

American Trans Air
USA
1973 – present

logo: circa 1980s – present

Ansett
Australia
1936 – present

logo: circa 1969 – 1982

Ansett
Australia
1936 – present

logo: 1982 – present

AOM - French Airlines
France
1993 – present

logo: current

Ariana Afghan Airlines
Afghanistan
1955 – present

logo: circa 1970s – present

Asiana *
South Korea
1988 – present

logo: circa 1991 – 1994+

ATI
(Aero Trasporti Italiani)
Italy
1963 – present

logo: 1963 – circa 1970s

ATI
(Aero Trasporti Italiani)
Italy
1963 – present

logo: circa 1980s – present

Australian Airlines *
Australia
1986 – 1993
(taken over by Qantas)

logo: 1986 – 1993

Austrian Airlines
Austria
1958 – present

logo: circa 1960s – present

Avensa *
(Aerovias Venezolanas SA)
Venezuela
1943 – present

logo: current

Avianca Columbia *
(Aerovias Nacionales de Columbia)
Columbia
1940 – present

logo: circa 1950s – circa mid-1970s

additional china topmark:
"PROPIEDAD AVIANCA"

Avianca Columbia *
(Aerovias Nacionales de Columbia)
Columbia
1940 – present

logo: circa mid-1970s – present

additional china topmark: "Avianca"

Aviateca Airlines
Guatemala
1945 – present

logo: circa 1990s – present

Balkan-Bulgarian Airlines *
Bulgaria
1968 – 1994+

logo: 1968 – 1987; also
used by predecessor,
Bulgarian Civil Air Transport

Balkan-Bulgarian Airlines *
Bulgaria
1968 – 1994+

logo: 1988 – present

Biman Bangladesh Airlines
Bangladesh
1972 – present

logo: 1972 – present

Bonanza Air Lines
USA
1945 – 1968
(merged with Pacific Airlines and West
Coast Airlines to become Air West,
which became Hughes Airwest in 1970)

logo: circa 1950s – 1968

Braniff Airways
USA
1930 – 1965

logo: early 1930s – 1940s

Braniff Airways
(unofficially called Braniff
International Airways, 1948 – 1965)
USA
1930 – 1965

logo: mid-1940s – 1965

Braniff Airways *
(unofficially called Braniff
International Airways, 1948 – 1965)
USA
1930 – 1965

china topmark shown: 1959 – 1965

Braniff International Airways
USA
1965 – 1982
Braniff Inc.: 1984 – 1989

logo: 1965 – 1984; used
concurrently with logo at right

Braniff International Airways *
USA
1965 – 1982
Braniff Inc.: 1984 – 1989

logo: 1965 – 1989

Britannia Airways
Great Britain
1964 – present

logo: 1964 – present

Britannia Airways *
Great Britain
1964 – present

china topmark shown: 1980s

British Airways
Great Britain
1972 – present

logo: 1974 – present

British Airways *
Great Britain
1972 – present

china topmark shown: 1974 – 1988

British Caledonian Airways
(Caledonian/BUA 1970 – 1972)
Great Britain
1972 – 1987
(taken over by British Airways)

logo: 1972 – late 1970s; also
used by predecessor, the initial
Caledonian Airways, 1961 – 1970

British Caledonian Airways
(Caledonian/BUA 1970-1972)
Great Britain
1972 – 1987
(taken over by British Airways)

logo: circa 1980 – 1987

British European Airways
(BEA) *
Great Britain
1946 – 1974
(merged with BOAC to form
British Airways in 1972)

logo: 1959 – 1968

china topmark variations:
"BRITISH EUROPEAN AIRWAYS"
with logo; also inverted logo

British European Airways
(BEA) *
Great Britain
1946 – 1974
(merged with BOAC to form
British Airways in 1972; BEA name
and logo used until 1974)

logo: 1968 – 1974
(note: the initials BEA in serif type
were used in the early 1990s by Birm-
ingham European Airways, which
merged with Brymon to beome Brymon
European Airways, 1993 – present)

British Midland Airways
Great Britain
1964 – present

logo: current

British Overseas Airways
(BOAC) *
Great Britain
1940 – 1974
(merged with BEA to form British Airways in 1972; BOAC
name and logo used until 1974)

logo: "Speedbird," 1940 – 1974; also
used by predecessor, Imperial Airways

china topmark: angle and
position of bird varies slightly

British United Airways (BUA)
Great Britain
1960 – 1970
(merged with Caledonian Airways to
form Caledonian/BUA, which became
British Caledonian Airways in 1972)

logo: 1966 – 1970

British West Indian Airways
Trinidad and Tobago
1941 – 1980
(merged with Trinidad and Tobago Air
Services to form BWIA International)

logo: circa 1950s – early 1960s

china topmark: "BWIA" inside sunburst

BWIA International Airways *
Trinidad and Tobago
1980 – present

logo: early 1960s – present

CAAC
(Civil Aviation Administration of China)
China
1954 – 1989
(reorganized into several airlines
including Air China)

logo: circa 1960s – circa 1970s

CAAC *
(Civil Aviation Administration of China)
China
1954 – 1889
(reorganized into several
airlines including Air China)

logo: circa 1980s

china topmark: winged
logo opposite "CAAC"

Caledonian Airways
Great Britain
1987 – present

logo: 1987 – present

(note: the initial Caledonian Airways,
1961 – 1970, merged with British United Airways to form Caledonian/BUA,
1970 – 1972, which became British
Caledonian Airways, 1972 – 1987)

Cameroon Airlines
Cameroon
1971 – present

logo: 1970s

Cameroon Airlines
Cameroon
1971 – present

logo: 1980s – present

Canadian Airlines International *
Canada
1987 – present

logo: 1987 – present

Canadian Pacific Air Lines *
Canada
1942 – 1968
(became CP Air)

logo: 1946 – early 1960s

china topmark: full color goose
below "Canadian Pacific"

Canadian Pacific Air Lines *
Canada
1942 – 1968
(became CP Air)

logo: early 1960s – 1968

china topmark: logo
without "Canadian Pacific"

Capital Airlines
USA
1948 – 1961
(taken over by United Air Lines)

logo: 1948 – 1961

Carnival Air Lines *
USA
1989 – present

logo: 1989 – present

CATHAY PACIFIC

Cathay Pacific Airways
Hong Kong
1946 – present

logo: current

Cathay Pacific Airways *
Hong Kong
1946 – present

china topmark shown: current (1996)

Cayman Airways *
British West Indies
1968 – present

logo: current (1996)

Ceskoslovenské - CSA *
(Czechoslovak Airlines)
Czechoslovakia / Czech Republic
1946 – 1995

Czech Airlines *
Czech Republic
1995 – present

logo: circa 1960s – present

China Airlines *
Republic of China
1959 – present

logo: circa 1960s – present

additional china topmark:
"CHINA AIRLINES"

China Eastern Airlines
Republic of China
1988 – present

logo: 1988 – present

China Northern Airlines
Republic of China
1989 – circa 1995

logo: 1989 – circa 1995

China Southern Airlines
Republic of China
1989 – present

logo: 1989 – present

China Southwest Airlines
Republic of China
1989 – present

logo: 1989 – present

Commercial Airways
South Africa
1967 – present

Condor Flugdienst
Germany
1961 – present

logo: circa 1970s – present

Continental Airlines
USA
1937 – present

logo: 1940s – mid-1950s

Continental Airlines *
USA
1937 – present

logo without oval and with
"AIRLINES" on lower portion of
eagle: mid-1950s – 1965

china topmark shown: 1959 – 1965

Continental Airlines *
USA
1937 – present

logo: 1965 – 1991

china topmarks:
gold logo, 1966 – 1970
embossed logo, 1968 – 1972
red logo, 1983 – 1992

additional china topmark:
white on white pattern with stylized
"CA" repeated near edge, 1970 – 1979

Continental Airlines
USA
1937 – present

logo: 1991 – present

COPA Panama *
(Compania Panamena de Aviacion SA)
Panama
1944 – present

logo: current

CP Air *
Canada
1968 – 1986
(became Canadian Pacific once
again, which merged with Pacific
Western to form Canadian Airlines
International in 1987)

logo: 1968 – 1986

Cubana
(Compania Nacional Cubana de
Aviacion, 1932 – 1945; Compania
Cubana de Aviacion, 1945 – 1959)
Cuba
1932 – 1959
(became Empresa Consolidada
Cubana de Aviacion)

Cubana *
(Empresa Consolidada Cubana
de Aviacion)
Cuba
1959 – present

logo: circa late 1960s – present

Cyprus Airways *
Cyprus
1947 – present

logo: 1960s – present

china topmark variations: "Cyprus
Airways" at right of logo or
logo enclosed in ornate frame

Dan Air
Great Britain
1953 – 1993
(taken over by British Airways)

logo: mid-1950s – 1994

Delta Air Corporation
USA
1930 – 1945

logo: 1930s – 1952

Delta Air Lines
USA
1945 – present

logo: 1952 – 1953 and circa 1955 – early
1960s; used concurrently with first logo
on the following page in early 1960s

logo variation: C & S (for Chicago and
Southern Airlines) appears below
Delta, 1953 – circa 1955

Delta Air Lines *
USA
1945 – present

logo: 1960 – present

additional china topmark:
"Delta Air Lines" in script

Dragonair
Hong Kong
1985 – present

logo: 1985 – present

Dragonair *
Hong Kong
1985 – present

china topmark shown

East African Airways
Kenya, Uganda, and Tanzania
1946 – 1977
(replaced by Air Tanzania)

logo: at least 1962 – 1977

Eastern Air Lines
USA
1934 – 1991

logo: circa 1935 – mid-1950s

Eastern Air Lines
USA
1934 – 1991

logo: mid-1950s – late 1950s

Eastern Air Lines
USA
1934 – 1991

logo: early 1960s

Eastern Air Lines *
USA
1934 – 1991
(operations ceased in January 1991
due to bankruptcy; purchased
by Frank Lorenzo)

logo: 1965 – 1991

Eastern Provincial Airways
(EPA)
Canada
1949 – 1985
(taken over by CP Air)

East-West Airlines
Australia
1947 – 1993
(taken over by Ansett in 1987, but
not fully integrated until 1993)

Ecuatoriana Air Line *
Ecuador
1974 – present

logo: 1974 – present

china topmark variations: as shown
or "ECUATORIANA" below logo

Egypt Air *
Egypt
1971 – present

logo: 1971 – present

additional china topmark:
"EGYPTAIR"

El Al Israel Airlines *
Israel
1948 – present

logo: circa 1950s – 1962

china topmark: solid circle, rather than
outline as shown, with airline name
and Hebrew letters on lower portion

El Al Israel Airlines *
Israel
1948 – present

logo: 1962 – circa early 1980s

El Al Israel Airlines *
Israel
1948 – present

logo: circa early 1980s – present

Emirates *
United Arab Emirates
1985 – present

logo: 1985 – present

Ethiopian Airlines *
Ethiopia
1946 – present

logo: circa 1950s – present

china topmark:
logo with "ETHIOPIAN
AIRLINES" inside circle

additional china topmark:
"ETHIOPIAN"

EVA Air
Taiwan
1991 – present

logo: 1991 – present

Finnair *
Finland
1968 – present

logo: 1968 – present

Formosa Airlines
Taiwan
1987 – present

logo: 1987 – present

Frontier Airlines
USA
1950 – 1986
(taken over by Continental)

logo: 1950 – 1958

Frontier Airlines *
USA
1950 – 1986
(taken over by Continental)

logo: 1959 – circa late 1970s

china topmark: left side of
arrow is eliminated from logo

Frontier Airlines *
USA
1950 – 1986
(taken over by Texas Air Corp. and
phased into Continental)

logo: circa late 1970s – 1986

china topmark: embossed logo

Frontier Airlines
USA
1994 – present

logo: 1994 – present

Garuda Indonesian Airways
Indonesia
1950 – present

logo: 1950s – circa 1960s

garuda

Garuda Indonesian Airways *
Indonesia
1950 – present

logo: circa 1970s – 1985

china topmark:
logo above "indonesian airways"
centered on diagonal stripes

Garuda Indonesian Airways *
Indonesia
1950 – present

logo: 1985 – present;
with or without eye in bird

Ghana Airways *
Ghana
1958 – present

logo: circa 1960s – present

china topmark variations:
as shown or outlined rather than
solid stripes in "wings"

Gulf Air
Bahrain
1974 – present

logo: 1970s

Gulf Air *
Bahrain
1974 – present

logo: 1980s – present

additonal china topmark:
"GULF AIR"

Guyana Airways *
Guyana
1963 – present

logo: circa 1970s – present

china topmark:
"Guyana Airways" at left of logo

Hapag-Lloyd Flug
Germany
1972 – present

logo: 1974 – present

Hawaiian Airlines
USA
1941 – present

logo: circa 1950s – late 1960s

Hawaiian Airlines
USA
1941 – present

logo: late 1960s – 1975

Hawaiian Airlines *
USA (Hawaii)
1941 – present

logo: circa 1975 – present

Highland Express *
Scotland
1987

logo: 1987

Hughes Airwest
USA
1970 – 1980
(taken over by Republic Airlines)

logo: 1970 – 1980

Iberia Airlines *
(Lineas Aereas de Espana SA)
Spain
1940 – present

logo: 1950s – mid-1960s

Iberia Airlines *
(Lineas Aereas de Espana SA)
Spain
1940 – present

logo: mid-1960s – late 1970s

Iberia Airlines *
(Lineas Aereas de Espana SA)
Spain
1940 – present

logo: late 1970s – present

additonal china topmark: "*IBERIA*"
in outlined type

Icelandair
(Flugfelag Islands HF)
Iceland
1940 – present

logo: circa 1960s – circa 1970s

Icelandair
(Flugfelag Islands HF)
Iceland
1937 – present

logo: circa 1980 – present

Indian Airlines
India
1953 – present

logo: at least 1969 – present

Intair *
Canada
1988 – 1991

logo: 1988 – 1991

Iran Air *
Iran
1962 – present

logo: 1962 – present

Iraqi Airways *
Iraq
1945 – 1991+
(fleet grounded in 1991)

logo: circa 1960s – 1991+

Istanbul Airlines
Turkey
1985 – present

logo: 1985 – present

Japan Airlines *
Japan
1953 – present

logo: 1953 – present; used
concurrently with first logo on the
following page since 1988

Japan Airlines
(Air Lines becomes one word in 1988)
Japan
1953 – present

logo: 1988 – present; used concurrently with last logo on the previous page since 1988

Japan Air System
Japan
1988 – present

logo: 1988 – present

Japan Asia Airways
Japan
1975 – present

logo: 1975 – present

JAT - Yugoslav Airlines *
(Jugoslovenski Aerotransport)
Yugoslavia
1947 – 1994

logo: circa 1960s – 1994

Kenya Airways *
Kenya
1977 – present

logo: 1977 – present

KLM Royal Dutch Airlines *
(Koninklijke Luchtvaart Maatschappij)
The Netherlands
1919 – present

logo: at least 1938 – 1958

KLM Royal Dutch Airlines
The Netherlands
1919 – present

logo: 1958 – 1964

KLM Royal Dutch Airlines *
The Netherlands
1919 – present

logo: 1964 – present

china topmark variations:
as shown or outlined letters

Korean Air Lines *
Korea
1962 – 1984
(became Korean Air)

logo: 1962 – 1984

Korean Air *
Korea
1984 – present

logo without horizontal lines:
1984 – present

china topmark shown

Kuwait Airways *
Kuwait
1958 – present

logo: circa 1960s – present

LACSA
(Lineas Aereas Costarricenses SA)
Costa Rica
1945 – present

logo: 1945 – circa 1960s

LACSA *
(Lineas Aereas Costarricenses SA)
Costa Rica
1945 – present

logo: at least 1983 – present

LADECO *
(Linea Aérea del Cobre)
Chile
1958 – present

logo: circa 1960s – 1990

china topmark variations: as shown
or with "*LADECO*" above "LINEA
AÉREA DEL COBRE SA"
at right of logo

LADECO
(Linea Aerea del Cobre)
Chile
1958 – present

logo: 1990 – present

LAI
(Linee Aeree Italiane SpA)
Italy
1947 – 1957
(taken over by Alitalia)

Laker Airways *
Great Britain
1966 – 1982

china topmark shown: used on
"Royal Service" china, 1978 – 1982

LAM
(Linhas Aereas Mocambique)
Mozambique
1980 – present

logo: 1980 – present; used concurrently with logo at right since 1993

LAM *
(Linhas Aereas Mocambique)
Mozambique
1980 – present

logo: 1993 – present

LAN Chile *
(Lineas Nacional de Chile)
Chile
1932 – present

logo: circa 1960s

LAN Chile *
(Lineas Nacional de Chile)
Chile
1932 – present

logo: late 1960s – present

china topmark:
"LAN-CHILE" below logo

additional china topmark: "Lan Chile"

Lauda Air
Austria
1979 – present

logo: current

china topmark:
embossed winged runner

Libyan Arab Airlines
Libya
1969 – present

logo: 1969 – present

Loftleidir *
(Icelandic Airlines)
Iceland
1944 – 1979
(merged with Icelandair in 1973, but
not fully taken over until 1979)

logo: circa 1950s – 1970s

LOT *
(Polskie Linie Lotnicze)
Poland
1929 – present

logo: circa 1960s – present

LTU
(Lufttransport Union)
Germany
1956 – present

logo: current (1996)

Lufthansa *
(Deutsche Lufthansa AG)
Germany
1954 – present

logo: 1954 – present; also used by predecessor, Deutsche Luft Hansa, 1930s –
1940s; surrounded by circle in 1930s
and after 1964

china topmark variations: as shown,
logo inside circle, or logo above
"Senator" on shield ("Senator Service,"
1958 – 1960s)

Luftschiffbau Zeppelin *
Germany
1928 – 1937

china topmark shown:
used on Graf Zeppelin, 1928 – 1937

Luxair
(Luxembourg Airlines)
Luxembourg
1961 – present

logo: 1961 – present

Maersk Air *
Denmark
1969 – present

logo: 1969 – present; this logo also
used by A. P. Moller shipping
company (Maersk Line)

Malaysian Airline System *
(formerly Malaysian Airways, 1963 –
1967, and Malaysian-Singapore
Airlines, 1967 – 1972)
Malaysia
1972 – 1987
(became Malaysia Airlines)

logo: 1972 – 1987

Malaysia Airlines *
Malaysia
1987 – present

logo: 1987 – present

Malev-Hungarian Airlines *
(Magyar Legiközlekedesi Vollat)
Hungary
1954 – present

china topmark shown: 1960s

Malev-Hungarian Airlines
(Magyar Legiközlekedesi Vollat)
Hungary
1954 – present

logo: circa 1960s – circa 1970s

Malev-Hungarian Airlines
(Magyar Legiközlekedesi Vollat)
Hungary
1954 – present

logo: circa 1980s – present

Malta Airways
Malta
1946 – 1973
(succeeded by Air Malta)

Mandarin Airlines *
Taiwan
1991 – present

logo: 1991 – present

Manx Airlines
Great Britain
1982 – present

logo: 1982 – present

Markair *
USA
1984 – present

logo: 1984 – 1995

Martinair *
The Netherlands
1968 – present

logo: early 1970s – present

china topmark: logo surrounded
by geometric design

McClain Airlines *
USA
October 1986 – February 1987 and
October 1987 – May 1988

china topmark:
"McClain Airlines" below logo on
cup only; other pieces decorated with
cobalt band between gold lines

Mexicana Airlines
(Compania Mexicana de Aviacion)
Mexico
1924 – present

logo: at least 1943 – 1968

Mexicana Airlines
Mexico
1924 – present

logo: 1968 – present

china topmark: "*mexicana*"

MGM Grand Air *
USA
1987 – 1994
(renamed Champion Air)

logo: 1987 – 1994

Middle East Airlines SA
(MEA) *
Lebanon
1945 – present

logo: circa 1960s – present

china topmark variations:
as shown or with "MEA"
at right of logo

Midwest Express Airlines *
USA
1983 – present

logo: 1983 – present

additional china topmarks: "Good
Morning!" in script, "*MIDWEST*
Express" ("Express" in script), or
"MIDWEST EXPRESS AIRLINES"

Mohawk Airlines
USA
origin 1945 – 1972
(taken over by Allegheny Airlines)

Monarch Airlines
Great Britain
1968 – present

logo: circa 1980s – present

Morris Air
USA
1992 – 1995
(taken over by Southwest Airlines)

Mount Cook Airlines
New Zealand
1937 – present

logo: circa 1970s – present

National Airlines
USA
1934 – 1980
(taken over by Pan Am)

logo: circa 1936 – 1950

National Airlines
USA
1934 – 1980
(taken over by Pan Am)

logo: 1950 – circa 1964

National Airlines
USA
1934 – 1980
(taken over by Pan Am)

logo: circa 1964 – 1968

National Airlines *
USA
1934 – 1980
(taken over by Pan Am)

logo: 1968 – 1980

New York Airways
USA
1949 – 1987
(taken over by Continental)

logo: 1970s – 1987

New Zealand National Airways
New Zealand
1945 – 1978
(taken over by Air New Zealand)

logo: circa 1960s – 1978

Nigeria Airways *
Nigeria
1958 – present

logo: circa 1960s – late 1970s

Nigeria Airways
Nigeria
1958 – present

logo: circa 1980s

Nigeria Airways *
Nigeria
1958 – present

china topmark shown

china topmark variations: logo with
italic (as shown) or straight "N,"
each with "*NIGERIA*" above and
"*AIRWAYS*" below logo

Nigeria Airways *
Nigeria
1958 – present

logo: circa early 1990s – present

china topmark: "*NIGERIA*" above
and "*AIRWAYS*" below logo

Northeast Airlines *
USA
1940 – 1972
(taken over by Delta Air Lines)

logo without oval or "Northeast":
circa early 1960s – 1972

china topmark variations: as shown
or without "NORTHEAST";
early 1960s

Northeast Airlines *
USA
1940 – 1972
(taken over by Delta Air Lines)

china topmark shown:
circa late 1960s – 1972

Northwest Airlines
USA
1934 – present

logo: mid-1930s – 1940s

Northwest Airlines *
(known as Northwest Orient Airlines
1947 – 1986)
USA
1934 – present

logo: 1948 – circa 1959

china topmark: "NORTHWEST"
above and "AIRLINES" below logo

Northwest Airlines *
(known as Northwest Orient Airlines
1947 – 1986)
USA
1934 – present

logo: early 1960s – 1969

Northwest Airlines *
USA
1934 – present
(known as Northwest Orient Airlines
1947 – 1986)

logo: 1969 – 1989

china topmark variations: as shown or
"Regal Imperial" in script below logo

Northwest Airlines
USA
1934 – present

logo: 1989 – present

Oasis International Airlines
Spain
1989 – present

logo: 1989 – present

Olympic Airways
/ Olympic Aviation
Greece
1957/1971 – present

logo: 1960s/1971 – present
(originally without plane at top right)

china topmark:
"OLYMPIC" above "AIRWAYS"

Ozark Air Lines
USA
1944 – 1986
(taken over by TWA)

logo: circa 1960s – 1986

Pacific Air Lines
USA
1958 – 1968
(merged with West Coast Airlines and
Bonanza Air Lines to become Air West,
which became Hughes Airwest in 1970)

logo: as shown, 1958 – 1966;
with angular eagle, 1967 – 1968

Pacific Western Airlines
Canada
1953 – 1987
(merged with Canadian Pacific to
form Canadian Airlines International)

logo: circa 1970s – 1987

Pakistan International Airlines *
Pakistan
1954 – present

logo: circa mid-1970s – present

Panagra
(Pan American Grace Airways)
USA
1930 – 1967
(taken over by Braniff)

logo: circa 1930s – circa 1956

Pan American Airways *
USA
1927 – 1948

logo: early 1930s – 1957

china topmark variations: "*PAA*" at left
of logo, rather than on wing, with
globe that resembles Panagra's globe
logo on 1930s – circa 1941 china or as
shown on mid-1940s china

Pan American World Airways
USA
1948 – 1991 and 1996 – present
(taken over by Delta Airlines in 1991;
name/logo purchased and airline
began operating again in 1996)

logo: 1958 – 1991 and 1996 – present

Pan American World Airways *
USA
1948 – 1991 and 1996 – present
(taken over by Delta Airlines in 1991;
name / logo purchased and airline
began operating again in 1996)

logo: 1958 – 1991 and 1996 – present

china topmark:
as shown on 1996+ china

People Express
USA
1981 – 1986
(taken over by Continental)

logo: 1981 – 1986

Philippine Air Lines *
Philippines
1946 – present

logo: at least 1963 – 1986

Philippine Air Lines
Philippines
1946 – present

logo: 1986 – present

Piedmont Airlines *
USA
1948 – 1989
(taken over by US Air in 1986 and
fully integrated by 1989)

logo: circa 1960s – 1989

Polynesian Airlines
Western Samoa
1959 – present

logo: 1980s – present; same logo
without horizontal lines in 1970s

Portugalia *
Portugal
1989 – present

logo: 1989 – present

Qantas Airways *
(Qantas Empire Airways, 1934 –
1967)
Australia
1967 – present
logo: 1959 – 1985

china topmark variations:
as shown or logo inside circle

Qantas Airways
Australia
1967 – present

logo: 1985 – present

Quebecair
Canada
1953 – 1987
(merged with Quebec Aviation and
Nordair Metro to form Inter-Canadian,
which became Intair shortly thereafter)

Regent Air *
USA
1983 – 1986

logo: 1983 – 1986

Republic Airlines
USA
1979 – 1986

(taken over by Northwest airlines)

logo: 1979 – 1986; also used by pre-
decessors, Wisconsin Central
Airlines, 1948 – 1952, and North
Central Airlines, 1952 – 1979

RenoAir

Reno Air
USA
1992 – present

logo: current

Rich International Airways
USA
1971 – present
(passenger service began in 1982)

logo: circa 1980s – present

Royal Air Maroc *
Morocco
1957 – present

logo: current

Royal Brunei Airlines *
Brunei
1975 – present

logo: 1975 – present; early version
does not include diagonal stripes

china topmark:
"*ROYAL BRUNEI*" below logo

additional china topmark:
"Royal Brunei"

Royal Jordanian Airlines *
Jordan
1986 – present

logo: 1986 – present

china topmark:
"ROYAL JORDANIAN" below logo

Royal Nepal Airlines *
Nepal
1958 – present

logo: current (1996)

Sabena World Airlines
Belgium
1923 – present

logos on left and right
used concurrently:
circa mid-1950s – early 1970s

Sabena World Airlines *
Belgium
1923 – present

logo on left: early 1970s – 1993;
1993+ logo has repeated wavy
horizontal lines through circle

china topmark variations:
as shown on left and right

SAETA SA *
(Ecuatoriana de Transportes Aereos)
Ecuador
1967 – present

logo: current

Saudia *
(Saudi Arabian Airlines)
Saudi Arabia
1945 – present

logo: circa 1960s – present

Scandinavian Airlines System
Sweden, Denmark, and Norway
1946 – present

logo: circa 1950s – circa late 1960s;
used concurrently with logo at right

Scandinavian Airlines System *
Sweden, Denmark, and Norway
1946 – present

logo: circa 1950s – present
with the following variations –
S•A•S , mid-1950s
/ / / SAS, 1983 – present

SilkAir *
Singapore
1991 – present

logo: 1991 – present

china topmark: logo incorporated in
border design, though somewhat
difficult to recognize

Singapore Airlines *
Singapore
1972 – present

logo: 1972 – present

Sobelair
(subsidiary of Sabena)
Belgium
1946 – present

logo: 1984 – present

South African Airways *
Republic of South Africa
1934 – present

logo: circa 1960s – present

china topmark variations:
as shown, with round cut diamond at
upper left of logo, or detailed logo

Southern Airways
USA
1949 – 1979
(merged with North Central Airlines
to form Republic Airlines)

logo: 1972 – 1979

Spanair
Spain
1987 – present

logo: 1987 – present

Standard Airways
USA
1960s
(worldwide charters)

Sudan Airways
Sudan
1946 – 1994+

logo: 1970s;
without "rays" in 1960s

Sudan Airways *
Sudan
1946 – 1994+

logo: 1980s – 1994+

Suidwes Lugdiens
South Africa
1959 – 1975+

logo: circa 1970s

Sun Express
Turkey
1989 – present

logo: 1989 – present

Swissair *
Switzerland
1931 – present

logo: 1952 – late 1970s

Swissair
Switzerland
1931 – present

logo: late 1970s – present

Syrian Arab Airlines
Syria
1961 – present

logo: 1960s

Syrian Arab Airlines
(Syrianair)
Syria
1961 – present

logo: circa 1970s – present

TAAG - Angola Airlines *
Angola
1975 – present

logo: 1975 – present

Talair
Papua New Guinea
1975 – 1993

logo: 1975 – 1993

TAP - Air Portugal *
Portugal
1979 – present

logo: 1975 – present; came into use
while known as Transportes Aereos
Portugueses - TAP

china topmark: "AIR" above
"PORTUGAL" at right of logo

Texas International Airlines *
USA
1968 – 1982
(taken over by Continental Airlines)

china topmark shown

Thai Airways International *
Thailand
1959 – present

logo: 1975 – present

china topmark variations:
as shown or "Thai" only

Tower Air *
USA
1983 – present

logo: current shown at top

china topmark variations:
current topmark shown at top and
previous topmark shown below

Transamerica Airlines *
USA
1979 – 1986

logo: mid-1970s – 1986;
came into use while known as
Trans International Airlines

Trans-Australia Airlines
Australia
1946 – 1986
(became Australian Airlines)

logo: circa 1950s – 1970s

Trans-Australia Airlines *
Australia
1946 – 1986
(became Australian Airlines)

logo: 1980 – 1986

Trans Brasil *
Brazil
1972 – present

logo: 1972 – present

Trans-Canada Air Lines (TCA)
Canada
1937 – 1964
(became Air Canada)

logo: 1937 – 1940s

Trans-Canada Air Lines (TCA)
Canada
1937 – 1964
(became Air Canada)

logo: early 1950s;
used concurrently with logo at right

Trans-Canada Air Lines (TCA)
Canada
1937 – 1964
(became Air Canada)

logo: late 1940s – 1964

china topmark: "TCA" in outlined
type (*see photograph on page 72*)
on detailed maple leaf

Transcontinental and Western Air
USA
1930 – 1950
(became Trans World Airlines)

logo: 1933 – 1945; many variations including outlined letters, outlined circle, and so forth

Transcontinental and Western Air
USA
1930 – 1950
(became Trans World Airlines)

logo: 1948 – 1950; with arrow pointing from left to right behind logo, 1945 – 1948

Trans International Airlines *
USA
1960 – 1979
(became Transamerica Airlines)

logo: 1960 – mid-1970s
(*see Transamerica Airlines for mid-1970s – 1979 logo*)

Transportes Aereos Portugueses
Portugal
1945 – 1979
(became TAP - Air Portugal)

logo: circa 1960s – 1975, *see TAP - Air Portugal for 1975 – 1979 logo*

Trans World Airlines *
USA
1950 – present

logo: 1960 – 1974

Trans World Airlines *
USA
1950 – present

logo: 1950 – 1960 and 1974 – present

china topmark variations:
as shown on sauce (butter) only or enclosed in ornate gold frame

additional china topmark: "RA" enclosed in ornate gold frame used for Royal Ambassador Service

Trans World Airlines
USA
1950 – present

logo: 1995 – present (1996); used concurrently with logo at left

Tunis Air
Tunisia
1948 – present

logo: circa 1960s

TunisAir
Tunisia
1948 – present

logo: 1990 – present

logo variation: on rectangle, rounded at upper right and lower left, without horizontal lines, late 1960s – 1990

Tunisavia
Tunisia
1974 – present

logo: 1974 – present

Turkish Airlines (THY) *
Turkey
1956 – present

logo: circa 1960s – present

Uganda Airlines
Uganda
1976 – present

logo: 1976 – present

Union de Transports Aériens *
France
1963 – 1992
(taken over by Air France; fully integrated by 1994)

logo: 1963 – 1994

United Air Lines *
USA
1931 – present

topmark shown: embossed on plastic plates and cups, 1930s – 1940s

United Air Lines *
USA
1931 – 1974
(became United Airlines)

logo: 1937 – 1953

logo variations: star or U.S. map replaces "MAINLINERS"; also logo at right

topmarked on salt and pepper only with star replacing "MAINLINERS"

United Air Lines
USA
1931 – 1974
(became United Airlines)

logo: 1942 – 1953;

variation of logo at left
china topmark: "UNITED AIR LINES"

United Air Lines
USA
1931 – 1974
(became United Airlines)

logo: 1954 – 1961

United Air Lines *
USA
1931 – 1974
(became United Airlines)

logo: 1961 – 1974

china topmark:
logo inside oval

additional china topmark:
"RED CARPET ROOM" at right of
logo on airport lounge china, 1960s

United Airlines *
USA
1974 – present

logo: 1974 – present

china topmark:
"UNITED" below logo

additional china topmarks:
"RED CARPET CLUB," 1970s, or
"The RED CARPET Club," 1980s –
1990s, on airport lounge china

United Air Services
South Africa
1965 – 1975+

United Arab Airlines
Egypt
1958 – 1971
(became Egypt Air)

logo: circa 1960s – 1971

US AIR *
USA
1979 – 1996
(became U.S. Airways)

logo: 1979 – 1989

US AIR *
USA
1979 – 1996
(became U.S. Airways)

logo: 1990 – 1996

VARIG *
(Viãcao Aérea Rio-Grandense)
Brazil
1927 – present

logo: circa 1950s – present
(used concurrently with next logo)

VARIG *
(Viãcao Aérea Rio-Grandense)
Brazil
1927 – present

logo: mid-1960s – present

china topmark:
"VARIG" below partially inverted logo

VASP *
(Viacao Aerea Sao Paulo SA)
Brazil
1933 – present

logo: circa 1980s – present

china topmark:
"VASP" as shown, but without graphic

VIASA *
(Venezolana Internacional de
Avacion SA)
Venezuela
1961 – present

logo: 1961 – present

china topmark variations: as shown
or logo surrounded by oval

Vietnam Airlines *
Vietnam
1990 – present

logo: 1990 – present

china topmark:
"*VIETNAM*" above
"*AIRLINES*" below logo

Virgin Atlantic Airways *
Great Britain
1984 – present

logo: 1984 – present

Viva Air *
Spain
1988 – present

logo: 1988 – present

Wardair *
Canada
1952 – 1989
(taken over by Canadian Airlines
International)

china topmark shown: circa 1950s

Wardair
Canada
1952 – 1989
(taken over by Canadian Airlines
International)

logo: circa 1960s – circa 1970s

West Coast Airlines
USA
1946 – 1968
(merged with Bonanza Air Lines and
Pacific Air Lines to become Air West)

logo: 1950s

West Coast Airlines
USA
1946 – 1968
(merged with Bonanza Air Lines
and Pacific Air Lines
to become Air West)

logo: 1960s

Western Air Lines
USA
1941 – 1987
(taken over by Delta Air Lines)

logo: 1940s

Western Airlines
USA
1941 – 1987
(taken over by Delta Air Lines)

logo: 1950s – 1960s
with many minor variations

Western Airlines
USA
1941 – 1987
(taken over by Delta Air Lines)

logo: 1970s – 1987

Wien Air Alaska
USA
1936 – 1968 and 1973 – 1986
(merged with Northern Consolidated
to form Wien Consolidated in 1968,
which became Wien Air Alaska once
again in 1973, and was taken
over by Markair in 1986)

logo: circa 1950s – 1960s

World Airways
USA
1948 – 1994+

logo: circa 1960s – circa 1988

World Airways *
USA
1948 – present

logo: circa 1988 – present

Xiamen Airlines
China
1991 – present

logo: 1991 – present

Yemenia *
(Yemen Airways Corp.)
Yemen
1972 – 1994+

logo: circa 1970s – 1994+

china topmark: logo inside
oval with "Yemenia" at left
and Arabic letters at right

Zambia Airways *
Zambia
1964 – present

logo: circa 1970s – present

Our Customer List Includes...

A successful line of dinnerware for inflight meal service must be functional, durable and sophisticated in both pattern and shape design. Our list of satisfied customers, including carriers from all over the globe, is a powerful testimonial to Noritake's record of successfully meeting the exacting needs of the world's premier airlines.

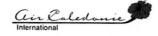

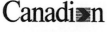

Airline Section Bibliography

Air Travel Bargins
by Jim Woodman
© 1968
Simon & Schuster

The Air Traveler's Handbook
Edited by Helen Armstrong
© 1989
St. Martin's Press

The Aircraft Encyclopedia
by Roy Braybrook
© 1985
Simon and Schuster Juvenile Divison

The Airline Builders
by Oliver E. Allen
© 1981
Time-Life Books, Alexandria, Virginia

Airlines Worldwide
by B. I. Hengi
© 1994
Midland Publishing

Airliners from 1919 to the Present Day
by Kenneth Munson
© 1972 and 1975
Peerage Books

Airplanes — From the Dawn of Flight to Present Day
by Enzo Angelucci
© 1971
McGraw-Hill Book Company

Boeing 707
by P .R. Smith
© 1991
Airlife Publishing Ltd.

Boeing 474
by Hiroshi Seo
© 1984
Jane's Publishing Company Ltd.

ButterPat World
by Richard W. Luckin
© 1996, 1st edition
R.K. Publishing

Classic Jetliners
by Mark Wagner and Guy Norris
© 1994
Osprey Aerospace

Commercial Aircraft
by Michael J. Taylor
© 1983
Hamlyn Publishing Group Ltd.

Commercial Aircraft & Airline Markings
by Christy Campbell
© 1992
Chancellor Press

Commercial Aviation Collectibles
by Richard R. Wallin
© 1990
Wallace-Homestead Book Company

Deregulation Knockouts - Round One
by Tom W. Norwood
© 1996
Airways International

Dinner in the Clouds
by Glenn I Howe
early 1990s
Zeta Publishers

Faded Glory — Airline Colour Schemes of the Past
by John K. Morton
© 1991
Airlife Publishing Ltd.

Flying Colours
by John K. Morton
© 1994
Motorbooks International

Fokker F27/Fairchild FH227/Fokker F50
by Wolfgang Kathe
© 1995
Airlife Publishing Ltd.

Footsteps in the Sky
by Helen E. McLaughlin
© 1994
State of the Art, Ltd

From Jenny to Jet
complied by Don C. Wigton
© 1963
Bonanza Books

The Hamline Guide to Commercial Aircraft & Airline Markings
by Christy Campbell
© 1992
Reed Internatinal Books Ltd.

The Illustrated Encyclopedia of Propeller Airliners
Editor-in-chief: Bill Gunston
© 1980, Phoebus Publishing Company
Exeter Books, New York

The International Encyclopedia of Aviation
General editor: David Monday
Assitant compiler: Jane's All The World Aircraft
© 1977, Octopus Books Limited
Crown Publishers, Inc., New York

Interavia 500 World Airline Leaders 1991/1992
by Jane's Information Group Ltd.
© 1991
Interavia SA, Switzerland

JP Airline — Fleets Interanational 88, 92, and 94/95
by U. Klee
© 1988, 1992, and 1994
Bucher Publications

Nostalgia North Americana
by Donald Thomas
©1990
Published in Dunedin, Florida

The Observer's World Airlines and Airliners Directory
by William Green and Gordon Swanborough
© 1975
Fredrick Warne & Co. Ltd.

Poster Art of the Airlines
by Donald Thomas
© 1989
Published in Dunedin, Florida

The Sky's the Limit — A History of the U.S. Airlines
by Arch Whitehouse
© 1971
The Macmillan Company

Skyliners Volume 1: North America
by George W. Hamlin
© 1991
World Transport Press, Inc.

Vintage Glory
by Adrian M. Balch
© 1994
Airlife Publishing Ltd.

World Airline Colours 4
by Nigel M. Tomkins
© 1987
Browcom Publishing

World Aviation Directory
Aviation Week Group
© 1992
McGraw-Hill

World's Air Fleets
by David W. Wragg
© 1969
Ian Allan Ltd.

The World's Airlines
by R. E. G. Davies
© 1964
Oxford University Press

Airline brochures, 1980s – 1990s

Captain's Log, World Airline Historical Society, 1988 – present

National Geographic and other magazine advertisments, 1920 – present

Dining on the Seas.....

Photo courtesy of Arabia

Collecting Ship China

Lured by tales of the high seas, the arm-chair sailor with eyes closed, savors the scent of salty air while riding the waves on a paddle steamer or aboard a luxury ocean liner…this is the stuff of which many a ship china collector is made. That is, they were enticed by shipping history before they began acquiring ship china. Others started with railroad china and broadened their collections to include ship and perhaps airline and military ware. Then there are those who initially sought heavy gauge rolled-edge restaurant china. Whatever the case, ship china ranks high in the field of commercial china.

Pre-1900 paddle steamer and ocean liner china is available, but difficult to find and fairly expensive. Undoubtedly the most popular is ocean liner china produced from the turn of the century until the 1960s, when airliners and cruise ships replaced nearly all of the great liners. However, custom decorated tableware used by worldwide freighter, container ship, tanker, ferryboat, cruise ship, and modern riverboat lines or any form of commercial water-going transportation is collectible; in fact, eagerly sought.

Ship Line History

Ship lines are formed as demand increases and operations cease in times of economic decline or war. Nations requisition their country's ships during wars (Cunard's QE2 participated as recently as 1982 in the Falkland Islands war) and a great percentage are lost. Line and company names change as ownership changes. Few lines are still owned by individuals, families, or small companies. Nearly all have been taken over by shipping conglomerates. While the United States maintains a substantial military fleet, our merchant fleet is considerably smaller than it was prior to WWII, consisting primarily of freighters, tankers, and container ships.

Brief ship line histories which in most cases list the full line name, company name, dates of operation, line service (e.g., passenger or freight), and other historical information are included in the Ship China Topmarks segment (pages 152 – 185). While this information is avidly sought by those involved in the hobby, it is difficult to obtain. The data presented herein was tediously gathered from dozens of references (*see ship section bibliography*), in addition to hundreds of magazine advertisements and cruise line brochures, then carefully analyzed. Unfortunately details tend to vary from one source to another, thus the rendering is as accurate as possible based on available references.

If you wish to locate the history of a particular ship line or company, refer to the alphabetical ship line listing in the index under "ship china."

Note: the home country of several cruise lines is unknown, because their ships are registered in Liberia and other countries and each line is listed at offices in a number of cities around the world.

Recognizing Ship China

No one will ever know precisely how many topmarked ship china patterns have been produced. Undoubtedly there are thousands.

Look for a belt or life-ring logo or a flag or pennant topmark. Also watch for the initials "SS" and the words "Line," "Navigation," "Steamship," "Shipping," "Transport," "Transportation," "Tanker," "Marine," and "Packet," as well as foreign equivalents such as "Linie," "Lijn," "Linien," "Navigazione," "Stoomvaart," "Stoomboot," "Maritimi," "Maritimes," and "Paketvaart."

When china is topmarked with one of these words or any initials, check the alphabetical Ship China Topmarks list on pages 152 – 185. If the topmark is one of the 280 listed, the information offered will identify the ship line and should narrow down usage dates.

In addition, ship china may be topmarked with a flag or logo that has no initials or words. One-hundred sixty-two of these artistic devices are illustrated on the Ship Line Logos, Flags, and China Topmarks table on pages 186 – 196, along with line name, country, and dates of operation.

Current Topmarked Ship China

Many lines no longer order topmarked china due to the initial expense, as well as the passenger's temptation to acquire a souvenir. However various upscale cruise lines, in addition to a surprising number of freight lines continue to uphold a prestigious corporate image by serving meals on high quality topmarked china. Examples of such ware are illustrated on pages 120 – 126.

Courtesy of Cunard

Cunard Royal Viking china

Ship China Manufacturers

Because thousands of lines have operated since the mid-1800s and ship china has been manufactured in several different bodies (i.e., varying gauges of vitrified china, bone china, porcelain, and even earthenware), it is quite likely that nearly all commercial as well as numerous household china manufacturers have produced china for a shipping concern at one time or another.

Each of the following companies, listed after their country, have made ware for a number of ship lines:

Great Britain: Dunn, Bennett & Co.; Grindley Hotelware; John Maddock & Sons; Minton; Royal Doulton; Ridgway
Germany: Bauscher; Hutschenreuther; Schönwald
Italy: Richard-Ginori
Norway: Porsgrund
United States: Buffalo; Greenwood; Jackson; Homer Laughlin; Maddock; Mayer; Scammell; Shenango; Sterling; Syracuse; Union Porcelain Works

Transportation Shows

Though there are no known annual ship memorabilia shows, ship china is available at transportation shows. These events usually offer a large selection of railroad and airline, as well as ship collectibles. Currently there are annual transportation shows in the following cities:

Dallas, Texas (Arlington or Irving, Texas), in March or April
Baltimore, Maryland (Timonium, Maryland), in May
St. Charles, Illinois, in June
Gaithersburg, Maryland, in November
Denver, Colorado, in July

Dates and specifics of these and other transportation shows are advertised in the World Airline Historical Society's *Captain's Log*, the Railroad Collectors Association's *Railroadiana Express,* and occasionally the Steamship Historical Society's *Steamboat Bill*. Advertising flyers, some with admission discount coupons, may be available at your local antique shows and shops a month or two prior to a show.

Ship China References

See the Ship Section Bibliography on page 197 for ship line and shipping references.

Steamship Historical Society of America

"The society was established in 1935 to bring together amateur and professional historians interested in the history of steam navigation. Membership is growing steadily and encompasses all interested in steam and other power driven vessels. Members are invited to contribute to *Steamboat Bill*, make use of our extensive marine library and photo collection, participate in local chapter activities, as well as national meetings held at fresh and salt water ports of maritime interest." (*quoted from the application card*)

Members receive an 84 page quarterly magazine *Steamboat Bill*. Features include historical and up-to-date ship and ship line information, ship related book reviews and an occasional article covering ship china.
For information write to:
Steamship Historical Society of America, Inc.
300 Ray Drive, Suite #4
Providence, RI 02906

Ship Line Advertisements

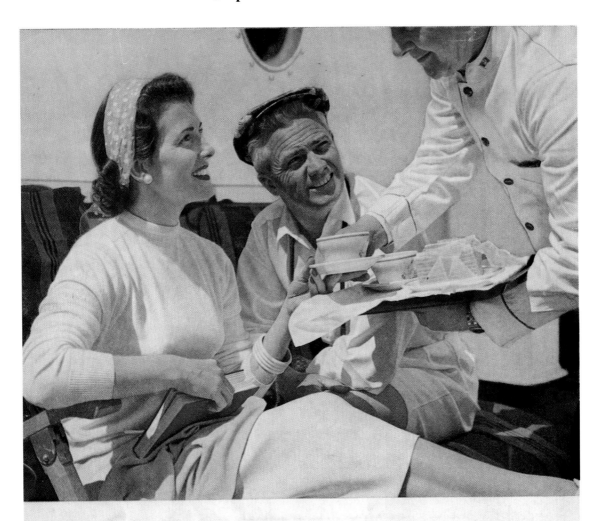

Sail Mooremack and own the sun!

Take a real rest! The kind you get *only* on a sea voyage in the warm, relaxing, summer sun! Mooremack has it—every day.

Pull up a deck chair near these sun worshippers. Sail the smoothest seas this side of paradise, on a 38-day Mooremack Luxury Cruise to South America! Aboard ship, you'll enjoy solid relaxation—or be as gay as you wish. You'll make stimulating new friends . . . spend days and nights ashore in exotic ports of call . . . sleep the whole night through in your spacious outside stateroom.

Arrange this really exciting vacation in the sun today—through your travel agent!

MOOREMACK TO SOUTH AMERICA

Harbor Policeman
. . . Barbados

Mosaic Promenade
. . . Rio

MOORE-McCORMACK *Lines*

Five Broadway,
New York 4, N. Y.

38-day cruises to South America and return—S.S. ARGENTINA . . . S.S. BRAZIL . . . cruises from $1,110. These 33,000-ton liners sail every three weeks from New York to: **TRINIDAD · BARBADOS · BAHIA · RIO DE JANEIRO · SANTOS (São Paulo) · MONTEVIDEO · BUENOS AIRES**

1957 Moore-McCormack Lines advertisement

Clipper Line's *Stella Polaris* dining room, 1960

Grace Line's SS *Santa Rosa* dining room, circa 1939

Fun runs an exciting pace.

sailing to and from *Hawaii* on the palatial LURLINE

Ship life is a shining parade of bright, gay hours

THE LURLINE IS HAWAII

On the LURLINE, you have scores of opportunities for lasting friendships to flower. With your new friends you discover why the LURLINE makes your trip a foretaste of Hawaii, as delightful as Hawaii itself. ■ You enjoy food that has the famous Matson touch. You move from outdoor sports to indoor games, spend your evenings at the movies or night club, or watch the stars above a moonlit sea. ■ Plan to go this spring when Hawaii is at her loveliest and you have a wider choice of hotel accommodations. Be sure to book round trip and redouble your pleasure. *It's twice the fun to sail the* LURLINE *both ways.* See your Travel Agent or any Matson Lines office: New York, Chicago, San Francisco, Seattle, Portland, Los Angeles, San Diego, Honolulu.

THE LURLINE SAILS FROM SAN FRANCISCO AND LOS ANGELES ALTERNATELY

For the finest travel, the **LURLINE**...
for the finest freight service, the
Matson Cargo Fleet...to and from Hawaii

Matson Lines

Matson Lines advertisement, 1954

P & O, The British Cruise Line, 1970 advertisement features "Canberra" pattern china, a blue maze design on white body.

Courtesy of Cunard

Dining room on Cunard's *Aquitania*, 1920s

Sitmar advertisement, 1979;
"Fairwind" pattern

Courtesy of Cunard

Afternoon tea on Cunard's *Caronia* in the early 1950s

The setting for shipboard dining is matched only by the cuisine itself.

Sundecks and pool are designed for outdoor living at its best.

Resort at Sea

To

**BRAZIL
URUGUAY
ARGENTINA**

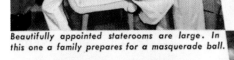

Beautifully appointed staterooms are large. In this one a family prepares for a masquerade ball.

How can you visit some of the most fascinating lands in the world and still enjoy the luxurious services of one resort hotel? The answer of course is to take a Delta Line cruise to South America. The sister ships, Del Norte, Del Sud and Del Mar are air-conditioned and feature the finest accommodations afloat today. Delta cruises sail from New Orleans every two weeks and the passenger list is limited to one hundred and twenty, ideal for shipboard social events.

For full information, see your travel agent.

Delta Line

MISSISSIPPI SHIPPING CO., INC., NEW ORLEANS

New York   Chicago   Washington
St. Louis   San Francisco   Los Angeles

Route of the Liners • DEL NORTE • DEL SUD • DEL MAR

Delta Line advertisement, 1957

French Line advertisement, 1952

French Line advertisement, 1951;
"Normandie" pattern

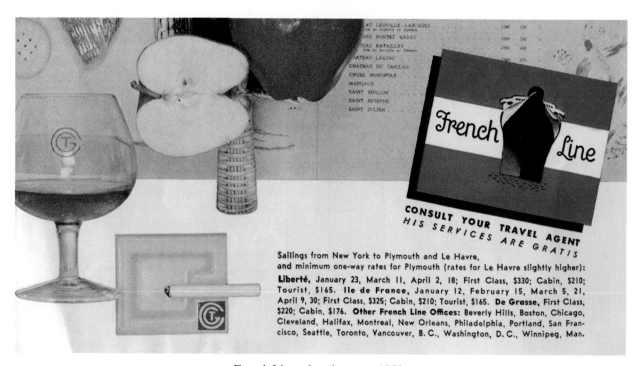

French Line advertisement, 1952

Welcome to Mark Twain's America

From 1811 to the turn of the century—in the great scheme of things, it's but a blink on the pages of history. In America it was the era of the paddlewheel steamboat —one of the first American inventions of world significance and one that was directly responsible for a period of unprecedented progress. From the Appalachians to the Rocky Mountains, it accelerated the development of the American frontier. The great inland rivers became the main highways, and anything from chickens to a dismantled merry-go-round could be waiting on the banks for shipment.

By 1825, steamboats travelled as much as a hundred miles a day, and to a generation dependent on the stagecoach or keelboat, they had revolutionary consequences. Within a few years of their introduction, villages grew into towns, towns became cities, and the course of American history was changed forever. The steamboat opened up a vast continent previously inaccessible other than on long overland treks through dangerous territory. In the

Robert Fulton, builder of the first steamboat.

At the turn of the century, a leisurely game of cards on deck was as much a part of Steamboatin' as it is today.

Courtesy of Delta Queen Steamboat Co.

span of just a few decades, long before trains became commonplace, the steamboat did more to advance American society than any other technological innovation—then or since. Then, as now, the magic of Steamboatin' held a special place in the hearts of the American people.

During the "Golden Age of Steamboatin'," paddlewheelers were much more than a means of transportation. By the standards of the day, they were incredibly fast and marvelously comfortable. Competition for passengers was so intense that every vessel went to extraordinary lengths to offer superior service,

exquisite cuisine and the most luxurious accommodations. There was also something incredibly special about the steamboat's influence on everyday life. Here was a vessel that brought the mail and critically important supplies. A "bale-boat" that transported cotton and other products to market. A showboat that provided dazzling entertainment. A floating palace that connected ports a thousand miles apart and fired the imagination of Mark Twain, who drew directly from his experiences as a steamboat pilot to create an uncannily accurate portrait of 19th-century America.

That portrait—the places and the people—can still be experienced in heritage-filled vacations aboard the steamboats of The Delta Queen Steamboat Co. Since 1890, the company has continued the uniquely American tradition of Steamboatin' at its best, offering memorable journeys on America's historic rivers. Journeys just like they used to be, and still are...aboard an all-American paddlewheel steamboat!

The J. M. White

The Great Steamboat Race of 1870 between the *Natchez* and *Rob't E. Lee*

Steamboatin'– the experience of a lifetime.

From the moment you step aboard, you enter a world far removed from today's fast-paced, jet-propelled society. Amid the atmosphere of an authentically detailed, all-American paddlewheel steamboat, time seems suspended. The gentle sound of the paddlewheel soothes and relaxes. And, as Mark Twain once described an early morning on the Mississippi, "the tranquility is profound and infinitely satisfying."

Here, as you float down one of America's great inland rivers at a lazy eight or nine miles per hour, it's easy to let your imagination run free and reflect on the amazing history witnessed along these waterways. Your journey may take you in the wake of explorers, pioneers, and settlers. Around the bend, a mist-shrouded Civil War monument may come into view. Upriver, the stately columns of an antebellum mansion might suddenly appear from behind moss-covered live oaks sweeping the shore.

"We have fallen in love with river cruising…this is a beautiful country, and there's nothing like seeing it from the deck of a steamboat."

Tom Gilpen *San Marcos, California*

Steamboatin' is rich in old-fashioned, friendly service.

Three glorious ways to see America's great rivers: Steamboatin' on the legendary *Delta Queen*, the magnificent *Mississippi Queen*, and the grand *American Queen*!

Food, glorious food! Your all-American steamboat crew serves four sumptuous meals a day, including a mouth-watering five-course dinner, and a tantalizing Moonlight Buffet–not to mention delightful treats like afternoon tea.

Courtesy of Delta Queen Steamboat Co.

As china patterns are discontinued and replaced, some of the current china shown
on this and the following pages will undoubtedly reach the secondary market.

Courtesy of Holland America Line

Holland American Line cruise ship dining room in 1996
brochure; china is decorated with current logo as shown on postcard at right.

Holland America Line's MS *Nieuw Amsterdam*, christened in 1983

Courtesy of Seabourn Cruise Line

Seabourn Cruise Line's room service and cafe pattern, 1995 brochure

Seabourn Cruise Line's dining room pattern, 1995 brochure

Seabourn Cruise Line's *Seabourn Pride*

Seabourn Cruise Line's *Seabourn Pride*
dining room, 1996 brochure

Seabourn Cruise Line's dining room pattern, 1996 brochure

Caravelle Dining Room on Dolphin Cruise Line's
SS *OceanBreeze*; Dolphin logo topmarked china shown on
tables and above, 1995 brochure.

Orient Lines' china topmarked with line logo, 1995
(*see logo on Ship Line Logos, Flags, and China Topmarks table*)

1996 Ivaran Lines' china topmarked with line flag
(white C on red flag with black pole; three red lines on rim)

Courtesy of Crystal Cruises

Crystal Cruises' Bistro and Crystal Dining Room china, 1995

Courtesy of Crystal Cruises

Crystal Dining Room, 1995

Courtesy of Crystal Cruises

Crystal Dining Room china, 1994; "Structura Gold" pattern on top of "Blue Medici" pattern "buffet plate" by Villeroy & Boch

Courtesy of Crystal Cruises

Celebrity Cruises' china topmarked with line logo, 1994

Courtesy of Crystal Cruises

Crystal Cruises' Palm Court china, 1995

China by Arabia used on the *Silja Serenade*,
an overnight ferry, owned by Silja Line, 1994

Cunard's *Royal Viking Sagafjord* dining room, 1995

Carnival Cruise Lines china, 1995:
"Nottingham Burgundy" stock pattern by Rego China

Cunard's *Royal Viking Sun* Garden Cafe, 1996

Cunard's *Royal Viking Sun* room service

Veranda on Cunard's *Royal Viking Sagafjord*, 1995

Cunard's *Royal Viking Sun* Garden Cafe

Courtesy of Cunard

Queens Room china on Cunard's *Queen Elizabeth 2*

Courtesy of Royal Doulton

Cunard's *Queen Elizabeth 2* china by Royal Doulton, 1995

Courtesy of Cunard

Cunard's silverplated flatware and hollow ware, 1996

Courtesy of Cunard

Cunard "QE2" pattern, 1993

Courtesy of Cunard

Queens Grill china on Cunard's *Queen Elizabeth 2*
1996; black band and gold lines with gold Cunard logo
(lion either with or without wreath and large crown)

Princess Cruises blue lined china, 1995

Princess Cruises advertisement, 1979

American President Lines advertisement, 1968

Captain's Gala Dinner.

Caspian Sevruga Malossol Caviar on Ice
Throne, American Dressing

Shrimp Cocktail, Louis Dressing

Liver Paté, Strasbourg

Fresh Fruit Cup with Triple Sec

•

Beef Consommé with Profiteroles

Cream of Tomato Soup

Petite Marmite Henry IV

•

Eleonora Salad, Balsamic Dressing

Ravioli, Porcini Mushroom Sauce

Broiled Rock Lobster Tail with Melted
Butter, Rice Pilaf

Baked Salmon en Croute,
Hollandaise Sauce,
Steamed Potatoes

Roast Royal Pheasant Flambé
with Cognac Souvaroff

Tournedos of Beef Tenderloin
Montmorency

•

Selection of Vegetables

•

Chocolate Souffle, Vanilla Sauce

Hazelnut Chocolate Cake

Coupe Jubilee

Petit Fours

•

Assorted Cheese Tray with Crackers

Fresh Seasonal Fruit Basket

•

Coffee – Tea – Espresso

Princess Cruises china and menu, 1994

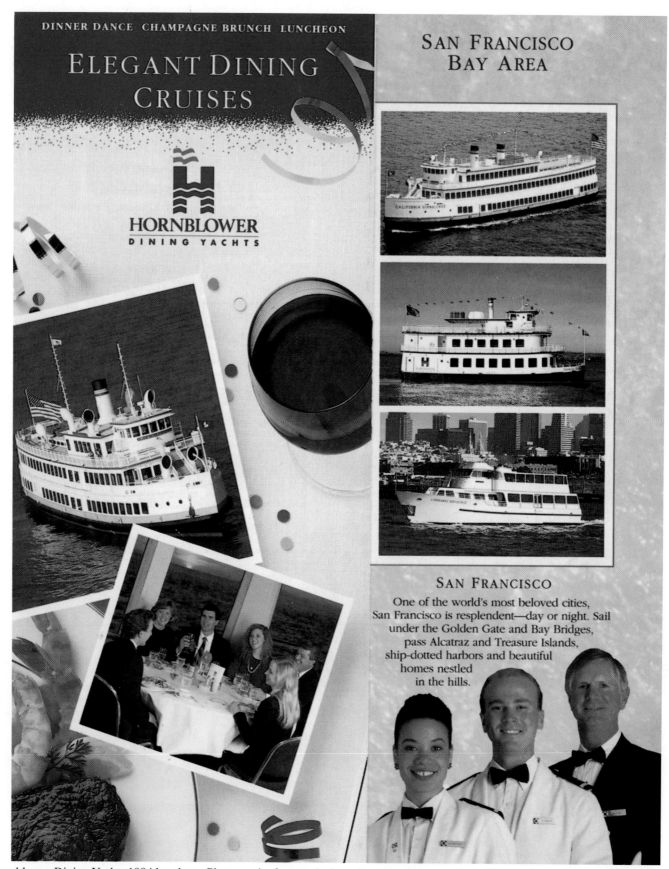

Hornblower Dining Yachts 1994 brochure. Photograph of topmarked service plate shown on Rego Corporation catalog page in Volume 3.

Ship China and Value Ranges

Pattern Names and Codes

Pattern names and codes (ship line or company code and dash number) as listed in *ButterPat World* by Richard W. Luckin are used here to promote continuity in the hobby. Many additional patterns were named by ship line and china expert Daniel Krummes of California and assigned an existing or new ship line or company code, as appropriate, and a sequential dash number.

Manufacturers

Although many patterns were produced by several manufacturers, in most cases only the maker of the photographed piece is noted.

China Backstamps

The manufacturer's name (usually shortened to one word) and manufacturer's trade name (if any; e.g., *Old Ivory*) are listed preceding the acronym "b/s" for backstamp. If the piece is also bottom marked with the ship line or company name, initials, flag, or logo, that information follows the manufacturer's name or tradename. "No b/s" indicates that the illustrated piece has neither a manufacturer nor a ship line or company backstamp.

Ship Usage of Stock Patterns

While ship usage of all illustrated stock patterns has been verified, each was undoubtedly used in at least some and possibly many restaurants, hotels, and other foodservice concerns. Proof that individual stock pattern pieces were actually produced for ship use is impossible to establish unless ware is backstamped with a ship line or company name, initials, logo, or flag. Without proof, value is reduced considerably. However, due to increased demand as ware representative of a particular ship line, the value is slightly higher than non-ship related stock patterns. *See definition of stock pattern and custom pattern in Introduction.*

Dates

Decades and date ranges refer to period in which the pattern was used by the ship line, unless otherwise indicated. Date codes are those marked on illustrated pieces.

Value Ranges

Each value range reflects the *illustrated piece only*: pattern, item, and size, as well as ship line or company backstamp or lack of same. Any variance can change the value considerably. Pieces are assumed to be in good condition without cracks, chips, or excessive wear.

Because the asking price of ship china varies greatly from source to source and region to region, it is difficult to offer accurate values. However in an attempt to be as realistic as possible, prices gathered from collector shops, transportation shows, and mail order lists, along with estimates offered by experts from various regions of the United States were combined and averaged. Final figures were reverified by additional ship china specialists. Again, please keep in mind that prices vary a great deal and that actual selling prices are ultimately determined by the requirements of the seller, along with the desire and willingness of the buyer. *Also see Factors in Determining Values in Introduction.*

Comments on individual values would be welcomed for value range listings in future editions.

Photographs

Photographs are in alphabetical order by ship line or company, then in date of usage order. Ship line souvenirs and advertising pieces appear at the end of the ship china photograph segment.

Alaksa Commercial Company "Goldrush" pattern 9½ long platter (ACC-1); John Maddock & Sons b/s; 1890s; $200.00 – 225.00.

Larry Paul Collection

Alaska Steamship Co. "Yukon" pattern 5" plate (ALS-1); Buffalo b/s; circa 1920s; $45.00 – 60.00.

Larry Paul Collection

Alcoa Steamship Co. "Alcoa Cavalier" pattern fruit (ALC-1); Syracuse b/s; 1960 date code; $30.00 – 40.00.

Larry Paul Collection

American Export Lines "Independence" pattern 9¼" long platter (AEL-2); stock pattern; Mayer and American Export Lines b/s; 1951 date code; $25.00 – 35.00 ship line b/s; $7.00 – 10.00 not ship line b/s.

Larry Paul Collection

American Export Lines "Signal Flags" pattern cocoa pot (AEL-3); flags spell out AEL (flags on larger pieces spell out American Export Lines); Mayer and American Export Lines b/s; 1952 date code; $90.00 – 110.00.

Jim Pratt Collection

American Export Lines "Exeter" pattern 4½" high pitcher (AEL-4); Mayer and American Export Lines b/s; 1960 date code; $18.00 – 22.00 ship line b/s; $9.00 – 12.00 not ship line b/s.

Larry Paul Collection

American Export-Isbrandtsen Lines "Constitution" pattern 10¼" service plate (AEIL-1); Sterling and American Export-Isbrandtsen Lines b/s; 1960s; $50.00 – 65.00+.

American President Lines "President Wilson" pattern butter (APL-1); Shenango b/s; circa late 1930s – early 1940s; $35.00 – 45.00.

American President Lines "APL Eagle I" pattern room service sugar (APL-2); made by Syracuse, though no manufacturer b/s; 1946 – early 1960s; $20.00 – 25.00.

American President Lines "APL Eagle II" pattern cup & saucer (APL-3); Pyroceram body; Corning and American President Lines b/s; 1960s – 1972 on passenger liners; may still be used on freighters; $30.00 – 40.00.

Larry Paul Collection

American Republics Line "Brazil" pattern logo close-up on 10" long celery (ARL-1); Syracuse Old Ivory b/s; 1947 date code; $30.00 – 40.00.

Larry Paul Collection

Baltimore Mail Line "City of Baltimore" pattern 7¼" plate (BML-1); Scammell Trenton b/s; circa 1930s; $35.00 – 45.00.

Larry Paul Collection

Baltimore Steam Packet Co. "Old Bay Line" pattern handled bouillon (SAL-10); Scammell Ivory Lamberton b/s; circa 1930s; $65.00 – 80.00.

Bowater Steamship Co. "Alice Bowater" pattern 8" plate (BOW-1a); John Maddock & Sons Ltd. b/s; circa 1940s; $25.00 – 35.00.

California Navigation & Improvement Co. "Stockton" pattern 9½" long platter (CN&I-1); John Maddock & Sons Ltd. b/s; circa early 1900s; $150.00 – 175.00.

Richard W. Luckin Collection

Canadian National Steamship "Maritime" pattern 9" long platter (CN-10); Theodore Haviland and Canadian National Railways b/s; 1928 – 1958 on West Indies service; $65.00 – 85.00.

Canadian National Steamship "Prince George" pattern (CN-16); either Royal Doulton (1938 date code) or Grindley Hotelware, along with Canadian National System b/s. Cream pitcher, $40.00 – 50.00; sauce or butter pot, $28.00 – 35.00.

Richard W. Luckin Collection

Canadian Pacific "Floral Oyster" pattern oyster (CP-12.1); Spode and Canadian Pacific Ocean Services b/s; pattern registered 1913; used on transatlantic ships; $80.00 – 100.00.

Canadian Pacific British Columbia Coastal Steamships "Empress" pattern 6½" plate (CP-11); Grindley Duraline and B.C.C.S. b/s; 1920s – 1930s; pattern also used on Canadian Pacific's transatlantic and transpacific service and b/s accordingly; $40.00 – 50.00.

August Riccono Collection

The Charente Steamship Co. Ltd. "Statesman" pattern cup & saucer (CSC-1); Nesbitt & Co. Ltd. b/s; circa 1930s; $55.00 – 70.00.

Larry Paul Collection

Chesapeake Steamship Co. "Chesapeake Steamship" pattern cake cover (SR-3); no b/s; circa 1930s; $95.00 – 110.00.

Chevron Shipping Co. "San Francisco" pattern saucer (CHV-1); ware may also have been used in company cafeteria or executive dining room; Mosa b/s; circa 1980s. Saucer, $11.00 – 14.00; cup & saucer, $22.00 – 30.00.

Larry Paul Collection

Cleveland and Buffalo Transit Co. (C & B Line) "City of Erie" pattern saucer (C&B-1); O.P.CO. b/s; 1906 date code. Saucer, $30.00 – 35.00; cup & saucer, $80.00 – 100.00.

Clipper Line (of Sweden) "Stella Polaris" pattern souvenir (CLP-1); Rorstrand b/s; 1969 date code; $9.00 – 11.00.

Larry Paul Collection

Clyde Line "Clyde" pattern 8¾" long platter (CLY-1c); Iroquois b/s; 1910s – 1920s; $75.00 – 95.00.

Larry Paul Collection

Colonial Line "Lexington" pattern 12½" long platter (COL-1); Warwick b/s; circa 1920s; $60.00 – 75.00.

Commodore Cruise Line "Boheme" pattern 10¼" plate (CCL-1); Homer Laughlin b/s; 1986 date code; $18.00 – 24.00.

Larry Paul Collection

Delta Queen Steamboat Co "Delta Queen" pattern 10½" plate (DLT-1); Mayer and Delta Queen Steamboat Co. b/s; circa 1980s; $22.00 – 28.00.

Larry Paul Collection

Delta Queen Steamboat Co. "Mississippi Queen" pattern 10¾" service plate (DLT-2); Syracuse b/s; 1987 date code; $40.00 – 50.00.

Larry Paul Collection

Detroit and Cleveland Navigation Co. "City of Detroit" pattern 6½" high pitcher (D&CN-1); handle behind pitcher; no b/s; circa 1900 – 1910s; pattern also used by predecessor, Detroit and Cleveland Steam Navigation, 1880s – 1890s; $200.00 – 250.00.

August Riccono Collection

Detroit & Cleveland Navigation Co. "Greater Detroit" pattern cream pitcher (D&CN-2); no b/s; circa 1930s; $40.00 – 50.00.

August Riccono Collection

Dollar Steamship Line "President Hoover" pattern double-egg cup (DOL-1); made by Syracuse, though not b/s; late 1920s – 1930s; $80.00 – 100.00.

Eastern Steamship Lines "Eastern Green" pattern double-egg cup (EAS-1); made by Buffalo, though no b/s; 1920s; $50.00 – 60.00.

Elders & Fyffes Ltd. "Golfito" pattern A.D. cup & saucer (E&F-1); Dunn Bennett & Co. b/s; circa 1950s; $60.00 – 80.00.

Empress Cruise Lines "Empress Cruise" pattern cup (ECL-1); Victoria Porcelain b/s; mid-1990s. Cup, $9.00 – 12.00; cup & saucer, $18.00 – 24.00.

Epirotiki Lines "Oceanos" pattern A.D. cup & saucer (EPL-1); Grindley Duraline b/s; 1977 date code; $30.00 – 40.00.

Farrell Lines "African Enterprise" pattern cup (FAR-1); Syracuse Syralite b/s; 1969 date code. Cup, $18.00 – 24.00; cup & saucer, $40.00 – 50.00.

French Line (Compagnie Générale Transatlantique) "Normandie" pattern cup (CGT-2a); Haviland b/s; 1935 – 1974. Cup, $65.00 – 75.00; cup & saucer, $135.00 – 165.00.

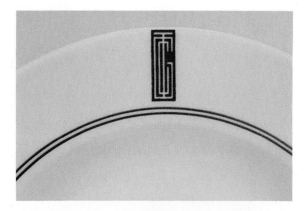

French Line (Compagnie Générale Transatlantique) "Ile de France" pattern 9" soup plate (CGT-3); GDA b/s; late 1940s – early 1950s; $70.00 – 90.00.

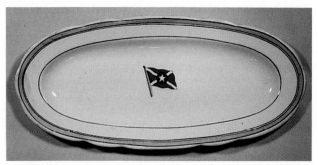

Larry Paul Collection

Great Northern Pacific Steamship Co. "Pacific Coast" pattern 10¼" long corn tray (GN-10); O.P.CO. b/s; 1916 date code; 85.00 – 100.00.

August Riccono Collection

Hamburg-South American Line "Monte Cervantes" pattern 8" plate (HSA-1); no b/s; circa 1920s – early 1930s; $90.00 – 110.00.

August Riccono Collection

Grace Line "Santa Barbara" pattern 6" high pitcher (GRA-2); Syracuse and Grace Steamship Co. b/s; 1942 date code; $125.00 – 160.00.

Larry Paul Collection

Hamburg-Atlantic Line "Hanseatic" pattern 4¼" long tray (HAL-1); Bauscher b/s; late 1950s – 1966; $20.00 – 25.00.

Hellenic Lines Ltd. "Hellenic Lines" pattern ashtray (HEL-2); Ionia Hellas b/s; circa 1970s; $14.00 – 18.00.

Larry Paul Collection

Holland America Line "Diamond NASM" pattern 2½" high egg stand (HOL-1); stylized gold NASM (Nederlandsch-Amerikaansche Stoomvaart Maatschappij) logo; Mosa b/s; circa 1950s; $30.00 – 40.00.

Holland America Line "Rotterdam" pattern 8" pickle (HOL-2); gold NASM (Nederlandsch-Amerikaansche Stoomvaart Maatschappij) script initials; Mosa b/s; 1970 date code; $25.00 – 30.00.

Home Lines "Oceanic" pattern 9½" plate (HOM-1); Richard Ginori b/s; circa 1980s; $18.00 – 22.00.

International Mercantile Marine Co. "Panama Pacific" pattern 6¼" plate (IMMC-1); Buffalo b/s; 1920s – early 1930s; $60.00 – 85.00.

Jim Pratt Collection

Italian Line "Rex" pattern cup & saucer (ITL-1); cabin or second class pattern; Richard Ginori b/s; 1936 date code; though cup is shown on plain saucer, value is for decorated; $60.00 – 75.00.

August Riccono Collection

Italian Line "Roma" pattern A.D. cup & saucer (ITL-2); Richard Ginori b/s; 1939 and 1940 date codes; $75.00 – 95.00.

Italian Line "Giulio Cesare" pattern saucer (ITL-3); Schönwald b/s; circa 1950s – 1960s. Saucer, $20.00 – 25.00; cup & saucer, $45.00 – 60.00.

Knutsen O.A.S. "Knutsen" pattern butter (KNU-1a); Fuji Trading Co. b/s; $24.00 – 30.00.

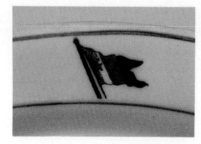

Larry Paul Collection

Mallory Line "San Marcos" pattern 7¼" long platter (MAL-3); McNicol b/s; circa 1910s – 1920s; $60.00 – 80.00.

August Riccono Collection

Wilh Jebsen "Atlantic" pattern cup (WJT-1); handle behind cup; M King & Co., The Pottery, North Shields b/s; circa 1920s. Cup, $15.00 – 20.00; cup & saucer, $35.00 – 45.00.

Luckenbach Line "Edgar Luckenbach" pattern 7¼" plate (LUC-1); McNicol b/s; circa 1930s; $28.00 – 35.00.

August Riccono Collection

Manitou Steamship Company "Manitou Chief" pattern A. D. cup & saucer; red decoration (MAN-1a); orange decoration (MAN-1b); Union Porcelain Works b/s; circa 1890s; $250.00 – 275.00+.

Jim Pratt Collection

Matson Lines "Matsonia" pattern 8" long platter (MAT-2); Wood & Sons Ltd. and S.S. Matsonia b/s; 1922 date code; $85.00 – 100.00.

Matson Lines "Lurline" pattern 12" long silver-plated platter (MAT-1); International Silver Co. b/s; 1926 date code; $50.00 – 65.00.

Larry Paul Collection

Merchants and Miners Transportation Co. "Chatham" pattern 6¼" plate (MMTC-2); Scammell Trenton b/s; circa late 1920s; $50.00 – 65.00.

Larry Paul Collection

Moore-McCormack Lines "Rio" pattern celery (MML-1); Sterling and Moore McCormack Lines b/s; circa 1950s; $45.00 – 60.00.

August Riccono Collection

NYK Line (Nippon Yusen Kaisha) "Kamakaura Maru" pattern A.D. cup & saucer (NYK-2); Sango b/s; $45.00 – 60.00.

Jim Pratt Collection

NYK Line (Nippon Yusen Kaisha) "Nitta Maru" pattern rice bowl (NYK-3); Mino and NYK logo b/s; $24.00 – 30.00.

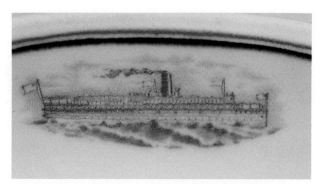

Larry Paul Collection

Norfolk and Washington Steamship Co. "Southland" pattern 10¼" platter (N&WSC-2); Scammell Lamberton b/s; circa 1920s; $100.00 – 125.00.

North German Lloyd (Norddeutscher Lloyd) "Dresden" pattern cream pitcher (NGL-2); Bauscher b/s; dated 1938; $65.00 – 85.00.

Norwegian American Cruises "Fjord Club" pattern peanut holder (NAC-2); Porsgrund and NAC b/s; early 1980s; $9.00 – 12.00.

August Riccono Collection

North German Lloyd (Norddeutscher Lloyd) "Kaiser Whilhem II" pattern mug (NGL-5); no manufacturer or ship line b/s; pre-1915; $75.00 – 95.00.

Norwegian American Cruises "Vistafjord" pattern ashtray (NAC-1); Pillivuyt b/s; 1981 date code; $9.00 – 12.00.

Larry Paul Collection

Ocean Steamship Co. of Savannah "Savannah" pattern A.D. cup (CG-2); handle behind cup; made by Buffalo, though no b/s; 1920s – 1930s. A.D. cup, $55.00 – 70.00; A.D. cup & saucer, $125.00 – 160.00.

Pacific Far East Line "Philippine Bear" pattern ashtray (PFEL-1); Syracuse Econo-Rim b/s; 1955 date code; $30.00 – 40.00.

Pacific Far East Line "Philippine Bear" pattern ashtray (PFEL-1a); Jyota b/s; 1950s – 1960s; $38.00 – 45.00.

Panama Line (Panama Railroad Steamship Co.) "Ancon" pattern " long plain white platter (PAN-2); Mayer and Panama Line /s; 1930s; $10.00 – 15.00.

Larry Paul Collection

Peninsular and Occidental Steamship Co. "SS Miami" pattern cream pitcher (FEC-9); John Maddock & Sons b/s; circa 1900s – 1910s; $150.00 – 200.00.

Larry Paul Collection

eninsular and Occidental Steamship Co. "Peninsular" pattern reamer (FEC-6); Buffalo Old Ivory b/s; circa 1930s; $75.00 – 00.00.

Pere Marquette "Autoferry" pattern cup (PM-1); Buffalo b/s; circa 1950s. Cup, $45.00 – 60.00; cup & saucer, $100.00 – 125.00.

Prudential Lines "Santa Magdalena" pattern 8" plate (PRD-1); Jackson b/s; 1978 date code; $22.00 – 28.00.

Rederi A.B. Transatlantic "Transatlantic" pattern 3" butter (RAB-1); Schönwald b/s; $24.00 – 30.00.

Rederiaktiebolaget Nordstjernan (Johnson Line) "Montevideo" pattern A.D. cup (RDN-1); handle behind cup; no b/s. A.D. cup, $10.00 – 15.00; A.D. cup & saucer, $25.00 – 35.00.

Rotterdamsche Lloyd "Baloeran" pattern egg stand (RDL-1); no b/s; 1930s; $30.00 – 40.00.

August Riccono Collection

Rotterdamsche Lloyd "Baloeran" pattern teapot (RDL-1); Mayer True Ivory b/s; 1930s; $80.00 – 100.00.

Royal Cruise Line "Crown Odyssey" pattern mug (RCRL-1); handle behind mug; Porsgrund b/s; 1982 date code; $12.00 – 15.00.

Royal Cruise Line "Golden Odyssey" pattern 4" butter (RCRL-2); Wedgwood b/s; 1980s; $10.00 – 12.50.

Royal Cruise Line "Royal Odyssey" pattern 6¾" plate (RCRL-3); Schönwald b/s; 1981 date code; $9.00 – 12.00.

Royal Viking Line "Royal Viking Sea" pattern cup (RVL-1); Mayer b/s; 1980s. Cup, $12.00 – 15.00; cup & saucer, $25.00 – 35.00.

Royal Viking "Royal Viking Sun" peanut holder (RVL-3); Porsgrund b/s; 1980s; $12.00 – 15.00.

Jim Pratt Collection

Royal Viking Line "Royal Viking Sky" pattern peanut holders; old logo (RVL-2); red logo (RVL-2a); Porsgrund b/s; 1985 and 1987 date codes; $11.00 – 14.00 each.

Salen Rederierna (Salen Line; Sven Salen A/B) "Salenia" pattern egg stand (SRE-1); Rorstrand b/s; 1932 date code; $25.00 – 32.00.

Sitmar Cruises; Richard-Ginori b/s; circa 1970s – 1988. "Fairwind" pattern bouillon & saucer (SIT-2), $40.00 – 50.00; ashtray, $9.00 – 12.00.

Sitmar Cruises "Fairwind" pattern 6" plate (SIT-2); Richard Ginori b/s; circa 1970s – l988; $20.00 – 25.00.

Star Clippers Inc. "Star Flyer" pattern cup (STR-1); Victoria Porcelain b/s; mid-1990s. Cup; $9.00 – 12.00. Cup & saucer; $18.00 – 24.00.

Southern Pacific Steamship Lines "Morgan Line" pattern (SP-8.2); stock pattern, 8" plate; McNicol and Southern Pacific S. S. Lines b/s; $90.00 – 110.00 ship line b/s; $9.00 – 12.00 not ship line b/s; sauceboat, no manufacturer b/s, $20.00 – 25.00 not ship line b/s.

States Line "California" pattern cup & saucer (STL-1); Sterling or Shenango b/s; 1970 and 1978 date codes; $30.00 – 40.00.

States Line "California" pattern 6¼" plate (STL-1); Jackson b/s; 1976 date code; $18.00 – 24.00.

Sun Line "Stella Solaris" pattern 6¼" plate (SNL-1); Richard Ginori b/s; circa 1980s; $18.00 – 22.00.

The Texas Co. "Texaco Michigan" pattern mug (TEX-1); Mayer b/s; circa 1940s; $125.00 – 175.00.

Ulysses Line "Calypso" pattern 9" long platter (ULL-1); J. H. Weatherby Falcon Ware b/s; 1979 date code; $18.00 – 22.00.

Union-Castle Line "Edinburgh Castle" pattern egg stand (UCL-1); no b/s; circa 1930s; $38.00 – 45.00.

Union Oil of California "Los Angeles" pattern 9" plate (UOC-1); Syracuse Syralite b/s; 1981 date code; $40.00 – 50.00.

United Fruit Co. "Castilla" pattern cream pitcher (UFC-3); Scammell Lamberton b/s; circa 1920s; $50.00 – 65.00.

Larry Paul Collection

United States Lines "Chapman" pattern butter (USL-1); Buffalo b/s; circa 1920s; $45.00 – 60.00.

Larry Paul Collection

United States Lines "Leviathan" pattern cream pitcher (USL-3); Jackson b/s; dated 1926; $75.00 – 95.00.

Larry Paul Collection

United States Lines "Manhattan" pattern soup (USL-4); Buffalo and United States Lines b/s; circa 1920s – 1930s; $60.00 – 80.00.

Larry Paul Collection

United States Lines "Manhattan" (USL-4); Buffalo and United States Lines b/s; circa 1920s – 1930s. Handled bouillon, $60.00 – 80.00; saucer, $35.00 – 45.00.

United States Lines "Kosher Service" pattern 7½" plate (USL-5); Mayer b/s; 1950 date code; $45.00 – 60.00.

Larry Paul Collection

United States Lines "Gray Star" pattern 6½" plate (USL-2); Sterling Lamberton and United States Lines b/s; 1952 – 1969; $24.00 – 30.00.

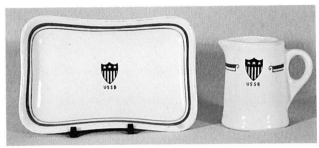

Jim Pratt Collection

United States Shipping Board "Centennial State" pattern (USSB-1); Shenango b/s. 1920s tray (1922 date code); $38.00 – 45.00. Cream pitcher; $65.00 – 80.00.

Larry Paul Collection

United States Shipping Board "Granite State" pattern cream pitcher (USSB-2a); no b/s; early 1920s; used on United States Lines ships; $80.00 – 100.00.

August Riccono Collection

Vaccaro Line (Standard Fruit & Steamship Co.) "Atlantida" pattern cream pitcher and saucer (VAC-1); Newport Pottery Co. Ltd. b/s; circa 1930s. Cream pitcher, $40.00 – 50.00; saucer, $20.00 – 25.00.

Larry Paul Collection

Virginia Ferry Corporation "Princess Anne" pattern 6¾" baker (PRR-19); Warwick b/s; dated 1936; $35.00 – 45.00.

August Riccono Collection

White Star Line (transatlantic line) "Brownfield-White Star" pattern 7¾" plate (WSL-2); no manufacturer or ship line b/s; dated 8/1906; $400.00+.

August Riccono Collection

White Star Line (transatlantic line) "Celtic" pattern 8¾" plate (WSL-3); no manufacturer or ship line b/s; dated 8/1906; $400.00+.

August Riccono Collection

White Star Line (Great Lakes line) "Tashmoo" pattern sauce-boat (WSLGL-2); no b/s; early 1900s; $125.00 – 175.00.

Ship Line Souvenirs and Advertising Pieces

(Note — ashtrays may have been used aboard ship.)

American President Lines ashtray; no b/s; 1970s; $10.00 – 12.50.

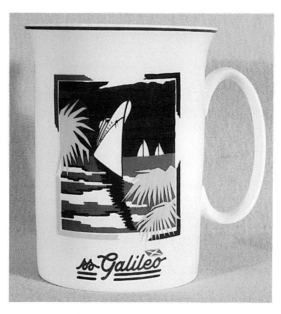

Chandris' SS *Galileo* (renamed SS *Meridan* in 1990) bone china souvenir mug; Roy Kirkham Staffordshire b/s; 1980s; $15.00 – 20.00.

Cunard's *Sea Goddess* 9" long souvenir; Hutschenreuther b/s; dated 1988; $14.00 – 18.00.

Cunard *QE2* world cruise captain's table souvenir 7" plate; Porsgrund b/s; dated 1989; $20.00 – 25.00.

French Line (Compagnie Generale Transatlantique) 4¼" souvenir; b/s not legible; circa 1930s – 1940s; $60.00 – 75.00.

German Atlantic Line 4" souvenir; Rosenthal b/s; late 1960s; $12.00 – 16.00.

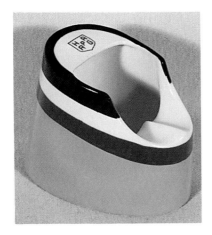

Hamburg-American Line (HAPAG – Hamburg Amerikanische Packetfahrt Aktien Gesselschaft) funnel ashtray; S.P.M. Walklure Bayreuth (First Bayreuth Porcelain) b/s; circa 1960s; $30.00 – 40.00.

Holland America Line ashtray; Mosa or Royal Sphinx b/s; 1960s; $15.00 – 20.00.

Holland America Cruises 8¼" souvenir plate; Bing & Grondahl b/s; dated 1979; $24.00 – 30.00.

Holland America Cruises 8¼" souvenir plate; Bing & Grondahl and Holland America b/s; dated 1981; $24.00 – 30.00.

Horn Blower Dining Yachts (San Francisco Bay) ashtray; no b/s; 1990s; $5.00 – 6.00.

Italian Line 3½" square tray; Verbano b/s; circa 1950s; $70.00 – 90.00.

Norwegian America Line MS *Sagafjord* 4" souvenir tray; Rosenthal Studio-Linie b/s; dated 1979; $9.00 – 12.00.

Orient Line ashtray; gold rim forms an "O"; "Orient Line" repeated in gold below rim; T.G. Green & Co. Ltd. b/s; circa 1960s; $18.00 – 22.00.

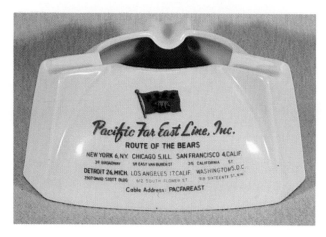

Pacific Far East Line ashtray; Jyota b/s; circa 1950s; $28.00 – 35.00.

Princess Cruises souvenir mug (although shown in use in 1994 cruise brochure); no b/s; 1990s; $6.00 – 8.00.

Royal Caribbean Cruise Line *Nordic Prince* ashtray; Schmidt Porcelana b/s; 1970s; $12.00 – 15.00.

Sitmar Cruises 8" souvenir plate; Richard Ginori b/s; 1980s; $18.00 – 24.00.

Sitmar Cruises ASTA '78 souvenir A.D. cup & saucer; Inter-American China b/s; dated 1978; $20.00 – 25.00.

Jim Pratt Collection

Swedish American Line pattern 3" high cream pitcher; no b/s; circa 1960s; reportedly sold in various sizes aboard ship; $25.00 – 32.00.

Swedish American Line ashtray; Made in Germany b/s; circa 1950s; $22.00 – 28.00.

Western Steamship Lines S.S. Azure Seas souvenir mug; Made In England b/s; early 1980s; $4.00 – 5.00.

Ship China Topmarks and Capsule Ship Line Histories

Use this list of initial and word topmarks to identify ship china. While thousands of topmarked ship patterns undoubtedly exist, the majority of the more common patterns are listed here, along with a small number of rare patterns.

For alphabetical purposes, the words "The," "Lines," and "Packet," and initials "SS" are disregarded. Initials precede full words. Should a topmark include both words and initials, it is generally listed alphabetically by the first letter of the first full word. In the case of superimposed initial china topmarks, it may be necessary to search for each letter alphabetically.

Where possible, words and initials are shown in a style and layout similar to that of the actual topmark. "Stylized initials" or "stylized type" in the description column indicates a variation of the type illustrated.

Additional ship china topmarks that have no initials or words are illustrated on the Ship Line Logos, Flags, and China Topmarks table, presented in alphabetical order by line or company name on pages following this list.

Brief ship line and company histories are presented here, because such information is extremely difficult to obtain; numerous references contain bits and pieces of often contradictory data, entire volumes yield minimal line information, and definitive references covering specific or multiple lines are often out of print. Using those works listed in the ship section bibliography, "facts" were compiled, compared, and analyzed. The results are offered here in the form of concise comments, in the hope that the information provides some assistance to the inquisitive reader. Year and decade date ranges refer to the period in which the respective line operated. A date range followed by an asterisk represents only the verifiable decades of operation; the line may have operated for years or decades before or after that period.

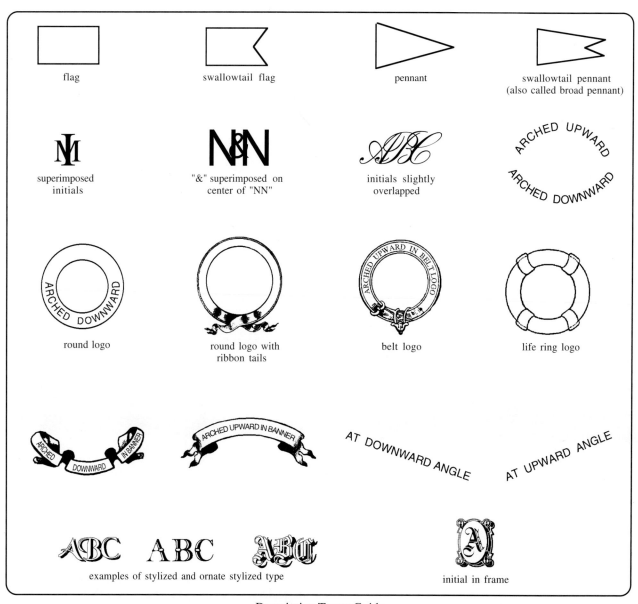

flag

swallowtail flag

pennant

swallowtail pennant
(also called broad pennant)

superimposed
initials

"&" superimposed on
center of "NN"

initials slightly
overlapped

ARCHED UPWARD
ARCHED DOWNWARD

round logo

round logo with
ribbon tails

belt logo

life ring logo

ARCHED DOWNWARD IN BANNER

ARCHED UPWARD IN BANNER

AT DOWNWARD ANGLE

AT UPWARD ANGLE

examples of stylized and ornate stylized type

initial in frame

Descriptive Terms Guide

Initials and Words	Description or Illustration	Line or Company Name and History
AB		American Banner Line; USA; 1958 – 1959; established by Arnold Bernstein, founder of the Bernstein Line of Germany (1926 – 1939); operated passenger service between New York and Amsterdam for less than two years; the line's only ship, *Atlantic*, was purchased by American Export Lines
A.C.Co.		Alaska Commercial Company; USA; 1867 – circa 1910; dominated the economic and political life of the Alaskan territory from 1870 to 1890; built trading posts and held a 20 year lease on the seal concession; offered San Francisco to Alaska passenger and freight service, with its heyday at the height of Alaskan gold rush in 1898
A D		Armement Deppe; Belgium; 1920s – 1960s*; freighter line
AG I	superimposed stylized initials inside circle	Atlantic, Gulf, and West Indies Steamship Lines; USA; 1907 – 1953; a holding company that owned and controlled several shipping lines including Clyde-Mallory Line, Porto Rico Line, Cuba Mail Line, and Southern Steam Ship Company
ANL	"ANL" in upper left section of flag; flag divided into rectangular four sections with rust colored cross	Australian National Line; Australia, 1956 – present
a p *L*	red logo; stylized initials on shield; halo of nine stars over shield; *see photograph*	American President Lines; USA; 1938 – present; originally the Dollar Line; taken over by the U. S. Maritime Commission in 1938 and renamed APL; offered transpacific ocean liner service until 1972; now (1996) operates freighters with 12 passenger limit to the Orient, as well as container ships
A R LINES		American Republics Line; USA; 1915 – 1958; initially backed by J. P. Morgan; associated with Moore-McCormack Lines, Inc.; passenger service between New York and South America began in 1915; took over ships previously operated by the defunct Munson Line in 1938; advertised as the "Good Neighbor Fleet" 1938+
ADIRONDACK PL	"PL" on flag in center of knotted rope logo; "Adirondack" above rope	People's Line; USA; 1835 – 1902; owned by C.W. Morse; operated steamboats at night on the Hudson River between various points in New York; merged with Citizen's Line to become the Hudson Navigation Company (1902 – 1926)
SS ADMIRAL FARRAGUT	arched upward in belt logo; swallowtail pennant inside logo	SS *Admiral Farragut* was built in 1898 and initially chartered by the Boston Fruit Company (USA; 1885 – 1899), which merged with several lines to become the United Fruit Company in 1899; china with topmark described at left used during Boston Fruit operation; the SS *Admiral Farragut* was later owned by the American Mail Steamship Company (not to be confused with the American Mail Line), purchased by the Pacific Alaska Navigation Company in 1912 and operated by their Admiral Line (1913+); she was sold for scrap in 1934

THE ADMIRAL LINE P.S.S.CO.		Admiral Line (Pacific Steamship Company); USA; 1916 – 1936; company formed by a merger of Pacific Alaska Navigation, Admiral Line's original holding company (1913+), and Pacific Coast Steamship Company; operated passenger and freight service between Seattle and San Diego; ships also carried automobiles during the 1930s and perhaps earlier; during 1935 – 1936 remaining 13 ships were sold for scrap or further use by various lines; although Pacific Steamship's Admiral Line flag is illustrated in *Brown's Flags and Funnels* © 1951, shipping activity after 1936 is unknown
ALASKA A STEAMSHIP CO	"Alaska" arched upward and "Steamship Co." arched downward in circle logo; "A" on flag in center of logo; logo superimposed on diamond shape; similar to the following logo	Alaska Steamship Company; USA; 1895 – at least 1965; offered passenger and freight service between Alaska and Seattle, 1895 – 1954; initially operated a single ship, *Willapa*, a 136-passenger and freight steamer; absorbed the Northwestern Steamship Company in 1907; operated the Black Ball Line, 1902 – 1927; advertised inter-Alaskan port freight service in 1965
ALASKA STEAMSHIP CO A THE ALASKA LINE		Alaska Steamship Company (*see information in previous entry*)
ALGOMA CENTRAL MARINE		Algoma Central Railway Marine Division; Canada; 1965 – 1990; operated self-unloading bulk carriers on the Great Lakes and oceans; became Algoma Central Corporation in 1990, which continues to offer freight service on the Great Lakes according to 1996 *Poor's Register*
ALLAN LINE	1) "Allan Line" arched upward in center of elaborately decorated star 2) "Allan Line" arched downward in banner below crest 3) "Allan" and "Line" alternate as part of ornate border design	Allan Line (Montreal Ocean Steamship Co., 1854 – 1897; Allan Steamship Co. Ltd., 1897 – 1909); Canada; transatlantic passenger and freight service; absorbed by the Canadian Pacific Railway in 1909
AMERICAN EXPORT	"American Export" arched upward around illustration of ship	American Export Lines; USA; 1924 – 1962 and 1973 – circa 1978; previously Export Steamship Corp., 1919 – 1924; freighter operations until 1931; operated transatlantic cargo-passenger liners, the "Four Aces," between New York and the Mediterranean; merged with Isbrandtsen Lines to become American Export-Isbrandtsen Lines, 1962 – 1973; reverted to American Export Lines, Inc.; listed in *Brown's Flags and Funnels* © 1982 with illustration of new flag (AEL in center of diamond with red stripe above and blue stripe below), however shipping activity is unknown
AMERICAN EXPORT E LINES		American Export Lines (*see information in previous entry*)

AMERICAN EXPORT ISBRANDSTEN LINES INC.	"American Export Isbrandtsen Lines Inc." arched upward around illustration of ship; *see photograph*	American Export-Isbrandtsen Lines; 1962 – 1973; formed by merger of Isbrandtsen Lines and American Export Lines; operated transatlantic cargo-passenger liners, the "Four Aces," between New York and the Mediterranean until 1965; offered Mediterranean and Caribbean cruises on the *Atlantic*, the *Constitution* and the *Independence*, which were laid up in 1967, 1968, and 1969 respectively; American Export-Isbrandtsen Lines subsidiary, First Atomic Ship Transport, operated NS *Savannah* as a cargo vessel and goodwill ambassador under the joint administration of the United States Maritime Commission and the Atomic Energy Commission, 1965 – 1970
AMERICAN HAWAIIAN S.S. CO. **A H**	"American Hawaiian S.S. Co." arched upward in belt logo with flag in center; "AH" on flag	American Hawaiian Steamship Company; USA; 1920s – 1950s*; operated transpacific freighter services
A M E R I C A N L I N E	"American Line" arched upward in round logo with ties at bottom	American Line (American Steamship Company); USA; 1872 – 1923; purchased by Red Star Line in 1884 and International Mercantile Marine Company in 1902; transatlantic passenger service; last two ships were sold to the Panama Pacific Line in 1923
AMERICAN MAIL LINE		American Mail Line; USA; 1926 – 1974; formed as a Dollar Steamship Company subsidiary to operate five *President* liners Dollar purchased from the United States Shipping Board (Admiral Oriental Line of Pacific Steamship Co. had been managing operator of these ships for the USSB since 1921); offered passenger and freight services between Seattle and the Orient; passenger services were suspended in 1938 and line was reorganized in 1939; operated cargo vessels thereafter; absorbed by American President Lines in 1974
Aquarama	stylized script	SS *Aquarama* operated by the Michigan-Ohio Navigation Company between Detroit and Cleveland on Lake Erie, 1956 – 1962; carried both passengers and automobiles; advertised "ocean liner comfort, beautiful lounges, spacious decks…" in 1957
𝕾.𝕾. 𝔄𝔯𝔩𝔦𝔫𝔤𝔱𝔬𝔫	𝕾.𝕾. 𝔄𝔯𝔩𝔦𝔫𝔤𝔱𝔬𝔫	SS *Arlington*, steamship owned and operated by the New England Fuel and Transportation Company, circa 1910s – 1920s
ATLANTIC **WJ**	"Atlantic" arched upward in belt logo with flag in center; "WJ" on flag; *see photograph*	Wilh Jebsen; Norway; 1920s*; became Wilh and Paul Jebsen in circa 1950s and Paul Jebsen in the 1960s; both of Wilh Jebsen's successors used a red flag with a "J" in the center
B	orange "B" in blue flag	Brodin Line (Erik O. Brodin); Sweden; 1950 – 1960s*; managed Rederi Poseidon A/B (1950 – present) and Rederi Disa A/B; operated freighters between Europe and Great Lakes
B SERVICE SINCE 1840		Baltimore Steam Packet Co. (Old Bay Line); USA; 1840 – 1962; owned by the Seaboard Air Line Railroad; operated on the Chesapeake Bay between Norfolk, Virginia, and Baltimore, Maryland
𝔅 & 𝔓 𝕾𝕾 𝔠𝔬.	"B & P" above and "S S Co." below flag; solid red circle in center of flag	Boston and Philadelphia Steamship Company; USA; 1873 – 1907; Atlantic Coast passenger service

B D B	"BDB" below crossed hammers inside circle in center of flag	Reederei Blumenfeld (Bernhard Blumenfeld); Germany; 1920s – 1950s*; freighter operation
B I S N C o	in banner below crest	British India Line (British India Steam Navigation Co.); Great Britain; 1862 – 1980s; operated passenger and freight service between Great Britain, East Africa, India, and Australia; became a subsidiary of Peninsular & Oriental of Great Britain in the mid-1930s, but continued to use its own line name and logo
BPC S	BPC	Baltimore Steam Packet Co. (Old Bay Line); USA; 1840 – 1962; owned by the Seaboard Air Line Railroad; operated on the Chesapeake Bay between Norfolk, Virginia, and Baltimore, Maryland
BSPCo	stylized script initials overlap	Baltimore Steam Packet Co. (*see information in previous entry*)
B. T. C.	B.T.C.	British Tanker Company (later Corporation); Great Britain; 1920s – 1950s*; tanker operation; associated with British Petroleum in later years
BTCo	stylized superimposed initials	Bradley Transportation Company; USA; 1923 – 1952; operated freighters on the Great Lakes; controlled by United States Steel since 1928; became a division of USS in 1952; use of Bradley Transportation Division name was discontinued when its fleet merged with USS Pittsburgh Steamship Division's fleet to become United States Steel Great Lakes Fleet in 1967
THE BANK LINE	in banner, below flag	Bank Line (Andrew Weir and Co. Ltd.); Great Britain; 1905 – present; worldwide freighter services; currently (1995) operates freighters with limited passenger accommodations on around-the-world sailings from Great Britain, as well as U.S. east coast to South America voyages
BIBBY LINE	in banner, below hand holding knife	Bibby Line (Bibby Bros. / Bibby Steamship Co. Ltd. / Bibby Bros. & Co.); Great Britain; 1850 – 1980s*; Bibby Bros. began operating between Liverpool and the Mediterranean in 1850; sold its ships to Frederick Leyland and Company in 1873; the Bibby Steamship Co. Ltd. was founded in 1891; offered passenger and freight service between Great Britain and Burma; carried British troops in four wars
BLACK DIAMOND STEAMSHIP CO. LIMITED	arched upward in belt logo with flag in center; black diamond on flag	Black Diamond Steamship Ltd.; Canada; circa 1880s – circa 1910; freighter operation
Boston and Bangor Steamship	stylized type below detailed illustration of vessel	Boston and Bangor Steamship Company; USA; 1834 – 1901; operated passenger service between Boston, Massachusetts, and Bangor, Maine; purchased by C. W. Morse and merged with several other Atlantic coastal lines to become Eastern Steamship Company; operated as Eastern's Bangor Line until 1932
THE BRITISH SHIPOWNERS CO. LIMITED	"The British Shipowners Co. Limited" arched upward in round logo; red and white flag in center	British Shipowners Co. Limited; Great Britain; mid-to-late nineteenth century; Australian immigrant service
Bull Lines	stylized type	Bull Lines (A. H. Bull and Company); USA; 1902 – mid-1960s; initially operated cargo ships between New York and Puerto Rico; began overnight passenger service between the Virgin Islands in 1923; took over the defunct Insular Line's Baltimore, Maryland–San Juan route in 1930; offered passenger service on the *Puerto Rico* between New York and Puerto Rico, 1949 – 1951; thereafter, operated cargo service only

C		Clyde Line; USA; 1844 – 1928; operated steamers on the east coast; by 1872 the line extended passenger and freight service to Galveston, Texas; C. W. Morse, in an attempt to create a shipping cartel, formed the Eastern Steamship Company in 1901 (a combination of numerous U.S. Northern Atlantic coastal lines) and purchased the Clyde Line, along with the Porto Rico Line, Ward Line, and Mallory Line in 1906; when the scheme failed in 1908, these lines were purchased by Atlantic, Gulf, and West Indies Steamship Co., a holding company; in 1928 AGWI merged Clyde Line with Mallory Line to form Clyde-Mallory Line, which operated until 1942
C		Columbia Transportation Company; USA; 1931 – 1957; successor of the Columbia Steamship Co. (1920 – 1931); offered freight service and cruises on the Great Lakes; merged with Oglebay Norton Co. and operated as its Columbia Transportation Division, 1957 – 1994
"C,,	"C..	Costa Line (Giacomo Costa fu Andrea); Italy; 1924 – circa 1983; purchased its first freighter in 1924; began passenger service between Genoa and South America in 1948; offered Caribbean cruises from 1968; became Costa Cruises and moved its head office to Miami, Flordia, in 1983 Costa Cruises; circa 1983 – present; note – quotation marks removed from ship funnels in the early 1990s; current advertising logo consists of the letter C, superimposed on eight-point star, surrounded by a circle
C	"C," superimposed with scroll lines, below crown	Cosulich Line (Societa Triestina di Navigazione); Italy; 1918 – 1932; passenger service between New York or Boston and ports in the Mediterranean; merged with Navigazione Generale Italiana and Lloyd Sabaudo to form Italian Line in 1932
C	white "C" on red swallowtail flag	Cromwell Line (American Atlantic Screw Steamship Company of Georgia, 1858 – circa 1871; New York and New Orleans Steamship Company, circa 1871 – 1902); USA; initially passenger and freight service between New York and Savannah and later between New York and New Orleans; the line's three remaining ships were purchased by Southern Pacific Steamship Lines in 1902
C	red "C" inside white diamond on blue swallowtail pennant	Cuyamel Fruit Company; USA; circa early 1900s – 1929; operated fruit cargo vessels between New Orleans and Central America; absorbed by the United Fruit Company in 1929
C	red flag	Ivaran Lines; Norway; 1925 – present; cargo ships with limited passenger service; increased passenger capacity to 88 in 1988; currently (1996) offer cruises on container ships from New Jersey or Miami to South American east coast ports
C.A.V.N.	large red initials on diagonally divided flag: blue on upper left and yellow on lower right	Venezuelan Navigation Company (Compania Anonima Venezolana de Navegacion); Venezuela; 1950s – 1980s*; transatlantic freighters
C&B LINE	1) stylized type 2) stylized type on shield; *see photograph*	C & B Line (Cleveland and Buffalo Transit Co.); USA; 1892 – circa 1941; operated Great Lakes cruises between Buffalo, Cleveland, Ontario, and eventually Chicago; its liner-like steamer, *Seeandbee*, sailed from 1913 to circa 1941; liquidated in 1945

CC PACKET CO.	stylized blue type; "Packet Co." superimposed on "CC"	Carnival City Packet Company; USA; pre-1920s; offered passenger service on the Mississippi River
cGT		French Line (Campagnie Générale Transatlantique, 1861 – 1972; Campagnie Générale Maritime, 1972 – present); France; 1861 – present; operated transatlantic passenger liners until 1974; became Campagnie Générale Maritime after merging with Messageries Maritimes in 1972; offered auto-ferry services in the Mediterranean until at least 1980; continues to maintain French cargo fleet
CGT		French Line (*see information in previous entry*)
CGT		French Line (*see information in previous entry*)
cGT	superimposed ornate initials	French Line (*see information in previous entry*)
C.L.F.	white initials on red and blue horizontally striped flag	Compania La Flecha de Navegacion; Spain; circa 1880s – 1890s; offered passenger and freight service from Spain to the Caribbean
CM	red superimposed initials inside white circle on red flag	China Mail Line (China Mail Steamship Company); USA and China; 1915 – 1923; operated three ships between San Francisco, Hawaii, and the Orient; ceased operations in 1923, primarily due to drug smuggling charges
C.N. & I. Co.		California Navigation and Improvement Co.; USA; late 1800s – 1927; ran sternwheelers on the San Joaquin and Sacramento rivers, as well as the San Francisco Bay between Stockton and San Francisco; built the famous *Delta King*; in 1927 California Transportation Company, which had owned controlling interest since 1922, purchased CN&I
CPNCO	stylized initials; "CO" superimposed on center of superimposed "C," "P," and "N"	Canadian Pacific Navigation Company; 1883 – 1901; operated small steamers on Puget Sound and the British Columbia coast; purchased by Canadian Pacific Railway in the 1880s; operations taken over by CPR in 1901 and renamed British Columbia Coast Steamship in 1904
CSSC0		Chesapeake Steamship Co.; late 1800s – 1941; originally the Powhatan Steamboat Company, 1841 – late 1800s; operated on Chesapeake Bay between Baltimore, Maryland, and several ports in Virginia; owned by Southern Railway, 1896 – 1941; merged with Baltimore Steam Packet (Old Bay Line) in 1941
cT	red superimposed stylized initials inside white circle on red pennant	Compania Trasmediterranea; Spain; 1920s – 1980s*; European ferry operation
CALIFORNIA TRANSPORTATION COMPANY C.T.Co.	"California Transportation Company" arched upward in ring logo with flag in center; "C.T.Co." on flag	California Transportation Company (River Lines); USA; 1875 – circa 1940; Captains Anderson and Nelson began transporting freight on the rivers in circa 1855 and formed C.T.C. in 1875; operated sternwheelers on northern California rivers and San Francisco Bay between Sacramento, San Francisco, and Stockton; oversaw the construction of and upon completion operated the *Delta King* and *Delta Queen*; purchased California Navigation and Improvement Company in 1927

Canadian National System	centered on framed maple leaf	Canadian National Steamships; Canada; 1918 – 1976; operated passenger and freight service in the Canadian Maritime provinces, as well as on the east and west coast of the United States; attempted to compete with Canadian Pacific Steamship passenger service between Seattle, Victoria, and Vancouver, 1930 – 1931, employing the five-deck *Prince* steamships, but failed; West Indies division sailed between Boston and Bermuda, Halifax and Havana, and so forth, 1925 – 1958; advertised Vancouver to Skagway, Alaska, cruise on the *SS Prince George* in 1965; renamed CN Marine in 1976; absorbed by Marine Atlantic, Inc. in 1986; Maritime Atlantic currently transports passengers, automobiles, large transport trucks and truck trailers, containers, and freight cars among the Maritime provinces
CANADIAN PACIFIC B.C.C.S.S.	"Canadian Pacific B.C.C.S.S." arched upward in belt logo with red and white checkered flag in center	British Columbia Coast Steamship; Canada; 1904 – circa 1970s; Canadian Pacific Railway purchased Canadian Pacific Navigation in the 1880s and took it over in 1901; new ships were ordered and the company name was changed to B.C.C.S.S.; operated *Princess* steamers in the British Columbia area
CANADIAN PACIFIC RAILWAY	"Canadian Pacific Railway" arched upward in belt logo with checkered flag in center	Canadian Pacific (*see information in next entry*)
CANADIAN PACIFIC RAILWAY cPR	"Canadian Pacific Railway" arched upward in belt logo; stylized "CP" superimposed on stylized "R" in center of logo	Canadian Pacific (Canadian Pacific Railway Company until 1915; Canadian Pacific Ocean Services, Ltd., 1915 – 1921; Canadian Pacific Steamships, Ltd., 1921 – 1968; CP Ships, 1968+); Canada; the CPR marine department operated on the Great Lakes, 1882 – 1968; purchased Canadian Pacific Navigation Company in the 1880s, took over its operations 1901 and changed the name to British Columbia Coast Steamship in 1904; inaugurated transpacific sailings (British Columbia to the Orient) on its *Empress* ships in 1891 and added Australia and New Zealand destinations in 1894; purchased Elder Dempster's Beaver Line fleet in 1903 and used its ships for immigrant service from Great Britain to Canada; absorbed the Allan Line in 1909; ships served in both WWI and WWII; began operating container ships in 1971; last passenger liner, *Empress of Canada*, was sold in 1972 to became Carnival Cruise Line's *Mardi Gras*; entered a joint container ship venture with Compagnie Maritime Belge in 1984
CANADIAN PACIFIC RAILWAY Co.	"Canadian Pacific Railway Co." arched upward in belt logo with checkered flag in center	Canadian Pacific (*see information in previous entry*)
CHAMPLAIN TRANSPORTATION COMPANY	"Champlain Transportation Company" in banner below complex graphic including anchor on shield below ship, flanked by a sailor on left and right	Champlain Transportation Company; USA; 1826 – 1937; operated sidewheelers on Lake Champlain; controlled by the Delaware and Hudson Railroad 1868+
THE CHARENTE STEAMSHIP Co LTD	1) "The Charente Steamship Co. Ltd." arched upward in belt logo with red and white flag in center; *see photograph* 2) "The Charente Steamship Co. Ltd." arched downward in banner below red and white flag	Charente Steamship Company (Thomas and James Harrison Ltd.); Great Britain; circa 1830 – circa 1940s; operated global freighters

CHESAPEAKE AND OHIO RAILWAY TRAIN FERRY SERVICE	illustration of ship on lake between the words "Chesapeake and" and "Ohio Railway"; "Train Ferry Service" below ship	Chesapeake and Ohio Railway Train Ferry Service; USA; 1957 – 1973; originally a Pere Marquette Railway operation, it was taken over by C & O Railway ten years after the two lines merged in 1947; operated auto-ferries on Lake Michigan; taken over by Chessie System in 1973; purchased by Michigan-Wisconsin Transportation Co. in 1983; various routes were discontinued between 1980 and 1990, however ferries were still operating in the early 1990s
Chevron	**Chevron**	Chevron Shipping Co.; USA; circa 1970s – present; operates tankers; previously Standard Oil of California
CHINA UNION LINES	"China Union Lines" opposite red, white, and blue vertically striped flag	China Union Lines; Taiwan; circa 1980s – present; operates freighters
CLIPPER LINE	"Clipper Line" arched downward below logo	Clipper Line; Sweden; 1952 – 1969; offered cruises on the yacht-like *Stella Polaris* from New Orleans to the West Indies, Caribbean, Mediterranean, or Scandinavia; purchased the Incres Line of Panama in 1964; shape of shield and spear is identical on Clipper Line and Incres Line china topmarks; note — this line is not associated The Clipper Line of the Wisconsin and Michigan Steamship Co., 1934+, or the Clipper Cruise Line, 1983+
THE CLIPPER LINE	"The Clipper" arched upward and "Line" arched downward in red life ring logo with nautical artwork in center; logo superimposed on blue rectangular illustration of lake	Clipper Line (Wisconsin and Michigan Steamship Co.); USA; 1934 – at least 1990; established by a merger of the Wisconsin and Michigan Transportation Company (1925 – 1934) and the Michigan Salt Transportation Company; advertised "auto-tourist route across Lake Michigan" on the SS *Milwaukee Clipper* (1941 – 1970; now a floating exhibit on Lake Michigan) between Milwaukee, Wisconsin, and Muskegon, Michigan, in the 1950s and 1960s
C COLONIAL LINE	white "C" inside circle in center of flag; four stars, one in each corner of the flag; "Colonial Line" below flag; *see photograph*	Colonial Line; USA; 1910 – 1942; operated between New York City and Providence, Rhode Island
COLUMBUS LINE	below silhouette of ship	Columbus Line; Germany; division of Hamburg Sud Amerika (1871 – present); currently (1995) operates freighters with limited passenger accommodations from Florida, through the Panama Canal, or Los Angeles to Australia and New Zealand
COMMODORE CRUISE LINE	"Commodore Cruise Line" below illustrated logo; *see photograph*	Commodore Cruise Line; 1966 – present; offers Caribbean and Central American cruises; owned by Effjohn International 1987 – 1995; temporarily merged with B.S.L. Cruises and Crown Cruise Lines while those lines were under Effjohn ownership, however all lines retained separate identities; Effjohn sold Commodore to Miami investors in 1995
Commodore The Happy Ships *Cruises*	*Commodore* The Happy Ships *Cruises*	Commodore Cruise Line (*see information in previous entry*)

COMPANHIA DE NAVEGACAO LLOYD BRASILEIRO	arched upward in round logo with flag in center	Lloyd Brasileiro Patrimonio Nacional (Lloyd Brasileiro Navigation Company); Brazil; 1890 – present; formed by a merger of Brazilian government subsidized lines; operates South American coastal and transatlantic passenger and freight service
H CONCORDIA LINE	"H" in flag; "Concordia Line" below flag	Christian Haaland (Concordia Line); Norway; 1920s – 1980s*; operated freighters
COSENS & COMPANY LIMITED	arched upward in belt logo with flag in center; three horizontal stripes on flag with solid circle on center stipe	Cosens and Co. Ltd.; Great Britain; 1845 – 1950s; originally Weymouth, Bournemouth & Swanage Steam Packet Co.; operated passenger and freight service in the English Channel between British and French ports; offered day trips in the same area during the latter years
THE CUNARD STEAM SHIP COMPANY LIMITED	logo: 1880 – at least 1960s	Cunard Line (British and North American Royal Mail Steam Packet Company, 1840 – circa 1880s; Cunard Steam Ship Co., circa 1880s – 1934; Cunard White Star, 1934 – 1950; Cunard, 1950 – present); Great Britain; 1840 – present; began transatlantic mail and passenger service in 1840; merged with White Star Line in 1934; Cunard's most famous passenger liners, *Queen Mary* (1937 – 1967) and *Queen Elizabeth* (1938 – 1968), transported numerous troops during WWII; transatlantic passenger service was primarily replaced by cruises in the 1970s; the *Queen Elizabeth II* (QE2, 1969 – present) served in the Falklands War in 1982; Cunard purchased Norwegian American Cruises (NAC) in 1983 and referred to it as Cunard NAC until circa 1990 when NAC was dropped from the name; marketed Effjohn's Crown Cruise Line ships, known as Cunard Crown Cruise Line, since 1993; bought Royal Viking Line, now known as Cunard Royal Viking, in 1994
CUNARD	**CUNARD**	Cunard Line (*see information in previous entry*)
D&C	1) **D&C** 2) white stylized script initials on cobalt blue flag; *see photograph*	D & C Lake Lines (Detroit and Cleveland Navigation Company); USA; 1898 – 1951; succeeded the Detroit and Cleveland Steam Navigation Company (1868 – 1898); operated luxurious passenger steamships on the Great Lakes; offered cruises with stops at Buffalo, Niagara Falls, Cleveland, Detroit, Chicago, Mackinac Island, and St. Ignace
DFDS	overlapped initials	United Steamship Company (Det Forenede Dampskibsselskab); Denmark; 1866 – present; initially operated between Great Britain and Denmark; owned and operated 16 container ships and 12 passenger ships in the Atlantic, Baltic Sea, North Sea, and Mediterranean in the 1980s; owned Scandinavian World Cruises (1980 – 1983), whose *Scandinavia* carried 1600 passengers and 400 cars between New York and the Bahamas every five days
DAY LINE	on center stripe of swallowtail pennant	Hudson River Day Line; USA; 1863 – 1980s; service originated in 1826 using barges owned by Abram Van Santvoord; line formed in 1863; advertised daily excursions between New York City and Albany on steel steamers with "magnificent scenery" in 1926; offered "150 mile full day excursions" on a 308 foot long steamship between New York City and Poughkeepsie in the 1960s

DAY LINE	cobalt blue type on white center stripe of swallowtail flag; red strip on top and bottom of flag	Hudson River Day Line (*see information in previous entry*)
Delta Line		Delta Line (Mississippi Shipping Co. 1919 – 1961; Delta Steamship Lines Inc., 1961+); USA; 1932 – 1980s; operated freighters between New Orleans and South America since 1919; Delta Line name introduced in 1932; began cruises from New Orleans to South America on "Del" passenger-cargo liners in 1940; service discontinued during WWII, but operated "Del" ships again, 1946 – 1967; purchased *Santa* liners from Prudential Line in 1978 and offered cruises from Vancouver, through the Panama Canal and around South America until 1983; thereafter Delta operated cargo-only container ships
DET OSTASIATISKE KOMPAGN	"Det Ostasiatiske Kompagn" below blue and white flag; flag has chained anchor on right and "OK" on lower left	East Asiatic Company Ltd. (Det Ostasiatiske Kompagn); Denmark; late 1800s – 1980s*; advertised services from Baltic and North European ports to Bangkok in 1909; offered transatlantic services 1946 – 1952; later sailed from Denmark to India, Australia, and the Far East and other worldwide destinations
DOLLAR STEAMSHIP LINE $		Dollar Steamship Company; USA; 1901 – 1938; named after its founder, Robert Dollar; began hauling lumber on a steam schooner six years before the company was organized; offered transatlantic, transpacific, and worldwide passenger voyages, 1910+; acquired ten *President* liners from the United States Shipping Board in 1926 (Pacific Mail Steamship Co. and Admiral Oriental Line of Pacific Steamship Co. had been managing operators of these ships for the USSB since 1921); Dollar formed American Mail Line in 1926 to operate five of the *President* liners; after bankruptcy and reorganization, Dollar Steamship became American President Lines in 1938
DOMINION LINE	"Dominion Line" in banner below red pennant or flag; blue dot inside white diamond in center of pennant or flag	Dominion Line (Liverpool and Mississippi Steamship Co., 1870 – 1872; Mississippi and Dominion Steamship Co., 1872 – 1894; British & North Atlantic Steam Navigation, 1894 – 1921); USA; 1870 – 1926; initially involved in cotton trade between New Orleans and Great Britain; began a Canadian route in 1871; operated transatlantic passenger service between Canada and Great Britain; purchased by International Mercantile Marine Company in 1902; began White Star-Dominion Line Joint Service in 1909; though all remaining Dominion ships were transferred to the Leyland Line in 1921, White Star-Dominion Line Joint Service continued until 1926, when White Star Line was purchased by Royal Mail Steam Packet Company
E	 cobalt blue and white	Hellenic Lines; Greece; 1934 – 1983; operated freighters; do not confuse with the original American Export flag, which is red and white with a blue "E" and has no stripes
E.I.N.	cobalt blue initials on white horizontal center stripe of flag	Empresa Insulana de Navegaco; Portugal; 1950s – 1960s*; operated passenger ships from Portugal to the Azores (Portuguese islands, approximately 1500 miles west of Portugal)
ENE	blue initials in red outlined pennant	Empresa Nacional Elcana de la Marina Mercante; Spain; 1950s and 1960s*; operated freighters

EASTERN STEAMSHIP LINES INC.		Eastern Steamship (Eastern Steamship Company, 1901 – 1909; Eastern Steamship Corporation, 1909 – 1917; Eastern Steamship Lines, 1917 – 1954); USA; 1901 – 1954; C. W. Morse combined Portland Steam Packet Co., Boston and Bangor Steamship Co. (Bangor Line, to 1932), International Steamship Co., and other lines operating on the northern Atlantic coast (Boston to Canadian Maritime Provinces) to form Eastern; many of the companies continued to operate under their original line names; the Metropolitan Steamship Company joined Eastern in 1911 and operated as the Metropolitan Line to 1941; Old Dominion Line was purchased in 1923; Eastern offered U.S. east coast passenger services, including Yarmouth summer and Caribbean winter sailings; all ships were taken over for war services; the *Evangeline* and *Yarmouth* resumed the Yarmouth route in 1947; the line's last two ships, along with the line name were sold in 1954; china topmarked with logo at left circa 1920s – 1930s Eastern Steamship Lines (Eastern Shipping Corp.); USA; 1954 – 1986; initially offered cruises from Miami to Havana and Nassau; concentrated on the Caribbean, 1960s – 1980s; formed Western Steamship Lines in 1980 (sailed from San Pedro to Ensenada); Eastern Steamship, Western Steamship, and Sundance Cruises merged to form Admiral Cruises in 1986
E̲ASTERN STEAMSHI**P** LINES INC.	E̲ASTERN STEAMSHI**P** LINES INC.	Eastern Steamship Company; USA; 1901 – 1953 (*see information in previous entry*); china topmarked with logo at left used in 1920s
E & F ELDERS & FYFFES L^TD	 cobalt blue flag; "Elders & Fyffes Ltd." in banner below flag	Elders and Fyffes Ltd.; Great Britain; circa late 1800s – present; associated with United Fruit Company in 1903; purchased ships from that company in 1957; operates refrigerated cargo vessels with limited passenger service between England, Central America, the West Indies, and the Caribbean
JRE HALL LINE ELLERMAN'S HALL LINE	"JRE" on pennant above flag; "Hall Line" on flag; "Ellerman's Hall Line" in banner below flag	Ellerman's Hall Line (Ellerman Lines Ltd.); Great Britain; 1901 – at least 1960s; operated freighters between Great Britain, India, and Africa; "JRE" in pennant represents John R. Ellerman, the line's owner
EPIROTIKI LINES PIRAEUS	"Epirotiki Lines" in stylized type inside oval; "Piraeus" at lower right of oval; *see photograph*	Epirotiki Lines; Greece; roots from 1850s; owned by the Greek Potamianos family; offered Aegean cruises as early as 1930 and in 1954 began regularly scheduled cruises in that area; operated 10 cruise ships (owned and chartered) in the 1980s and six in the 1990s; merged with Sun Line Cruises to form Royal Olympic Cruises in 1995, but continues to use the Epirotiki name and logo in 1996

Esso		Standard Oil Company; New Jersey and New York, USA / multinational; 1892 – 1972; operated oil tankers on the Great Lakes, as well as worldwide; line flag was blue with a white "S" in the center through at least the 1920s; by 1950 (and perhaps as early as 1930) the company used a white flag with "Esso" enclosed in an oval in the center; a new logo, Exxon, was designed in 1966, but apparently was not used until 1972 when Standard Oil became the Exxon Corporation and the shipping division known as Exxon Transportation Co. (note —Esso logo was also used by Transportadora de Petroleos of Brazil, Ostlandske of Norway, Esso Transportation Co. Ltd. of Great Britain, Panama Transport Co. of Panama, and others; still in use by Esso Petroleum Co. Ltd. of Great Britain and perhaps others)
FALL RIVER LINE		Fall River Line; USA; 1847 – 1937; began as the Bay State Steamboat Company in 1847; operated overnight steamers between Fall River and other locations in Massachusetts including Martha's Vineyard; owned by New York, New Haven & Hartford Railroad, 1892+; managed by the New Haven railroad Marine District, 1898+; merged with several lines and operated as New England Navigation Company, 1904 – 1912, and New England Steamship Company, 1912 – 1937
FALL RIVER LINE		Fall River Line (*see information in previous entry*)
Ford	stylized script type; with or without surrounding oval; rotunda illustrated in center of some large pieces	Ford Motor Company, Marine Division; USA; 1924 – 1989; operated steamships on the Great Lakes from the Dearborn, Michigan, Ford plant; managed by Rouge Steel Company, a Ford subsidiary, 1982 – 1989; fleet purchased by Lakes Shipping, an Interlake Steamship subsidiary, in 1989; china pattern used on ships, as well as in company executive dining rooms and possibly cafeterias
F FURNESS LINE	white "F" in center of blue swallow-tail pennant; "Furness Line" in banner below pennant	Furness Lines; Great Britain; operated steamships from Britain to North America in the late 1800s; merged with two other lines in 1896 to form the Wilson & Furness-Leyland Line Ltd.; became Furness, Withy, and Co. Ltd. in early 1900s; purchased George Warren & Company (1865+) in 1912, renamed it Furness-Warren Line and offered passenger service between Great Britain, New Foundland, Nova Scotia, and Boston until 1962; the Furness-Bermuda Line offered Bermuda-Nassau cruises, 1919 – 1960s; Furness, Withy & Co. advertised regular sailings from the Great Lakes to Great Britain in 1960s; the large Furness Withy Group operated a number of lines, offering worldwide passenger and cargo services until circa 1970s
GL	superimposed squared initials	Great Lakes Steamship Company; Inc., USA; 1911 – 1957; established through the merger of six companies; operated steamers on the Great Lakes; fleet purchased by Wilson Marine Transit Co.
GTP		Grand Trunk Pacific Steamship Co.; Canada; 1910 – 1920; operated passenger steamers between Seattle, Washington, Vancouver Island, British Columbia, and Alaska

G.T.P	stylized script initials	Canadian National's trainferry, SS *City of Grand Rapids* used this pattern in circa 1970 according to *Dining on Rails* by Richard W. Luckin; Grand Trunk Pacific Railway also used this china pattern on trains in early 1900s.
GEORGIAN BAY LINE	below funnel; funnel partially superimposed on half-circle of stars	Chicago, Duluth, and Georgian Bay Transit Company; USA; 1913 – 1967; known as Georgian Bay Line since 1934; operated cruises on liner-like steamships on the Great Lakes between Buffalo, Cleveland, Detroit, Duluth, and Chicago; added Montreal via the Saint Lawrence Seaway in latter years
THE GEORGIAN BAY LINE	in pennant below ship wheel; anchor and two ships in center of ship wheel	Chicago, Duluth and Georgian Bay Transit Company (*see information in previous entry*)
GOODRICH STEAMSHIP LINES	GOODRICH STEAMSHIP LINES variation: inverted logo	Goodrich Steamship Lines (Goodrich Transit Company); USA; 1906 – 1933; succeeded the Goodrich Transportation Company, 1868 – 1906; operated freight and passenger ships on the Great Lakes; advertised "a week's cruise from Chicago through beautiful Green Bay to Mackinac Island, the Soo, North Channel, thirty thousand islands of Green Bay…" in 1914
gRACe	(GRACE logo)	Grace Line (W.R. Grace and Company); USA; 1892 – 1970; initially operated freighters between New York and South American ports; began United States east coast, around South America to U.S. west coast passenger-cargo service in 1913; operated the famous "*Santa*" liners from U.S. east or west coast ports, through the Panama Canal and around South American from 1919; in 1926 established Panama Mail Steamship Company, which became Grace-Panama Mail Line in 1930, to operate North, South, and Central America inter-coastal service; that service was abandoned in 1936, in favor of a weekly Caribbean route and Panama Mail was dropped from the line name; Grace also offered Caribbean cruises in the 1950s and 1960s; Prudential purchased a controlling interest in Grace Lines, which became Prudential-Grace Lines in 1970; Grace was removed from line name in 1974
GRAND TRUNK G. T. P. PACIFIC S. S. Co.	"Grand Trunk" arched upward and "Pacific S.S.Co." arched downward in round logo with maple leaf in center; "G.T.P." on bar superimposed across entire logo	Grand Trunk Pacific Steamship Co.; Canada; 1910 – 1920; operated passenger steamers between Seattle, Washington, Vancouver Island, British Columbia, and Alaska
GREAT NORTHERN STEAMSHIP CO.	(illustrated flag) "Great Northern Steamship Co." arched upward above illustrated flag	Great Northern Steamship Company; USA; 1900 – 1915; established by James Hill of Great Northern Railway; the SS *Minnesota* sailed on her first voyage from Seattle, Washington, to Japan in 1905; her final crossing was in 1915 and she was sold in 1917; the line also owned the *Dakota*, 1905 – 1907
• GUION • LINE •	in banner, superimposed on crossed flag poles, below American and British flag	Guion Line (Liverpool and Great Western Steamship Co.); Great Britain; 1866 – 1894; transatlantic passenger service between Great Britain and New York
GULF	blue type on orange circle	Gulf Oil Corporation; multinational; at least 1920s – present; originally Gulf Refining Company; operates oil tankers on the Great Lakes and worldwide

H A L		Hamburg-American Line (*see information in next entry*)
H A P A G	or centered in flag or ornate decoration	Hamburg-American Line (Hamburg Amerikanische Packet-fahrt Aktien Gesselschaft / HAPAG); Germany; 1856 – 1970; transatlantic passenger service; merged with North German Lloyd to form Hapag-Lloyd in 1970 For reference only: Hapag-Lloyd; Germany; 1970 – present; operates freighters and cargo ships worldwide; initially offered cruises on the *Kungsholm I*, replaced by *Europa* in 1982 and later added the *MS Bremen*
H A P A G	as shown superimposed on anchor	Hamburg-American Line (*see information in previous entry*)
HNCo	superimposed initials on center horizontal stripe of flag	Hudson Navigation Company; USA; 1902 – 1926; operated steamboats on the Hudson River; became Hudson River Navigation Company, 1926 – 1939
H S D G	logo consists of three crossed flags and anchor superimposed on lower two-thirds of ship wheel; flag on right is divided into four triangular portions with "H" on top white, "S" on red left, "D" on red right, and "G" on bottom white portion; *see photograph on page 136*	Hamburg-South American Line (Hamburg-Sudamerikanische Damps.); Germany; 1871 – present; passenger and freight service between Germany and South America, 1871 – 1964; Nazi's sponsored indoctrination cruises in the Baltic Sea during the 1930s; currently (1995) operates freighters with limited passenger accommodations from Germany to Israel and Cyprus, as well between Auckland and Hong Kong
HARRISON LINE	"Harrison Line" arched downward in banner below flag	Harrison Line (Thomas and James Harrison Ltd.); Great Britain; circa 1940s – present; worldwide freighter operation; currently (1995) operates freighters with limited passenger accommodations from Great Britain to the West Indies, Central America, and South America
E **HELLENIC LINES LTD.**	 "Hellenic Lines Ltd." below flag	Hellenic Lines; Greece; 1934 – 1983; operated freighters
HOULDER BROTHERS & CO. AUSTRALIAN AND NEW ZEALAND LINE OF PACKETS	arched upward in logo with flag in center	Houlder Brothers & Co.; Great Britain; 1849 – at least 1980s; associated with Furness Lines; operated between Great Britain and Australia, New Zealand, South America, and Africa
HUDDART PARKER LINE H P	"Huddart Parker Line" arched upward in belt logo with flag in center; "H" and "P" in left and right triangular quadrants of flag respectively	Huddart Parker Ltd.; Australia; 1884 – at least 1960s; freight and passenger ships between New Zealand and Australia
I	1) "I" inside diamond 2) "I" inside diamond on red and black steamer funnel	Inland Steamship Company; USA; 1924 – present; owned by the Inland Steel Company (1917 – present); operates freighter and passenger service on the Great Lakes; *SS Wilfred Sykes*, flagship in 1949; *SS Edward L Ryerson*, new flagship in 1960

IMM**C**		International Mercantile Marine Company; USA; 1902 – circa 1936; founded by J.P. Morgan Jr. with a capital investment of $120 million, in an effort to dominate the North Atlantic shipping industry; owned numerous ship lines including the American Line, Red Star Line, White Star Line, Atlantic Transport Line, Dominion Line, Leyland Line, Panama Pacific Line, and in later years the United States Lines; regularly transferred ships from one line to another; china may have been used on ships of any line owned by IMMC
IO **LTD.**		Imperial Oil Company, Ltd., marine division; Canada; 1920s – 1970s*; operated oil tankers on the Great Lakes; apparently taken over by ESSO in the 1970s
INLAND	"Inland" superimposed on red diamond	Inland Steamship Company; USA; 1924 – present; owned by the Inland Steel Company (1917 – present); operates freighter and passenger service on the Great Lakes; *SS Wilfred Sykes*, flagship in 1949; *SS Edward L Ryerson*, new flagship in 1960
INTER ISLAND STEAM NAVIGATION CO LTD.	arched upward in round logo; flag superimposed on volcano in center of logo	Inter-Island Steam Navigation Company, Ltd.; USA; 1883 – 1947; operated Hawaiian inter-island passenger service; merged with Wilder's Steamship Company in 1904; the line's 19 ships were taken over for military service in 1941; only one returned, continuing the inter-island service, 1946 – 1947
ITALIA	 also non-script serif type below various crowns; *see photographs*	Italian Line (Italia Flotte Riunite/Italia SA); Italy; 1932 – present; formed by the merger of Navigazione Generale Italiana, Lloyd Sabaudo, and the Cosulich Line; became a part of the Finmare Group, the Italian state-owned shipping organization (ship lines, as well as shipbuilding yards), in the 1930s; operated transatlantic ocean liners; made its final crossing in 1976; advertised "Asiapac" joint service with Lloyd Triestino in 1995, sailing from Toronto, Canada, through the Panama Canal to the Orient
J.C.J.L.		Java-China-Japan Line; The Netherlands; 1903 – mid-1950s; operated freighter and passenger service between Holland and the Orient; became Koninklijke Java-China Paketvaart Lijnen (Royal Interocean Lines) in the mid-1950s
K	 black initial on white flag	Knut Knutsen O.A.S.; Norway; 1920s – 1980s*; cargo ships with limited passenger service operating between Norway and various ports in the Pacific
K	 white "K" on red swallowtail flag with blue band at top and bottom	A. F. Klaveness and Company; Norway; 1870 – present; operates freighters; along with Bergen Line and Nordenfjeldske, created the Royal Viking Line in 1970

LAKE TRIPS THAT HAVE NO EQUAL C. D. & G. B. T. Co.	"Lake Trips That Have No Equal" arched upward and "C. D. & G. B. T. Co." arched downward in ship wheel logo; ship on lake in center of logo	Chicago, Duluth and Georgian Bay Transit Company; USA; 1913 – 1967; known as Georgian Bay Line since 1934; operated cruises on liner-like steamships on the Great Lakes between Buffalo, Cleveland, Detroit, Duluth, and Chicago; added Montreal via the Saint Lawrence Seaway in latter years
LAMPORT & HOLT LINE L + H	"Lamport & Holt" arched upward in belt logo; "L + H" on flag in center of logo	Lamport and Holt Line; Great Britain; 1845 – at least 1980s; passenger and freight service between Great Britain, New York, and South America; became part of Vestey Group in 1974
LIVERPOOL, BRAZIL & RIVER PLATE STEAMERS **LH**	"Liverpool, Brazil & River Plate Steamers" arched upward in round logo; superimposed stylized "L" & "H" in center of logo	Lamport and Holt Line (*see information in previous entry*)
LIVERPOOL & N. WALES S.S. Co. Ltd	arched upward in cobalt blue belt logo with line pennant in center	Liverpool and North Wales Steamship Company Ltd.; Great Britain; early 1900s – 1960s*; operated on the east coast of Great Britain in the Liverpool Bay vicinity
LOS ANGELES STEAMSHIP CO.	"Los Angeles" arched upward and "Steamship Co." arched downward in round logo; flag in center of logo	Los Angeles Steamship Company; USA; 1920 – 1936; operated overnight express service between Los Angeles and San Francisco, 1921 – 1936; offered ocean liner passenger-cargo service between Los Angeles and Hawaii, 1922 – 1933; merged with Matson Line in 1930, but retained its own identity until service ceased; the SS *City of Los Angeles* served as a hotel during the San Diego Exposition of 1935 and sailed on occasional cruises until 1936
L Luckenbach Line	"L" inside circle on red swallowtail pennant; "Luckenbach Line" below pennant; *see photograph*	Luckenbach Line (Luckenbach Steamship Co.); USA; 1910s – 1960s*; operated freighters
M	or	Matson Lines (Matson Navigation Company); USA; 1901 – present; the original *Lurline* sailed from San Francisco to Hawaii 14 years before the company was incorporated; specialized in San Francisco and Los Angeles to Hawaii cruises, 1908 – 1971, except during WWII when all of Matson's ships served as troop transports; Atlantic coast – Hawaii service was inaugurated in 1921; Matson merged with Oceanic Line in 1926; advertised as Matson Line • Oceanic Line in the 1930s and as Matson Navigation Company, as well as Oceanic Steamship Company 1930s – 1959; Pacific Far East Lines took over its last two cruise ships, SS *Mariposa* and SS *Monterey*, in 1971; currently operates freighters and container ships
M	 flag: blue on upper left and red on lower right	Moltzau and Christensen; Norway; 1950s and 1960s*; passenger and freight operations

M		Morgan Line; USA; 1834 – 1941; named after its founder, Charles Morgan; initially operated sternwheelers between New York and Charleston; in 1837 its *Columbia* was the first steamer to sail to Galveston, Texas, and New Orleans; New York – New Orleans service began in 1848; offered passenger service between New York, New Orleans, and ports in Texas by 1856; purchased by Southern Pacific Steamship Company in 1885, giving the Southern Pacific Railroad access to eastern ports; began New Orleans – Havana service in 1900; purchased the Cromwell Line in 1902; only one ship remained in 1941, *Dixie*, and she was requisitioned by the government at the beginning of WWII
MM LINES	MM LINES	Moore-McCormack Lines; USA; 1913 – circa 1970s; initially known as Moore & McCormack; began freighter service between New York and Brazil in 1913; started cargo service between New York and Scandinavian ports in 1918; in 1927 established a subsidiary, American Scantic Line, which operated cargo ships on the North Atlantic and began passenger service in 1932; Moore-McCormack offered passenger-liner service on its "Good Neighbor Fleet" to South American ports, 1938 – 1960s; in the 1960s destinations included South America, Africa, Scandinavia, the Mediterranean, and the Caribbean; remaining ships were laid up in 1969 and purchased by Holland America Line in 1972; listed in *Brown's Flags and Funnels* © 1982, but shipping activities unknown
M.&M.T.CO.		Merchants and Miners Transportation Company; USA; 1852 – 1948; began operating sternwheelers between Boston and Baltimore in 1854; passenger service on two new side-wheelers was extended to Savannah in 1859; operated an iron screw steamer between New York and Philadelphia, 1880 – 1883; added a Philadelphia – Savannah route in 1900; purchased the Winsor Line in 1907; discontinued passenger service entirely in 1942 when ships were requisitioned for WWII duty; liquidated in 1948
M T M Co	stylized script type inside knotted rope	Merchants and Miners Transportation Company (*see information in previous entry*)
MAERSK	seven-sided star on blue square above "Maersk"	Maersk Line (A. P. Moller); Denmark; at least 1920s – present; worldwide freighter operation
S. S. Malden	S. S. Malden	SS *Malden*, steamship owned and operated by the New England Fuel and Transportation Company, circa 1910s – 1921
MALLORY	"Mallory" below pennant variation: without the word "Mallory"	Mallory Line (New York and Texas Steamship Company, 1886+); USA; 1867 – 1928; the Mallory family became involved in shipping as early as 1830; in addition to operating whalers, they built schooners, yachts, and steamships; passenger and freight service between New Orleans, Galveston, and New York began in 1867; forced out of New Orleans by pressure from the Morgan Line, however Morgan agreed to discontinue Galveston service; C. W. Morse, owner of Eastern Steamship Company, a combination of numerous U.S. Northern Atlantic coastal lines, 1901+, purchased the Mallory Line, along with the Porto Rico Line, Ward Line, and Clyde Line in 1906 in an attempt to form a shipping cartel; when the venture failed in 1908, Mallory and the latter lines were purchased by Atlantic, Gulf and West Indies Steamship Co., a holding company headed by Henry Mallory; AGWI merged Clyde Line with Mallory Line to form Clyde-Mallory Line in 1928

MALLORY LINE	 "Mallory Line" below pennant	Mallory Line (*see information in previous entry*)
MANITOU STEAMSHIP COMPANY CHICAGO		Mackinac Line (Manitou Steamship Company); USA; circa 1900 – circa 1908; offered passenger service on Lake Michigan; advertised "the Great Lake route to northern summer resorts," 1901 – 1903
MARINE DISTRICT NY NH & H	"Marine District" curved upward in belt logo; stylized initials ("& H" below "NY" superimposed on "NH") inside shield in center of logo	New Haven Railroad Marine District; USA; 1898 – 1904; marine division of the New York, New Haven, and Hartford Railroad, managed the railroad's ship lines; all lines merged in 1904 to form New England Navigation Company
N. B. S. Co. *MAYFLOWER*	"N. B. S. Co." arched slightly upward above "Mayflower"	Nantasket Beach Steamboat Company; USA; 1890s – 1930s; owned and operated the steamboat, *Mayflower*, in Boston Harbor
McCORMICK M STEAMSHIP COMPANY	"McCormick" arched upward and "Steamship Company" arched downward in round logo with flag in center; "M" on solid white circle inside star in center of flag	McCormick Steamship Company; USA; 1923 – 1941; the line's founder, C. McCormick, began operating a lumber mill before the turn of the century; a year before his steamship company was formed he had a controlling interest in five west coast lumber shipping lines, in addition to ship building firms who catered to the lumber industry; the McCormick Steamship Company operated cargo ships 1923+; biweekly passenger service between Portland and San Francisco began in 1924; in September of that year its passenger line was extended to Los Angeles; regular service was discontinued in 1928; McCormick merged with Pope and Talbot Lumber Company in 1934; operated irregular passenger service on cargo ships between Puget Sound and San Francisco, 1936 – 1937 and very limited service until 1941
• S • S • MIAMI •	below United States flag, P & O's swallowtail pennant, and British flag	SS *Miami*, owned by Peninsular & Occidental Steamship Co.; sailed between Miami and Nassau, circa 1910s – 1920s
N. B. S. Co. **Miles Standish**	"N. B. S. Co." arched slightly upward above ornate decoration' "Miles Standish" arched slightly downward below decoration	Nantasket Beach Steamboat Company; USA; 1890s – 1930s; owned and operated the steamboat, *Miles Standish*, 1895 – 1924
A. P. MOLLER KOBENHAVN	 "A.P. Moller" arched upward above and "Kobenhavn" arched downward below logo	A. P. Moller; Denmark; at least 1920s – present; worldwide operations, including freighter, tanker, and tramp lines; Kobenhavn is Dutch for Copenhagen, the location of Moller's home office
A. P. MOLLER MAERSK LINE	 "A.P. Moller" arched upward above and "Maersk Line" arched downward below logo	Maersk Line (A. P. Moller); Denmark; at least 1920s – present; worldwide freighter operation

MONTICELLO S. S. CO. **VALLEJO** MARE ISLAND SAN FRANCISCO	"Monticello S. S. Co." arched upward and "Mare Island San Francisco" arched downward in round logo; "Vallejo" superimposed diagonally across logo	Monticello Steamship Co.; USA; 1895 – 1927; operated ferries between Vallejo, Mare Island, St. Helena, Napa, Calistoga, and San Francisco (San Francisco Bay Area, California); purchased by Southern Pacific Railroad and became Golden Gate Ferries in 1927
MOOR LINE LIMITED R	"Moor Line Limited" arched upward in round logo with swallowtail flag in center; "R" on flag	Moor Line Limited (Runciman Shipping Co. Ltd); Great British; 1920s – 1960s*; tramp line (i.e., unscheduled, as required freighter services)
Moore and McCormack	**Moore and McCormack**	Moore-McCormack Lines; USA; 1913 – circa 1970s; initially known as Moore & McCormack; began freighter service between New York and Brazil in 1913; started cargo service between New York and Scandinavian ports in 1918; in 1927 established a subsidiary, American Scantic Line, which operated cargo ships on the North Atlantic and began passenger service in 1932; Moore-McCormack offered passenger-liner service on its "Good Neighbor Fleet" to South American ports, 1938 – 1960s; in the 1960s destinations included South America, Africa, Scandinavia, the Mediterranean, and the Caribbean; remaining ships were laid up in 1969 and purchased by Holland America Line in 1972; listed in *Brown's Flags and Funnels* © 1982, but shipping activities unknown
C. W. MORSE PL	"PL" on flag in center of knotted rope logo; "C. W. Morse" above logo	People's Line; USA; 1835 – 1902; owned by C. W. Morse; operated steamboats at night on the Hudson River between various points in New York; merged with Citizen's Line to become the Hudson Navigation Company (1902 – 1926)
MUNSON STEAMSHIP M LINE	"Munson Steamship" arched upward and "Line" arched downward in knotted rope logo with swallowtail flag in center; "M" on flag	Munson Steamship Company; USA; 1884 – 1938; initially a New York – Cuba freighter operation; Gulf of Mexico destinations were added in the 1890s; passenger service between New York and Cuba began in 1915; operated freight and passenger service between New York and east coast South American ports, 1919 – 1938, adding Bermuda and Nassau to the itinerary in the 1930s; ships taken over by the American Republics Line
N	(logo)	Stavros S. Niarchos; Greece / multinational; 1960s – present; operates tankers and freighters worldwide
NAC	(logo)	Norwegian American Cruises; Norway; 1980 – 1983; originally Norwegian America Line (NAL, 1910 – 1980), it was renamed to reflect its cruising operations; its ships, *Vistafjord* and *Sagafjord*, were purchased by Cunard in 1983; continued to use illustrated logo, operating as Cunard / NAC until circa 1990 when NAC was eliminated from name
N A L	(logo) red initials on red and white swallowtail flag	Norwegian America Line; Norway; 1910 – 1980; transatlantic passenger service, 1913 – 1971; cruises, 1971 – 1980; name changed to Norwegian American Cruises (NAC) in 1980

NASM	1) gold script initials; *see photograph* 2) 3) 4) white stylized "NA" above "SM" on gold diamond shape; *see photograph*	Nederlandsch-Amerikaansche Stoomvaart Maatschappij; The Netherlands; 1872 – 1972; known as Holland America Line, 1896 – 1972 and early 1980s – present, and Holland America Cruises, 1972 – early 1980s; offered transatlantic passenger service, 1872 – 1971, and cruises, 1971 – present; became a subsidiary of Carnival Cruise Lines in 1989
N E **Co.** **F T**	on white flag divided into quadrants with green cross; red initials in positions illustrated; "Co." on green circle in center of cross	New England Fuel and Transportation Company; USA; circa 1910 – 1926; owned and operated the steamships SS *Arlington* and SS *Malden*
NgI	superimposed stylized initials below crown	Navigazione Generale Italiana; Italy; 1870s – 1932; received subsidies from the Italian government as early at 1876; took over several shipping lines and its fleet numbered more than one-hundred in 1886; operated transatlantic passenger liners, particularly after WWI; merged with Lloyd Sabaudo and Cosulich Line to form Italian Line in 1932
N N **C O**		Northern Navigation Company; Canada; 1899 – 1983; absorbed North West Transportation Co. in 1900; Northern Navigation Co. of Ontario became Northern Navigation Company Ltd. in 1910; merged with Richelieu & Ontario Navigation Company, Niagara Navigation Company, and others to form Canada Steamship Lines, Ltd. in 1913 and become their Northern Navigation Division; offered passenger and freight service on the Great Lakes until 1949 and later freight only; advertised "Detroit-Duluth cruise" in 1949 and "package freight service" in 1965
N. P. **S. S. Co**	above crossed flags; United States flag on left; North Pacific's blue flag with red star on solid white circle in center at right	North Pacific Steamship Co.; USA; 1911 – 1917; operated passenger ships on U. S. west coast; became the Emerald Line in 1917
N. W. **TRANSPORTATION** **CO. LIMITED**	arched upward in belt logo below crown; ship at sea in center of logo	North West Transportation Co. Ltd. (Beatty Line); Canada; 1877 – 1900; passenger and freight service; advertised "The favorite lake route between the Northwest and Pacific Coast and all points in Canada and the eastern states" in circa 1896; absorbed by Northern Navigation Co. in 1900
N. Y. & C. M. **S. S. Co.** **W**	"N . Y. & C. M. S. S. Co." arched upward in belt logo with swallowtail flag in center; "W" inside circle on flag	Ward Line (New York and Cuba Mail Steamship Company); USA; 1877 – circa 1949; operated between New York and Cuba; C. W. Morse, in an attempt to form a shipping cartel, formed the Eastern Steamship Company in 1901 (a combination of numerous U.S. Northern Atlantic coastal lines) and purchased the Ward Line, along with the Porto Rico Line, Clyde Line, and Mallory Line in 1906; when the scheme failed in 1908, Ward Line was purchased by Atlantic, Gulf and West Indies Steamship Co., a holding company; due to several well publicized disasters of the 1930s, the line was advertised as the Cuba Mail Line in the 1940s; all ships served in WWII and none were returned; new ships were advertised in 1946 and service continued until circa 1949; while there was no official end of the line, AGWI, its holding company, went out of business in 1953

N. Y. K. LINE		Nippon Yusen Kaisha (N.Y.K. Line; Japan Mail Steamship Company Ltd.); Japan; 1895 – present; formed by a merger of two Japanese lines (1885+), with a total fleet of 58 steamers; offered freight, mail and passenger service, including around-the-world and Pacific cruises, 1900s – 1930s; fleet was virtually destroyed during WWII; currently a worldwide cargo operation; formed Crystal Cruises as a subsidiary in 1988
N.Y.P.& N.	**N.Y.P.&N.**	Virginia Ferry Corp.; USA; 1884 – circa 1960s; owned by Pennsylvania Railroad and operated by the New York, Philadelphia and Norfolk Railroad (initials on topmark); passenger and later car ferries ran between Norfolk and Cape Charles, Virginia, on the Chesapeake Bay
The **N**ew England avigation COMPANY	stylized type; "N" extends downward at left of "England" and "avigation"	New England Navigation Co.; USA; 1904 – 1912; formed by a merger of New York, New Haven and Hartford Railroad owned shipping lines; succeeded by the New England Steamship Company
The New England avigation Company	stylized script type; "N" extends downward at left of "avigation"	New England Navigation Co. (*see information in previous entry*)
THE NEW ENGLAND NAVIGATION COMPANY	in banner below crest	New England Navigation Co. (*see information in previous entry*)
The **N**ew **E**ngland **S**teamship COMPANY	stylized type	New England Steamship Co.; USA; 1912 – 1945; owned by New York, New Haven and Hartford Railroad; successor to the New England Navigation Company
N NIAGARA NAVIGATION COMPANY LIMITED	"Niagara Navigation Company Limited" on solid green circle in center of life ring; pennant superimposed on top portion of life ring; "N" on pennant	Niagara River Line (Niagara Navigation Company Limited); Canada; 1877 – 1913; operated freight and passenger service on the Niagara River; advertised "Niagara River Line steamers… Buffalo, Niagara Falls, Lewiston, Queenston, Niagara-on-the-Lake, and Toronto via the lower Niagara River and Lake Ontario" in 1905; merged with Richelieu & Ontario Navigation Company, Northern Navigation Company, and others to form Canada Steamship Lines, Ltd. in 1913
NORTH PACIFIC STEAMSHIP CO.	"North Pacific" arched upward and "Steamship Co." arched downward in round logo with flag in center; red star on solid white circle in center on blue flag	North Pacific Steamship Co.; USA; 1911 – 1917; operated passenger ships on U. S. west coast; became the Emerald Line in 1917
NORTHERN STEAMSHIP COMPANY N GREAT NORTHERN Ry. LINE	"Northern Steamship Company" in banner, superimposed on upper point of large star; "N" in center of star; "Great Northern Ry. Line" in banner, superimposed on lower points of star	Northern Steamship Company; USA; 1894 – 1916; owned and operated in conjunction with Great Northern Railway; offered passenger service on Great Lakes; advertised "A summer cruise on inland sea via the Great Lakes to the far West" in 1896 on the SS *North West* and SS *North Land*; absorbed by Great Lakes Transit Corporation in 1916
𝔑𝔬𝔯𝔴𝔦𝔠𝔥 𝔏𝔦𝔫𝔢	type arched slightly upward	Norwich Line (Norwich and New York Transportation Company); USA; 1860 – 1904; associated with New York, New Haven and Hartford Railroad; operated river steamers, including the *Atlantic*

O C **F Co**	initials on swallowtail flag in position shown at left	Ontario Car Ferry Co.; Canada; 1907 – 1950; auto-ferry operation on Lake Ontario between Rochester, New York, and Cobourg, Ontario, 1909+; owned by Buffalo, Rochester & Pittsburgh, and Canadian National railroads
O. D.	red initials in center of swallowtail flag; blue horizontal stripe at top and bottom of flag	Old Dominion Line (Old Dominion Steamship Company, 1867 – 1923; Eastern Steamship Company, 1923 – 1941); USA; 1867 – 1941; operated passenger and freight service between Norfolk, Virginia, and New York City; became a division of Eastern Steamship in 1923, but continued to operate as the Old Dominion Line until service was terminated in 1941
O H		Oostzee Steamship Company (Stoomvaart Maatschappij Oostzee; Vinke and Zonen) and Hillegersberg Steamship Company (Stoomvaart Maatschappij Hillegersberg; Vinke & Co.); The Netherlands; both companies operated 1920s – 1960*; joint freighter operation
OL		Oranje Line (Seatransport Company, Ltd., Anthony Veder and Company); The Netherlands; 1937 – 1970; transatlantic freighter operation, 1937 – 1953; passenger and freight service 1953+; offered Great Lakes – Saint Lawrence Seaway cruises after 1959
O **L**	"o" inside upper left portion of simple anchor; stylized "L" inside lower right portion of anchor	Orient Line (Orient Steam Navigation Company); Great Britain; 1878 – 1967; operated passenger service from Great Britain to Australia, New Zealand, and the North American west coast; merged with Peninsular and Oriental of Great Britain in 1960 to form P & O – Orient Lines; Orient Lines removed from name in 1967
O.R.&N.	*O.R.&N.*	Oregon Railway and Navigation Company; USA; 1879 – 1904; formed by a merger of the Oregon Steam Navigation Company and the Oregon Steamship Company; operated steamers between San Francisco and Portland, as well as on the Snake, Columbia, and Williamette rivers; the *T.J.Potter*, a floating palace, ran between Astoria and Portland, Oregon; company name was changed to San Francisco and Portland Steamship Company in 1904
O. R . & N. Co.	1) initials only 2) initials below brown flag; star in center of flag	Oregon Railway and Navigation Company (*see information in previous entry*)
O. S. S. Co.	**O. S. S. Co.**	Oceanic Line (Oceanic Steamship Company); USA; 1881 – 1971; established by Claus Spreckles to ship sugar from Hawaii to the United States; service between San Francisco and Hawaii began in 1883 and between San Francisco and Sydney, Australia, in 1885; merged with and became a subsidiary of Matson Line in 1926; advertised as Matson Line • Oceanic Line in the 1930s and as Matson Navigation Company, as well as Oceanic Steamship Company, 1930s – 1959; continued to operate transpacific passenger service under the Oceanic flag until 1971
O W & R R Co		Oregon-Washington Railroad & Navigation; USA; Union Pacific purchased and merged several railroad-navigation companies to form this company in 1910; operated steamships between San Francisco and Portland, as well as on the Snake, Columbia, and Williamette rivers

OCEAN STEAM SHIP COMPANY AH 1865	"Ocean Steam Ship Company" arched upward and "1865" arched downward in round logo with flag in center; slightly overlapped "AH" in center of flag	Ocean Steam Ship Company (Alfred Holt and Company); Great Britain; 1865 – 1903; passenger and freight service from Great Britain to worldwide ports; succeeded by Alfred Holt and Company's Blue Funnel Line, 1903 – 1980s*
OMNIUM TRANSPORTATION COMPANY O	"Omnium Transportation Company" arched upward in round logo with red pennant in center; "O" on pennant	Omnium Transportation Company; USA; freighters
OVE SKOU S COPENHAGEN	"Ove Skou" arched upward and "Copenhagen" arched downward in round logo with flag in center; white "S" on blue flag	Ove Skou; Denmark; 1950s – 1980s*; freighter operation
P		Panama Line (Panama Railroad Steamship Co., 1896 – 1951; Panama Canal Company, 1951 – 1981); USA; 1896 – 1981; originally owned by a French company, it was purchased by the United States government in 1904 and controlled for a period of time by the Isthmian Canal Commission; operated passenger and freight service between New York and Panama (Colón and later Cristobal), 1896 – 1961; transported government freight and passengers only between New Orleans and Panama, 1961 – 1981
P	"P" on swallowtail pennant	Pittsburgh Steamship Company; USA; 1899 – 1951; transported iron ore on the Great Lakes; a subsidiary of United States Steel since 1901, commonly referred to as the "Steel Trust Fleet"; became a division of USS in 1951; its fleet merged with USS Bradley Transportation Division's fleet to become United States Steel Great Lakes Fleet in 1967
P		Prudential Lines; USA; circa 1950s – present; Prudential purchased a controlling interest in Grace Lines and became Prudential-Grace Lines in 1970; Grace was removed from line name in 1974; advertised cruises from Rio de Janeiro, though the Strait of Magellan to Lima, Peru in 1976; continued to operate the famous *Santa* liners from U. S. west coast ports, through the Panama Canal and around South America until 1978 when Delta Line purchased the *Santa* ships; Prudential now (1996) operates freighters from the United States east coast to the Mediterranean with a limit of 12 passengers
P & O		Peninsular & Occidental Steamship Co.; USA; 1900 – 1968; established by merger of the Plant Line and the Florida East Coast Steamship Company; sailed from Miami and Tampa to Key West, Nassau, and Havana; advertised Miami to Nassau cruises (passengers, freight, and automobiles) on SS *Florida* in 1965
PCSSco	"P" and "C" superimposed; "SS" superimposed on "P" and "C"; "CO" superimposed on second "S"	Pacific Coast Steamship Company; USA; 1876 – 1916; offered passenger and freight service between Los Angeles and Alaska; merged with Pacific Alaska Navigation, Admiral Line's holding company, to form Pacific Steamship Company in 1916
P.C. S.S. Co.	arched slightly downward below line flag	Pacific Coast Steamship Company (*see information in previous entry*)

PFEL		Pacific Far East Line; USA; 1946 – 1978; operated cargo iners between the U.S. west coast, the Far East, and beginning in 1970 Australia and New Zealand; advertised "express freight • dry cargo • refrigeration • tanks • passengers" in 1965; took over Matson Lines' last two cruise ships, SS *Mariposa* and SS *Monterey*, in 1971 and offered cruises to Hawaii, New Zealand, Australia, Alaska, and Europe; filed for bankruptcy in 1978
P M	on round logo; circle divided into two sections by wavy vertical line; white "P" on rust left side; white "M" on black right side variation: "Canada" below logo	Pickands-Mather Company, circa 1883 – 1973; Pickands Mather & Company; 1973 – present; USA; operates freighters on the Great Lakes; after a long association, Interlake Steamship Company (1913 – present) merged with Pickands-Mather in 1966
PM Co.		Pickands-Mather and Company (*see information in previous entry*) Interlake Steamship Company, 1913 – present, a division of Pickands-Mather since 1966, also used china topmarked with this line flag according to *ButterPat World* by Richard W. Luckin
P M H	three pronged spear on and protruding above shield; "P" on left and "M" on right side of spear handle; "H" centered on lower portion spear handle	Polska Morska Handlowa; Poland; circa 1950s – circa 1980s; owned by Polish goverment; operated freighters
P M O	"P" on left and "M" on right side of spear handle; "O" centered on lower portion spear handle	Polish Ocean Lines; Poland; 1951 – mid-1980s; owned by Polish government; known as Gdynia-America Shipping Line, 1935 – 1951, which operated passenger service between Poland and New York catering to immigrants in the 1930s and 1947 – 1951; Polish Ocean Lines resumed transatlantic service in 1957; offered cruises between Poland and Canada, as well as Great Britain and the West Indies on the *Stefan Batory* in 1982
PMssc	"P" and "M" superimposed; "SS" superimposed on "P" and "M"; "C" superimposed on lower portion of "P"	Pacific Mail Steamship Company; USA; 1848 – 1926; initially operated steamers on the United States west coast and carried mail between Panama and Oregon; began transpacific freight and passenger service in 1867; took over San Francisco – Australia mail service in 1875 and withdrew in 1885; W. R. Grace and Company (Grace Line) acquired controlling interest in the line in 1916; Pacific Mail became managing operator of five *President* liners owned by the United States Shipping Board in 1921, offering transpacific service (west coast to the Orient via Hawaii); W. R. Grace and Co. established the Panama Mail Steamship Company in 1926 and transferred Pacific Mail's coastal ships to that line in the same year; Dollar Steamship Company purchased the *President* liners from the USSB and the "Pacific Mail name, house flag, and good will" in 1926
PACIFIC COAST STEAMSHIP CO.	"Pacific Coast" arched upward and "Steamship Co." arched downward in round logo with line flag in center	Pacific Coast Steamship Company; USA; 1876 – 1916; west coast service between San Francisco and Alaska; merged with Pacific Alaska Navigation, a holding company, to form Pacific Steamship Company (Admiral Line)
PACIFIC MAIL S. CO. S.	"Pacific Mail" arched upward and "S. CO. S." arched downward in round logo; horizontal stripes of line flag in center of logo	Pacific Mail Steamship Company (*see information under PMSSC topmark*)

PANAMA RAILROAD P STEAMSHIP LINE	"Panama Railroad" arched upward and "Steamship Line" arched downward in ship wheel logo with swallowtail flag in center; "P" on flag	Panama Line (Panama Railroad Steamship Co., 1896 – 1951; Panama Canal Company, 1951 – 1981); USA; 1896 – 1981; originally owned by a French company, it was purchased by the United States government in 1904 and controlled for a period of time by the Isthmian Canal Commission; operated passenger and freight service between New York and Panama (Colón and later Cristobal), 1896 – 1961; transported government freight and passengers only between New Orleans and Panama, 1961 – 1981
THE PENINSULAR & OCCIDENTAL STEAMSHIP COMPANY P & O	"Peninsular & Occidental Steamship Company" arched upward in round logo with diagonally checkered swallowtail pennant in center; "P & O" in center of pennant; *see photograph*	Peninsular & Occidental Steamship Co.; USA; 1900 – 1968; established by merger of the Plant Line and the Florida East Coast Steamship Company; sailed from Miami and Tampa to Key West, Nassau, and Havana; advertised Miami to Nassau cruises (passengers, freight, and automobiles) on SS *Florida* in 1965
PERE MARQUETTE	as shown or arched downward below illustration of ship; *see photograph*	Pere Marquette Railway Company; USA; 1899 – 1957; operated ferries and later auto-ferries on Lake Michigan between Ludington (a town originally known as Pere Marquette), Michigan, and various towns in Wisconsin; absorbed by Chesapeake & Ohio Railway 10 years after the two lines merged in 1947
PERE MARQUETTE SYSTEM	inside rectangle	Pere Marquette Railway Company (*see information in previous entry*)
PETROLEOS MEXICANOS VAPOR SAN RICARDO	"Petroleos Mexicanos" arched upward above "Vapor San Ricardo"	Petroleos Mexicanos; Mexico; oil tanker operation; 1950s – 1980s *
PITTSBURGH AND CINCINNATI PACKET LINE	arched upward in ship wheel logo; riverboat in center of logo	Pittsburgh and Cincinnati Packet Line; USA; circa 1880s – circa 1920s; operated stern wheelers on the Ohio River between Cincinnati, Ohio, and Pittsburgh, Pennsylvania
PORTLAND PSCo STEAMSHIP Co.	"Portland" arched upward and "Steamship Co." arched downward in round logo; stylized "P," "S," "C," and "o" superimposed in center of logo	Portland Steamship Company (initially Portland Steam Packet Company); USA; 1843 – 1901; operated passenger service between Boston, Massachusetts, and Portland, Maine; combined with several other lines to form Eastern Steamship Company in 1901
PORTO RICO LINE B	"Porto Rico Line" arched upward in round logo with ribbon tails at bottom; "B" on pennant in center of logo	Porto Rico Line (New York & Porto Rico Steamship Co.); USA; 1885 – 1949; offered freight (1885+) and passenger (1899+) service from New York to Florida, Texas, Puerto Rico, the Dominican Republic, Cuba, and Mexico; C. W. Morse, in an attempt to form a shipping cartel, formed the Eastern Steamship Company in 1901 (a combination of numerous U.S. Northern Atlantic coastal lines) and purchased the Porto Rico Line, along with the Clyde Line, Ward Line, and Mallory Line in 1906; when the scheme failed, Porto Rico Line was purchased by Atlantic, Gulf and West Indies Steamship Co., a holding company, in 1908; all but one ship was lost at sea by 1942; passenger and freight service began again in 1946, but operations were suspended and last ship was sold in 1949
PRINCESS ANNE	illustration of ship on ocean between the words "Princess" and "Anne"; *see photograph*	auto-ferry operated by the Virginia Ferry Corp.; USA; 1936+; ran between Norfolk and Cape Charles, Virginia, on the Chesapeake Bay

PUGET SOUND NAVIGATION COMPANY	arched upward in round logo with flag in center; star inside diamond in center of flag	Puget Sound Navigation Company; USA; 1903 – early 1950s; Charles Peabody of the Alaska Steamship Company purchased Thompson Steamboat Company and interest in La Conner Trading and Transportation Company in 1902; the two companies merged to form Puget Sound Navigation in 1903; ran ferries and inland waterway steamboat service on and in the vicinity of Puget Sound and British Columbia; operated the Black Ball Line passenger-auto ferries between Port Angeles and Victoria and on other routes, 1927 – mid-1950s; took over the Kitsap County Transportation Company in 1940; holdings purchased by the Washington State Toll Bridge Authority in the early 1950s
Q$_{E2}$	stylized type	*Queen Elizabeth II* (QE2), Cunard's current (1996) flagship, was launched in 1979
THE QUEBEC STEAMSHIP COMPANY		Quebec Steamship Company; Canada; 1880 – 1913; operated in the Maritime Provinces and on the St. Lawrence River; also offered passenger service from New York to Bermuda; merged with several lines to form the Canada Steamship Company in 1913
QUIS SEPARABIT	arched downward in banner below rising sun logo	Peninsular[1] and Oriental Steam Navigation Company (P & O); Great Britain; 1840 – present (roots extend to 1837); cargo and passenger-liner service from Great Britain to Australia, New Zealand, the Orient, North Africa, and India, as well as round-the-world cruises; formed P & O Group in early 1950s, which consists of numerous shipping concerns including Princess Cruises (began operating in 1965; owned by P & O 1974+), as well as a fleet of 25 tankers; merged with Orient Lines in 1960 to form P & O-Orient Lines; Orient Lines eliminated from name in 1967; P & O Cruises has offered worldwide cruises since mid 1970s

"Quis Separabit," P & O's motto, translates to "Who shall separate us?"

[1] Refers to Spanish peninsula where P & O operated its first chartered steamer from London to Spain in 1837 |
A R B T	 yellow "X" divides blue flag into triangular quadrants	Rederi Transatlantic A/B (G. Carlsson); Sweden; 1904 – present; operates freighters; joined the Swedish Bilspedition Group in 1988
RED COLLAR STEAMSHIP LINE	arched upward in round logo; ship funnel in center of logo	Red Collar Steamship Line; USA; circa 1910 – circa 1920; operated steamboats on a river and lake in Idaho
RED CROSS LINE		Red Cross Line; Canada / Great Britain; circa late 1800s – late 1930s; offered passenger and freight service between Halifax, Nova Scotia, and New York; operated New York to Caribbean cruises during the 1920s; became part of Furness Withy Group in 1929; operations ceased due to WWII

RED STAR LINE	red star on white swallowtail pennant	Red Star Line; 1872 – 1939; USA / Germany; transatlantic passenger service; purchased American Line in 1884; International Mercantile Marine Company bought Red Star, along with the American Line in 1902; the Red Star Line name and its two remaining ships were sold to Bernstein Line of Germany (1926 – 1939) in 1935; ships were purchased by Holland America Line in 1939 and service terminated shortly thereafter due to WWII
REDERIAKTIEBOLAGET NORDSTJERNAN J STOCKHOLM	"Rederiaktiebolaget Nordstjernan" arched slightly upward above flag; "J" inside white star in center of cobalt blue swallowtail flag; "Stockholm" arched slightly downward below flag; *see photograph*	Johnson Line (Rederiaktiebolaget Nordstjernan); Sweden; at least 1920s – present; owned by Axel Axelson Johnson; specialized in high speed cargo-liner services; merged with Effoa of Finland to form Effjohn International (also known as Rederi Effjohn of Scandinavia), one of Europe's largest passenger ship line holding companies; Effjohn owned Commodore Cruise Line, 1987 – 1995 (sold to Miami investors in 1995), B.S.L. (previously known as Bermuda Star Line), and Crown Cruise Line (1991 – 1993; purchased by Cunard) and currently owns Silja Line, which operates large ferries on Scandinavian coasts
REGULATOR R O N LINE	entirely inside logo: "Regulator" arched upward in top, "R," "O," and "N" are inside circle in center in positions shown, and "Line" arched downward in bottom	Regulator Line (Dalles, Portland and Astoria Navigation Company); USA: 1902 – 1915; operated sternwheelers between Portland and The Dalles on the Columbia River; originally owned by Columbia River and Northern Railway; taken over by Spokane, Portland and Seattle Railway, which operated the Regulator Line until 1915
RICHELIEU & ONTARIO NAVIGATION COMPANY RO	"Richelieu & Ontario Navigation Company" in ship wheel logo with superimposed stylized "R" and "O" in center; ship wheel superimposed on anchor	Richelieu & Ontario Navigation Company; Canada; 1875 – 1913; advertised excursion tours from Niagara Falls to Philadelphia in 1876, "palatial steamers between Niagara Falls, Toronto, Montreal," and so forth in 1890 and "Niagara to the seas, descriptive of that delightful trip down the River St. Lawrence and up the world-famed Saguenay" in 1897; merged with Niagara Navigation Company, Northern Navigation Company, and others to form Canada Steamship Lines, Ltd. in 1913
RIVIERA CRUISES	stylized type below ocean liner	Riviera Cruises; Italy; circa 1962 – 1964; its only ship, *Riviera Prima*, was sold in 1964
ROTTERDAMSCHE LLOYD RL	"Rotterdamsche Lloyd" arched upward in round logo with checkered flag in center; "RL" in center of flag; *see photographs*	Rotterdamsche Lloyd; The Netherlands; circa 1900 – circa 1963; advertised around-the-world tours in 1909; became Koninklijke Rotterdamsche (Royal Rotterdam) Lloyd after WWII; offered transatlantic immigrant service, 1951 – 1963; merged with Nederland Line to form Nedlloyd Lines in circa 1963
ROYAL MAIL STEAM PACKET CO.	"Royal Mail Steam Packet Co." in banner below British coat of arms	Royal Mail Steam Packet Company / Royal Mail Lines; Great Britain; 1839 – at least 1980s; began mail runs between Boston and Great Britain in 1840 and passenger service between South America and Great Britain in 1842; purchased White Star Line from International Mercantile Marine Company in 1926 and sold that line to Cunard in 1934; company name changed to Royal Mail Lines, Ltd. in 1931; operated passenger, cargo, and refrigerated cargo-liner services to South America, as well as the Caribbean and United States west coast until the mid-1960s; offered cargo service only thereafter
S		Sabine Transportation Company Inc.; USA; at least 1950s – present; operates towing vessels and freighters; listed in 1996 *Poor's Register* under "deep sea transportation of domestic freight"

S		Salen Rederierna A/B (Sven Salen Line); Sweden; 1916 – circa 1970s; name changed to Saleninvest A/B in circa 1970s, but line flag remained the same; operates general and refrigerated cargo ships
S		Showa Line; Japan; 1964 – present; part of the Japanese SMI Group; operates container ships, tankers, and passenger ships worldwide; formed Oceanic Cruises in 1989
S		Standard Oil Company; New Jersey and New York, USA / multinational; 1892 – 1972; operated oil tankers on the Great Lakes, as well as worldwide; line flag was blue with a white "S" in the center (as shown at left) through at least the 1920s; by 1950 (and perhaps as early as 1930) the company used a white flag with "ESSO" enclosed in an oval in the center; a new logo, Exxon, was designed in 1966, but apparently was not used until 1972 when Standard Oil became the Exxon Corporation and the shipping division known as Exxon Transportation Co.
S		Svea Line (Svea Rederi; Eman Hogberg); Sweden; at least 1920s – present; operates freighters in and near the Mediterranean
S		Stolt-Nielsen; USA / Norway; at least 1920s – present; operates tankers worldwide
S A **M L**	 three crowns on solid crcle in center of flag (not shown)	Swedish America Mexico Line; Sweden; 1950s *; operated freighters
THE **S F** Co.	inside diamond in positions shown on swallowtail flag	Shenango Furnace Company; USA; circa 1920s – circa 1930s; operated freight service on the Great Lakes
S I S Co.	initials enclosed in circle, "Co" superimposed on center of "I"	Interlake Steamship Company; USA; 1913 – present; operates freighters and passenger service on the Great Lakes; merged with Pickands Mather & Co. in 1966; Interlake's subsidiary, Lakes Shipping purchased the Ford Motor Company Marine Division fleet in 1989; Interlake has also used china topmarked with the Pickands Mather flag according to *ButterPat World* by Richard W. Luckin (*see PM flag topmark*)
SAFMARINE	 **SAFMARINE** "Safmarine" as shown or in script	South African Marine Corporation (better known as Safmarine); South Africa; circa 1950s – present; operated freighters and Union Castle passenger ships between South Africa and Great Britain; owned and operated United Cruise Lines (previously Astor United Cruises, 1982 – 1983), 1983 – circa 1986; UCL's only ship, *Astor*, cruised to South African ports and the Indian Ocean; currently (1995) operates freighters with limited passenger accommodations from Essex to South Africa

LGSCo. **Sagamore.**	*Sagamore.*	Lake George Steamboat Co.; USA; circa late 1800s – circa late 1930s; owned by the Delaware & Hudson Railway; operated the SS *Sagamore*, 1902 – 1937
SANDY HOOK New Jersey Central	all type on shield; "Sandy Hook" arched upward; "New Jersey Central" in a circle below	Sandy Hook line; USA; to circa 1918; operated ferries owned by Central Railroad of New Jersey in the New York Harbor; in circa 1918 the line's flagship, *Asbury Park*, was purchased by Monticello Steamship Company which operated on San Francisco Bay, 1895 – 1927
N S Savannah	stylized script type at right of nuclear symbol	NS *Savannah*; nuclear passenger and freight ship built by the United States Maritime Commission and jointly administered by the Atomic Energy Commission; launched in 1959; initially operated by States Line carrying passengers and limited cargo, 1960 – 1965; operated by an American Export-Isbrandtsen Lines' subsidiary as a cargo vessel and goodwill ambassador, 1965 – 1970; berthed in Savannah, Georgia, harbor, 1972 – 1981; on exhibit at Patriots Point Naval and Maritime Museum in Charleston, South Carolina, since 1981
O S S Co *Savannah Line*		Savannah Line (Ocean Steamship Company of Savannah); USA; 1872 – 1941; associated with the Central of Georgia Railroad; operated passenger and freight service between New York City, Boston, and Savannah, Georgia, until 1941
Silja Serenade	stylized type	*Silja Serenade*, 1990 – present; an overnight ferry operated by Silja Line of Norway; the line currently (1995) owns eight vessels with passenger capacities ranging from 1200 to 3000; its most popular route is between Stockholm and Helsinki
SINCLAIR	below oil rig	Sinclair Refining Company; USA; circa 1951 – circa 1969; operated oil tankers on the Great Lakes and in the Atlantic
SOUTHERN PACIFIC M S.S. LINES		Morgan Line; USA; 1834 – 1941; named after its founder, Charles Morgan; initially operated sternwheelers between New York and Charleston; in 1837 its *Columbia* was the first steamer to sail to Galveston, Texas, and New Orleans; New York – New Orleans service began in 1848; by 1856 offered passenger service between New York, New Orleans, and ports in Texas; purchased by Southern Pacific Steamship Company in 1885, giving the Southern Pacific Railroad access to eastern ports; began New Orleans – Havana service in 1900; purchased the Cromwell Line in 1902; only one ship remained in 1941, *Dixie*, and she was requisitioned by the government at the beginning of WWII
Standard Oil Co. **INDIANA**	"Standard Oil Co." as shown; "Indiana" in white letters on green scroll	Standard Oil Company of Indiana; USA; 1912 – 1962; operated oil tankers on the Great Lakes, as well as worldwide; china may also have been used in company cafeteria or executive dining room; fleet taken over by AMOCO (American Oil Company) and operated until the mid-1980s
STANDARD OIL COMPANY OF LOUISIANA	"Standard Oil Company" arched upward and "of Louisiana" arched downward in round logo with shield in center	Standard Oil Company of Louisiana; USA; at least 1920s – 1930s; operated on the Mississippi River; china may also have been used in company cafeteria or executive dining room

STAR CLIPPERS	 "Star Clippers" below logo	Star Clippers, Inc.; 1991 – present; offers Caribbean, Mediterranean, and transatlantic cruises on four-masted clipper ships
STATES **S** LINE	STATES **S** LINE	States Line (States Steamship Company); USA; 1932 – circa 1980s; operated cargo and passenger service on chartered ships between Portland or San Francisco and the Orient, 1932 – 1937; advertised single class passenger service from the U. S. west coast to the Orient and around-the-world on its *General* liners in the 1930s; due to loss of government subsidy in 1937 and WWII, service was discontinued until 1946 when the line reentered transpacific service; advertised "deluxe" passenger accommodations on voyages from the United States west coast to Hawaii, the Philippines, the Orient, and Southeast Asia in 1965; listed in *Brown's Flags and Funnels* ©1982, however shipping activity unknown
STOOMVAART MAATSCHAPPIJ NEDERLAND	"Stoomvaart Maatschappij" arched upward and "Nederland" arched downward in oval logo	Nederland Line (Nederlandsche Stoomvaart Maatschappij or Netherlands Steamship Company; also known as Royal Dutch Mail); The Netherlands; circa 1900 – circa 1963; advertised around-the-world tours in 1909; transported immigrants, 1951 – 1963; merged with Royal Rotterdamsche Lloyd to form Nedlloyd Lines in circa 1963
SUN LINE		Sun Line; Greece; 1958 – present; operates cruise ships in the Aegean Sea; merged with Epirotiki Lines to form Royal Olympic Cruises in 1995, but continues to use the Sun Line name and logo in 1996
SUNOCO		Sun Oil Company; USA; at least 1950s – circa 1970s; operated oil tankers; logo as shown at left in 1960s and 1970s; SUNOILS fitted to shape of diamond on 1950s logo; may have been known as the Sun Shipping Company, also of Philadelphia, in the 1920s
TEXACO **T**	star inside circle on flag; "Texaco" superimposed on top point of star; "T" in center of star; *see photograph*	Texaco (The Texas Company, circa 1930s – circa 1950s; Texaco Inc., circa 1960s – present); USA; operates oil tankers
tirrenia *navigazione*	green type	Tirrenia Line (Tirrenia Navigazione; Societa Tirrenia per Azioni di Navigazione); Italy; 1930s – 1980s *; became part of the Finmare Group, the Italian state-owned shipping organization (ship lines, as well as shipbuilding yards), in the 1930s; operated ferries on the Mediterranean
UFCo	overlapped stylized initials; "o" inside "C"; *see photograph*	United Fruit Company (*see information under "United Fruit Company" topmark*)
U. S. L. H. S.	**U. S. L. H. S.**	United States Light House Service (Bureau of Lighthouses); 1789 – 1939; consolidated with several other maritime services into the U.S. Coast Guard in 1939

U$_S$S		United States Steel Corporation; USA; Pittsburgh Steamship Company (1899 – 1951) became a subsidiary of USS in 1901 and a division in 1951; Bradley Transportation Company (1923 – 1952), controlled by United States Steel since 1928, became a division of that company in 1952; the United States Steel shipping division fleets merged in 1967 to become United States Steel Great Lakes Fleet, which operated until at least 1990
U S S B	**USSB** variation: without USSB; *see photographs*	United States Shipping Board; 1916 – 1934; set up to develop and maintain a strong merchant marine, as well as regulate ships involved in foreign and interstate commerce; abolished in 1933, effective March 1934; functions temporarily taken over by U.S. Department of Commerce; replaced by the U.S. Maritime Commission in 1936 Shipping Board Emergency Fleet Corp., 1917 – 1927, and United States Shipping Board Merchant Fleet Corp., 1927 – 1936; took over (enemy ships seized after WWI), ordered or purchased 2000+ ships for the USSB; also maintained and sold these vessels; ships were operated by various U.S. ship lines, referred to as "managing operators for USSB"; remaining property taken over by the U.S. Maritime Commission in 1936
U.S.S.C$\underline{o}$ of B.C. L^{TD}		Union Steamship Company, Ltd.; Canada; 1889 – 1950s; operated freight steamers on the British Columbia coast
union	"76" inside "o"	Union Oil Company of California (Unocal); USA; at least 1920s – present; operates oil tankers; "76" replaced "U.O.Co" on line flag in circa 1970s, though it had been used as advertising logo since at least the 1940s
UNION CASTLE LINE	1) "Union-Castle Line" in banner below flag 2) "Union-Castle Line" arched upward in belt logo; *see photograph*	Union-Castle Line (Union-Castle Mail Steamship Co. Ltd.); Great Britain; 1900 – at least 1980s; formed by merger of Union Steam Collier Co. (1853+) and Castle Mail Packet Co. (1872+); operated cargo, mail, and the leading passenger service between Great Britain and Africa including complete "Round-Africa" tours; when Union-Castle merged with Clan Line (worldwide cargo line) in 1956 both lines retained their own identity and the newly formed British Commonwealth Shipping Co. became their parent company; weekly mail service between Capetown and Southampton required eight ships in 1961; operated a large fleet of express liners in the mid-1960s; Union-Castles last passenger liner, *Windsor-Castle*, sailed until 1977; operated container ships until at least the 1980s
UNITED BALTIC CORPORATION LTD. U.B.C.	"United Baltic Corporation Ltd." arched upward in round logo with ribbon tails at bottom and flag in center; "U.B.C." on lower left of flag and anchor on right of flag	United Baltic Corp. Ltd.; Great Britain; 1920s – 1980s *; operated freighters between Great Britain and Baltic Sea ports
UNITED FRUIT COMPANY	blue and red swallowtail pennant with white diamond in center; "United Fruit Company" below pennant	United Fruit Company; USA; 1899 – circa late 1960s; formed by the merger of four fruit cargo lines, the largest of which was the Boston Fruit Company; operated refrigerated cargo vessels that accommodated 12 to 100 passengers; offered cruises from the United States to ports in Central America, northern South America, the West Indies, and the Caribbean on their ships, known as the "Great White Fleet," 1910s – 1930s; all ships were taken over for service WWII; advertised 12-passenger freighter cruises in 1965

UNITED STATES LIGHT HOUSE SERVICE	"United States" arched upward and "Light House Service" arched downward in round logo with lighthouse in center	United States Light House Service (Bureau of Lighthouses); 1789 – 1939; consolidated with several other maritime services into the U.S. Coast Guard in 1939
UNITED STATES LINES	"United States" arched upward and "Lines" arched downward in round logo with triangle in center; triangle divided into three curved sections; *see photograph*	United States Lines; USA; 1921 – circa 1990; established by the United States Shipping Board to operate government owned ships previously operated by the United States Mail Steamship Company (1919 – 1921), including the *George Washington* and *America* (former *Amerika*); a subsidiary of International Mercantile Marine Company, the United States Lines Company of Nevada, purchased United States Lines and the ships it had been managing from the USSB (with the *Manhattan* and *Washington* under construction) in 1931; maintained a 50 vessel fleet including cargo and passenger ships in the 1950s and 1960s; offered transatlantic passenger liner service until 1969 when its superliner flagship, *United States* (launched in 1952), was taken out of service; operated container ships until circa 1990
V		Incres Line; Panama; 1950 – 1975; offered transatlantic passenger service until 1952 and Bahamas cruises, 1952 – 1975; owned by Clipper Line of Sweden since 1964
V	white initial on blue flag	Sitmar Line (Societa Italiana Trasporti Marittimi); Italy; 1938 – 1968; founded by Alex Vlasov and remained a member of the Vlasov group; began transatlantic passenger service in 1947; became Sitmar Cruises in 1968; remaining ships purchased by Princess Cruises in 1988
V D S	red initials on white center diagonal stripe of flag; blue top and bottom diagonal stripes	Vesteraalens Dampskibsselskab; Norway; at least 1950s – present; worldwide freighter operation, in addition to mail and passenger service on Norway's coastline
VACCARO LINE V	"Vaccaro" arched upward and "Line" arched downward in life ring logo with swallowtail flag in center; "V" on flag; *see photograph*	Vaccaro Line (Standard Fruit and Steamship Company); USA; circa 1930s – circa 1950s; operated cargo ships with limited passenger service between New Orleans, New York, and Central America
VACCARO LINE STANDARD FRUIT & SS Co V	"Vaccaro Line" above logo; "Standard Fruit & SS Co" arched upward in belt logo with flag in center; "V" on flag	Vaccaro Line (*see information in previous entry*)
WSDL		White Star-Dominion Line joint service; USA; 1909 – 1926; offered transatlantic passenger service between Canada and Great Britain; joint service of these two lines, then owned by International Merchant Marine (IMMC), ended when the last Dominion ship was scrapped and White Star Line was purchased by Royal Mail Steam Packet Co.
W S L	initials on white star, inside circle on flag; *see photograph*	White Star Line (lake line); USA; 1896 – 1925; advertised excursions on the Detroit and St. Clair rivers in the early 1900s; operated passenger steamers on the Great Lakes between ports in Michigan, Ohio, and Ontario; succeeded by White Star Navigation, 1925 – 1930, followed by Tashmoo Transit Company in 1931 – 1936; note — there is no connection between this line and the transatlantic White Star Line

I W A P A M A	"I" in center of flag; "Wapama" in banner below flag	McCormick Steamship Company; USA; 1923 – 1941; the line's founder, C. McCormick, began operating a lumber mill before the turn of the century; in 1915 one of his companies, St. Helens Ship Building Co., built the *Wapama* for his fleet; a year before his steamship company was formed he had a controlling interest in five west coast lumber shipping lines, in addition to ship building firms who catered to the lumber industry; the McCormick Steamship Company operated cargo ships 1923+; offered biweekly passenger service between Portland, San Francisco, and Los Angeles, 1924 – 1928; merged with Pope and Talbot Lumber Company in 1934; operated irregular passenger service between Puget Sound and San Francisco, 1936 – 1937 and very limited service until 1941
WHITE STAR LINE	white star on red swallowtail pennant	White Star Line (transatlantic line); Great Britain / USA / Great Britain; 1849 – 1960; primarily transatlantic passenger service; operated as the White Star Line of Packets, 1849 – 1868; the Oceanic Steam Navigation Company was founded in 1869 by Thomas Ismay, who had owned the line since 1868; White Star Line was purchased by International Mercantile Marine Company in 1902; operated White Star-Dominion Line Joint Service (Canada to Great Britain) under the IMMC, 1909 – 1926; the famous White Star *Titanic* sank in 1912; advertised New York to the Mediterranean or West Indies cruises in the 1920s; the line was purchased by Royal Mail Steam Packet Co. in 1926; White Star merged with Cunard in 1934 to become Cunard White Star Ltd.; in 1950 Cunard dropped White Star from its name; the two remaining White Star ships retained the White Star livery as long as they sailed – the *Georgic II* until 1956 and the *Britannic II* until 1960
X	cobalt blue and white flag	Chandris, Inc., Greek; 1915 – present; family-run freight and cruise lines; first passenger ship sailed in 1922; operated in the Mediterranean in the 1930s; transatlantic immigrant passenger service began in 1959 and continued on an intermittent basis until 1973; established Chandris Fantasy Cruises in circa 1980 and Celebrity Cruises in 1989; the Chandris Group also owns large hotels in Greece
X		Celebrity Cruises; Greece; 1989 – present; upscale cruise line founded by Chandris, Inc.; offers Caribbean cruises, as well as cruises to Alaska and Bermuda
YARMOUTH STEAM SHIP Co Y.S.S.Co	"Yarmouth Steam Ship Co" arched upward in belt logo with cobalt blue flag in center; "Y.S.S.Co." on flag	Yarmouth Steam Ship Company; Canada; 1855 – 1912; operated between Boston and Yarmouth and Halifax, Nova Scotia; owned by Dominion Atlantic Railway, 1901 – 1912; taken over by Eastern Steamship Company in 1912
ZIM	‏צים‎ **ZIM**	Zim Lines (Zim Israel Navigation Company); Israel; 1948 – present; originally carried Hebrew immigrants to Israel; operated transatlantic passenger service, 1953 – 1967, as well as Mediterranean cruises in the 1960s; currently operates freighters worldwide

Ship Line Logos, Flags, and China Topmarks

Use these logos and flags to identify ship china and related collectibles, particularly glassware, hollow ware, and flatware.
A ship line or company name followed by an asterisk signifies that the illustrated logo or flag topmarks ship china.

Admiral Cruises Inc.
USA
1986 – 1992

Admiral Line *
(Pacific Steamship Co.)
USA
1916 – 1936

Alaska Commercial Co. *
USA
circa 1870 – circa 1910

Alaska Steamship Co. *
USA
1895 – at least 1965

Alcoa Steamship Co. *
USA
1940 – present

Algoma Central Railway
Marine Division *
1965 – 1990
Canada
(became Algoma Central Corporation)

American Banner Line *
USA
1958 – 1959

American Export Lines *
USA
1924 – 1962
(became American Export-Isbrandtsen Lines, 1962 – 1973; reverted to
American Export Lines in 1973, but
used a different flag)

American Hawaii Cruises
USA
1979 – present

American Mail Line *
USA
1925 – 1974

American President Lines *
USA
1938 – present
(container ships and freighters with
12 passenger limit since 1972)

American Republic Lines *
USA
1915 – 1958

Anchor Line *
(Erie & Western Transportation Co.)
USA
1865 – 1916
(taken over by Great
Lakes Transit Corp.)

Armement Deppe *
Belgium
at least 1920s – 1960s

Atlantic Container Line
Multinational
1984 – present

Baltimore Steam Packet
Company *
(Old Bay Line)
USA
1840 – 1962

Baltimore Steam Packet Company *
(Old Bay Line)
USA
1840 – 1962

British Tanker Corporation *
Great Britain
at least 1920s – 1950s

Brodin Line *
(Rederi Disa and Poseidon;
Erik O. Brodin)
Sweden
at least 1950s – 1960s

CP Ships
Canada
1968 – circa 1986

California Navigation and
Improvement Co. *
USA
late 1800s – 1927
(taken over by California
Transporation Co.)

California Transportation Co.
(River Lines)
USA
1875 – circa 1941

china topmark:
inverted flag in center of
life right logo

Canadian National Steamship *
Canada
1918 – 1976
(became CN Marine)

Canadian Pacific Steamship
Canada
1921 – 1968
(became CP Ships)

flag: 1946 – 1968

china topmark:
flag in center of belt logo

Carnival Cruise Lines
USA
1972 – present

Celebrity Cruises *
Greece
1989 – present

Chandris Lines *
Greece
1915 – present

Chandris Fantasy Cruises
Greece
1980 – present

Chesapeake Steamship Co. *
USA
circa mid-1800s – 1941
(merged with Baltimore
Steam Packet Co.)

Classical Cruises
USA
1990 – circa 1995

Clipper Cruise Line
USA
1983 – present

Clipper Line *
Sweden
1952 – 1969

Clyde Line *
USA
1844 – 1928
(merged with Mallory Line to form
Clyde-Mallory Line)

Clyde-Mallory Line *
USA
1928 – 1942

flag: red star on blue and white flag

Columbia Transportation Co. *
USA
1931 – 1994

Commodore Cruise Line *
Finland / Sweden
1966 – present

Commodore Cruise Line *
Finland / Sweden
1966 – present

Costa Line *
Italy
1924 – 1983

Costa Cruises
1983 – present

current logo: letter C, superimposed on
eight-pointed star, surrounded by circle

Crystal Cruises
Japan / USA
1988 – present

Cunard Line *
(British and North American Royal
Mail Steam Packet Company)
Great Britain
1841 – present

Cunard Line *
Great Britain
1841 – present

topmark variations: with and without
"CUNARD" below lion

Cunard Line *
Great Britain
1841 – present

Delta Line *
(Mississppi Shipping Co., 1919 –
1961 [Delta Line 1932+];
Delta Steamship Lines, 1961 – 1980s)
USA
1932 – 1980s

Delta Queen Steamboat Co.
(succeeded Greene Line, 1890 – 1973)
USA
1973 – present

Detroit & Cleveland
Navigation Co. *
USA
1898 – 1951

Dollar Steamship Company *
USA
1901 – 1938
(became American President Lines)

Dolphin Cruise Line *
multinational
1984 – present

Eastern Steamship Lines, Inc. *
USA
1901 – 1954
(line name sold; subsequent company offered cruises, 1954 – 1986)

Elders & Fyffes Ltd. *
Great Britain
circa late 1800s – present

Epirotiki Lines
Greece
1850s – present
(Royal Olympic Cruises
subsidiary, 1995+)

Evergreen Marine Corporation
(Evergreen Line)
Taiwan
circa 1980s – present

Evergreen Marine Corporation
(Evergreen Line)
Taiwan
circa 1980s – present

current logo: "EVERGREEN" may
be arched downward in lower portion of logo; otherwise logo is identical to their subsidiary, Eva Air

Fall River Line *
USA
late 1800s – 1904

Fall River Line *
USA
late 1800s – 1904

French Line *
(Campagnie Générale Transatlantique,
1861 – 1972; Campagnie Générale
Maritime, 1972 – present)
France
1861 – present

French Line *
(Campagnie Générale Transatlantique,
1861 – 1972; Campagnie Générale
Maritime, 1972 – present)
France
1861 – present

Furness, Withy & Co., Ltd.
Great Britain
circa 1902 – present

German-Atlantic Line *
(succeeded Hamburg-Atlantic
Line, 1957 – 1966)
Germany
1967 – 1973

Goodrich Steamship Lines *
USA
1856 – 1933

Grace Line *
Great Britain / USA (1913+)
1892 – 1970
(became Prudential-Grace Lines)

Grand Trunk Pacific *
Canada
1910 – 1920

Great Northern Steamship Co. *
USA
1900 – 1915

Great Northern Pacific
Steamship Co. *
USA
1915 – 1917

Greek Line *
(originally General Steam
Navigation of Greece)
Greece
1939 – 1975

logo: 1954 – 1975

Hamburg-American Line *
Germany
1856 – 1970
(merged with North German Lloyd
to form Hapag-Lloyd)

Hamburg-American Line *
Germany
1856 – 1970
(merged with North German Lloyd
to form Hapag-Lloyd)

logo: 1960s

Hamburg-Atlantic Line *
Germany
1957 – 1966
(became German-Atlantic Line)

Hapag-Lloyd *
Germany
1970 – present

china topmark variation:
inverted logo

Hellenic Lines Ltd. *
Greece
1934 – 1983

Hindustan Shipping Co. Ltd. *
Great Britain
at least 1920s – 1960s

flag colors (clockwise from top left):
blue, yellow, red, and white

Holland-America Line *
(Nederlandsch-Amerikaansche
Stoomvaart Maatschappi)
The Netherlands
1873 – 1972

Holland-America Line *
(Nederlandsch-Amerikaansche
Stoomvaart Maatschappi)
The Netherlands
1873 – 1972

Holland America Line *
The Netherlands
1873 – 1972 and early
1980s – present

logo: 1950s – 1972
& early 1980s – present

Note: known as Holland America
Cruises, 1972 – early 1980s;
used a different logo; *see logo
on 1979 souvenir plate photograph*

Home Lines *
Panama
1946 – circa 1988

china topmark: detailed,
rather than solid crown

Imperial Oil Co. Ltd. *
Canada
at least 1920s – 1950s

Incres Line *
Panama
1950 – circa late 1960s

International Mercantile
Marine Co. *
USA
1902 – circa 1936

Italian Line *
Italy 1932 – 1977

china topmark shown:
see photographs for variations

Ivaran Lines *
(originally Ivar An Christensen)
Norway
1925 – present

Java-China-Japan Line *
The Netherlands
1903 – mid-1950s
(became Royal Interocean Line)

A. F. Klaveness and Co. *
Norway
1870 – present

Knut Knutsen O. A. S. *
Norway
1920s – present

Lake George Steamboat Co. *
USA
circa late 1800s –
circa late 1930s

Maersk Line *
(A. P. Moller)
Denmark
1920s – present

Majesty Cruise Line
1992 – present

Mallory Line *
USA
1867 – 1928
(merged with Clyde Line to become
Clyde-Mallory Lines)

flag: red star; white, red, and
blue vertical stripes

Manitou Steamship Co. *
USA
1900 – 1908

Marine Atantic
(previously Canadian National
Steamships, 1918 – 1976 and CN
Marine, 1976 – 1986)
Canada
1986 – present

Matson Lines *
USA
1901 – 1971

Matson Lines *
USA
1901 – 1971

Merchant & Miners
Transportation Co. *
USA
1852 – 1948

Moltzau & Christensen *
Norway
at least 1950s – 1960s

flag: blue on left, red on right

McCormack Lines
USA
1913 – circa 1980s

Moore-McCormack Lines *
USA
1913 – circa 1980s

Morgan Line *
USA
(began operating in 1834;
owned and operated by
Southern Pacific, 1885 – 1941)
1834 – 1941

N. Y. K. Line *
(Nippon Yusen Kaisha)
Japan
1895 – present

Niarchos *
Greece
1960s – present

North German Lloyd *
(Norddeutscher Lloyd)
Germany
1958 – 1970
(merged with Hamburg-American to
form Hapag-Lloyd)

Northern Navigation Co. Ltd. *
Canada
1910 – 1983
(was Northern Navigation Company
of Ontario, 1899 – 1910)

Norwegian America Line *
Norway
1910 – 1980
(became Norwegian
American Cruises)

Norwegian American Cruises *
Norway
1980 – 1983
(became Cunard/NAC, 1983 – circa
1990; continued use of logo)

Norwegian Caribbean Lines
Norway
1966 – 1987
(became Norwegian Cruise Line)

Norwegian Cruise Line
Norway
1987 – present

Ocean Cruise Lines
1983 – 1994

Ocean Steamship Co.
of Savannah *
USA
1872 – 1939

Oceanic Cruises
(owned by Showa Line)
Japan
1989 – present

Oostzee S.S. Co. & Hillegersberg
S.S. Co. *
(joint operation)
The Netherlands
each company operated at least
1920s – 1960s

Oranje Line *
The Netherlands
1937 – 1970

Orient Lines *
Great Britain
1992 – present
(no connection with Orient Line,
1878 – 1967, also of Great Britain)

Pacific Far East Line *
USA
circa 1950s – 1978

Panama Line *
USA
1896 – 1981

Pearl Cruises
Denmark / Norway
1981 – 1995

Peninsular & Occidental
Steamship Co. *
USA
1900 – 1968

Pickands-Mather & Company *
USA
1883 – present

Premier Cruise Lines
("The Big Red Boat")
USA
1983 – present

Princess Cruises
(P & O Group since 1974)
Great Britain
1965 – present

Prudential Lines *
USA
circa 1950s – present

Radisson Diamond Cruise Ltd.
multinational
1992 – 1995
(merged with Seven Seas Cruise
Line to form Radisson Seven Seas
Cruises; above logo also represents Radisson's hotel chain)

Radisson Seven Seas Cruises
multinational
1995 – present

Red Cross Line *
Canada / Great Britain
circa 1850s – circa 1939

Red Star Line *
USA
1872 – 1939

pennant: red star on white

Rederi A.B. Transatlantic *
Sweden
1933 – present

Regency Cruises
1984 – 1995

Renaissance Cruises
Norway
1990 – present

Royal Caribbean Cruise Line
Norway
1969 – present

Royal Cruise Line *
Norway
1971 – present

Royal Mail Lines *
(originally Royal Mail Steam Packet
Company, 1839 – 1931)
Great Britain
1931 – 1969

Royal Viking Line *
1970 – 1994
(became Cunard Royal Viking in
1994; above logo remains in use)

Sabine Transportation Company *
USA
at least 1950s – present

SAFMARINE

Safmarine *
(South African Marine Corporation)
Union of South Africa
circa 1970s – present

Salen Rederierna A/B *
1916 – circa 1970s
Sweden

Saleninvest A/B
circa 1970s – circa early 1990s
Sweden

Seabourn Cruise Line *
Norway
1987 – present

Sealink *
Great Britain

logo used on Sealink china when it was owned by British Railways; pre-1990

Seawind Cruise Line
multinational
1991 – present

Shell Tankers *
multinational
at least 1950s – present

Showa Line *
Japan
1964 – present

Silversea Cruises
multinational
1993 – present

Sitmar Cruises *
(Societa Italiana Trasporti Marittimi;
Sitmar Line, 1938 – 1968)
Italy
1968 – 1988

Socony Mobil Oil Co. *
USA
mid-1950s – 1966
(was Socony-Vaccum Oil,
1931 – mid-1950s; became Mobil
Oil Corp., 1966)

Southern Pacific Steamship
Lines / Morgan Line *
USA 1885 – circa 1941

(also see Morgan Line)

Standard Oil Co. *
USA
1892 – 1972
(became Exxon Corporation)

Standard Oil Co. *
multinational
1892 – 1972
(USA companies became Exxon
Transportation Co., however Esso
Petroleum of London and perhaps
others still use the Esso flag)

logo: circa 1940s – 1972 in USA

Star Clippers *
1991 – present

STATES ⚓ LINE

States Line *
(States Steamship Lines)
USA
mid-1920s – circa 1980s

Stolt-Nielsen *
Norway
at least 1920s – present

Sun Line
Greece
1958 – present

early logo shown

Sun Line Cruises *
(Royal Olympic Cruises
subsidiary, 1995+)
Greece
1958 – present

current logo

Sun Oil Company *
USA
at least 1950s – 1970s

Svea Line *
(Stockholms Rederi) Sweden
at least 1920s – present

Swedish America Mexico Line *
Sweden
circa 1950s

Swedish American Line *
Sweden
1922 – 1975+
(listed in *Brown's Flags and Funnels*
© 1982, however shipping activi-
ty unknown)

Tidewater Oil Company *
USA

flag: orange and black

Ulysses Cruise Line *
Greece
1979 – 1984
(became Dolphin Cruise Line)

Union Castle Line *
USA
1900 – circa 1980s

United Fruit Company *
USA
1899 – circa 1960s

pennant: red and blue with white
diamond in center

United States Shipping Board *
USA
1916 – 1933
(replaced by U.S. Maritime
Commission in 1936)

United States Steel's shipping
divisions *
(Pittsburgh Steamship or
Bradley Transportation)
USA
1952 – 1967

United States Steel
Great Lakes Fleet *
USA
1967 – at least 1990

White Star Line *
Great Britain / USA
1850s – 1934
(operated as Cunard White
Star until 1949)

white star on red pennant

Windstar Sail Cruises
1984 – present

World Explorer Cruises
1978 – present

Zim Lines *
Israel
1948 – present

Zim Lines *
Israel
1948 – present

Courtesy of Cunard

Columbia Restaurant on *QE2*

Courtesy of Cunard

Queen Elizabeth 2

Ship Section Bibliography

Individual ship line historical information is extremely difficult to locate. Unfortunately dates tend to vary from one reference to another. The line data offered in this volume was tediously gathered from the following books, in addition to hundreds of magazine advertisements and cruise line brochures, and deciphered to the best of the author's ability.

American Passenger Ships – The Ocean Lines and Liners, 1873 – 1983
by Frederick E. Emmons
© 1985
Associated University Presses, Inc.

The American President Lines and Its Forebears
by John Niven
© 1987
University of Delaware Press

Berlitz Complete Guide to Cruising and Cruise Ships
by Douglas Ward
© 1994
Berlitz Publishing Company, New York

Brown's Flags and Funnels of British and Foreign Steamship Companies
Second, Fifth, and Sixth Edition
Compiled by Captain F. J, N. Wedge
© 1929, © 1951, © 1958, and © 1982
Brown, Son & Ferguson, Ltd..

ButterPat World
by Richard W. Luckin
© 1995
RK Publishing

Dining on Inland Seas
by Daniel C. Krummes
© 1997
Nautical Works Press

Dining on Rails
by Richard W. Luckin
© 1990, © 1998
RK Publishing

Fielding's Worldwide Cruises
Second and Fifth Edition
by Antoinette DeLand
© 1985 / 1991
William Morrow and Company, Inc.

Fielding's Worldwide Cruises 1995
by Anne Campbell
© 1994
William Morrow and Company, Inc.

Fielding's Worldwide Guide to Cruises
by Antoinette DeLand
© 1981, 1982
William Morrow and Company, Inc.

The First Great Ocean Liners, 1897 – 1927
by William H. Miller, Jr.
© 1984
Dover Publications, Inc., New York

Flags, Funnels and Hull Colours
by Colin Stewart
revised by John S. Styring
© 1963
Adlard Coles Ltd., London and
John de Graff Inc., New York

Flagships of the Line
by Milton H. Watson
© 1988
Patrick Stephens Limited

Fodor's 93 Cruises and Ports of Call
by Daniel and Sally Grotta
© 1992
Fodor's Travel Publications, Inc.

Great Cruise Ships and Ocean Liners From 1954 – 1986
by William H. Miller, Jr.
© 1988
Dover Publications, Inc., New York

The Great Luxury Liners 1927 – 1954
by William H. Miller, Jr.
© 1981
Dover Publications, Inc., New York

How to Identify and Price Ocean Liner Collectibles
by Karl D. Spence
© 1991

King and Queen of the River
by Stan Garvey
© 1995
River Heritage Press

A Maritime History of the Pacific Coast, 1540 – 1980
by James H. Hitchman
© 1990
University Press of America

Merchant Fleets in Profile
by Duncan Haws
© 1979
Patrick Stephens Ltd., Cambridge

Modern Cruise Ships, 1965 – 1990
by William H. Miller, Jr.
© 1992
Dover Publications, Inc., New York

Ocean Liners of the 20th Century
by Gordon Newell
© 1963
Superior Publishing Company, Seattle

Oceanliner Collectibles
by Karl D. Spence
© 1992

Oceanliner Collectibles, Volume 2
by Karl D. Spence
© 1996

Pacific Steamboats
by Gordon Newell
© 1958
Superior Publishing Company, Seattle

Shipping Literature of the Great Lakes
by Le Roy Barnett
© 1992
Michigan State University Press

Ships and the Sea (The Oxford Companion to)
Edited by Peter Kemp
© 1976
Oxford University Press

Stern's Guide to the Cruise Vacation
by Stephen B. Stern
© 1988

Sway of the Grand Saloon
by John Malcolm Brinnin
© 1971
Delecorte Press

The Total Traveler By Ship
by Ethel Blum
© 1993

Transatlantic Liners 1945 – 1980
by William H. Miller
© 1981
Arco Publishing, Inc., New York

The Unofficial Guide to Cruises
by Kay Showker with Bob Sehlinger
© 1995, First Edition
MacMillian, USA

The Western Ocean Packets
by Basil Lubbock
© 1988 (copy of 1925 original)
Dover Publications, Inc., New York

Western Ocean Passenger Lines and Liners
by Commander C. R. Vernon Gibbs
© 1989
Brown, Son & Fergusin, Ltd.

National Geographic and other magazine advertisements, 1910 – present

Cruise line brochures, 1990s

Steamboat Bill, Journal of the Steamship Historical Society of America, 1990s

Dinner on the Diner.....

American Railroad History

Nothing had a greater impact on land use and economic development in America between 1840 and 1950 than the railroads. When the gold and silver spikes were put in place at Promontory Summit in Utah on May 10, 1869, joining the rails of the Union Pacific and the Central Pacific, one of the gold spikes was engraved with the following, "May God continue the unity of our Country as this Railroad unites the two great Oceans of the world." A very few entrepreneurs became eminently wealthy and others were financially destroyed. While ordinary travelers depended on the trains as a means to journey from one place to another, wealthy patrons enjoyed luxurious holidays. Politicians used them as a means of campaigning. The railroads became an integral part of the U.S. mail system. Farmers and ranchers relied on the railroads to move their crops and live stock to market. Stores and catalog businesses counted on trains for delivery of merchandise. The livelihood of most families was in some way railroad dependent. Nearly everyone was affected in some way. But all this started to change in the 1950s when previous passengers began looking to the airlines for accelerated transportation or driving on interstate highways. And trucks became a more convenient way to transport interstate commerce. With only a few exceptions, most United States railroads went out of the passenger business on May 1, 1971. All that remains is Amtrak (the government owned and subsidized National Railroad Passenger Corporation), freight lines, local commuter trains, a number of short lines, excursion trains, and now and then a luxury train, such as the American Orient Express.

Collecting Railroad China

Most people are fascinated with the bygone era when hundreds of railroads offered efficient transit along with a pleasurable view of unfamiliar cities and the spacious diversified American countryside. Current means of transportation are neither as entertaining, nor as relaxing as a journey by rail. Because dining car meals were one of the most enjoyable events of train travel ("nothing could be finer"), collecting railroad china seems to somehow satisfy the yearning for those days that will never return. While the acquisition of this china is not as exciting as riding the rails (some would argue with that), it may fill the void with poignant memories.

I LOVE to dine at leisure
From a table set in style,
And enjoy my fresh-cooked dinner
With a fresh view every mile!

Value of Railroad China

American railroad china is the most highly valued of all commercial china. Some collectors are willing to drive hundreds of miles or fly from coast to coast to seek an elusive piece of this ware at an antique shop, auction, or railroad fair. To give you an idea of its worth, one collector said he recently sold the bulk of his collection in order to put a major down payment on a house! Not only is its value high, but buyers are easily found. Many collectors would not consider parting with a single piece, contributing to its rarity.

Railroad markings increase value. In general, collectors prefer pieces that are *both* railroad logo, name, or initial topmarked *and* railroad name or initial backstamped. Next they favor patterns that are railroad logo topmarked without a railroad backstamp, followed by railroad back stamped exclusive patterns, and finally non-railroad backstamped exclusive patterns or railroad backstamped stock patterns.

A.D. cup and saucer sets, coffee pots, teapots, cocoa pots, sauceboats, cream pitchers, creamers, sugars, and double egg cups are in higher demand because less were produced. Matching cups and saucers are difficult to locate, as they are often separated. Butter pats are especially popular, perhaps because of their small size.

Other than Canadian, the value of foreign railroad china remains relatively low in America at this time and will until demand increases.

Pattern rarity is a major factor in determining value, along with condition. *Also see Factors in Determining Value following the introduction.*

Pattern Terminology

Custom patterns
    1. Any pattern topmarked with a name, initials, or logo. Additional decoration, such as bands or intricate borders may be of custom or stock design. The word "Pullman" was added to the "Indian Tree" stock pattern. While the original stock pattern remained part of a standard product line, the addition of word "Pullman" created a custom pattern.
    2. Exclusive patterns do not have a logo, name, or initial topmark. After a design is submitted to and accepted by a customer, it is produced exclusively for that customer. Many exclusive designs are fairly distinctive. Several have overall decorations, for example Great Northern's "Glory of the West" pattern and Chicago, Milwaukee, St. Paul, and Pacific's "Traveler" pattern. Others are adaptations of stock patterns with altered colors or the addition or elimination of a decorative element such as a band or flower, for example Amtrak's "National" pattern which has only a custom colored band and line.

Stock patterns
    Part of a standard product line and available for purchase by any customer. Stock patterns used on railroad dining cars were most likely also used by numerous restaurants, hotels, and so forth. Therefore unless a stock pattern piece is railroad backstamped, proof of railroad usage is impossible.

A number of stock patterns are railroad backstamped, thus validating railroad usage of individual pieces. However some patterns, such as Kansas City Southern Railroad's "Roxbury," have never (according to current knowledge) been railroad backstamped. Though the pattern was used on the KCS for many years, railroad usage of any individual piece cannot be verified.

The Narrow Rim Designed for Dining Cars

"No product made a more significant contribution to the company's ability to survive the Depression and provide employment for its workers than the 'Econo-Rim' shape. Introduced in the Adobe body in 1933, the new shape was developed and patented to meet specific needs of the railroad industry, which was entering the era of fast streamlined trains. With narrower longer cars, the dining cars of newer trains were fitted with smaller tabletops. The new shape was designed to provide the space saving economies of a narrow rim without sacrificing any well space for foods. It was exactly what the railroads wanted. At the same time, the introduction of the 'Artint' process that provided color highlight to the new embossed rim design, further enhanced the appeal of the 'Econo-Rim' shape." (Quoted from the *History of Syracuse China.*) For an example, *see Chicago, Milwaukee, St. Paul, and Pacific's "Traveler" or "Peacock" pattern.*

Railroad China Manufacturers

Bauscher of Germany produced a considerable amount of high quality American railroad china. Many collectors consider Bauscher's ware superior to that made by American manufacturers, including Syracuse China who made the largest percentage of American railroad china. Shenango China also produced ware for numerous lines. Manufacturers of early railroad china include GDA Limoges, Greenwood, Grindley, Haviland, KT&T, Maddock (both the American and British companies), Mercer, Minton, Ridgway, Spode, and Union Porcelain. Later nearly all American commercial china firms produced ware for one or more lines. Well known companies include Buffalo, Fraunfelter, Hall, Iroquois, Jackson, Homer Laughlin, Mayer, McNicol, Scammell, Sterling, Walker, and Warwick, among others.

Reproductions and Fakes

As railroad china has increased in value so extensively during the last 30 years, numerous reproductions and fakes have appeared on the market. A reproduction is a copy of china that saw railroad usage. A fake is not a copy; either the pattern was never used on railroad china or the type of piece (for example, a creamer) was never used by the railroad whose topmark it bears.

Many reproductions are clearly marked and sold as such. Some collectors choose to purchase these, considering them representative of ware used by a particular railroad. Fake pieces, such as the creamer shown in the photograph at the right, were marked with a "NEW 1990" sticker and originally sold at a very modest price. The makers intent was not to fool the public. However, with the sticker no longer attached, an unaware collector may purchase it assuming it is genuine railroad china.

With the exception of gold and platinum and a few very early (pre-1920s) or recent (1975+) patterns, nearly all railroad china decoration was applied before glazing (underglaze) or fired in-glaze to resist wear. On the other hand, most fakes are decorated with low-fire ceramic enamel decals which can only be fired on-glaze. Therefore authenticity can sometimes be determined by examining the decoration. In addition nearly all railroad china backstamps are underglaze and should also be carefully scrutinized.

On-glaze fired enamel decals: the application of low-fire ceramic enamel decals is followed by a firing to burn off the lacquer film and adhere the decal to the china. The firing temperature is not high enough to sufficiently melt the glaze and allow the decal to sink below the surface (i.e., in-glaze). Therefore the low-fire enamel decals, which would begin to disintegrate if fired to a higher temperature, remain on top of the glaze. The somewhat glossy enamel look, often slightly pitted as if a needle had partially penetrated the decal, is quite obvious to both the eye and the touch. *For more information see Decals on pages 350 – 351.*

A familiarity with date codes and backstamps also helps. If china is topmarked with the name or logo of any railroad that went out of the passenger business on or before May 1, 1971, check for post-1970 date codes or recent manufacturer backstamps. In particular, watch for railroad topmarks on plain, lined, banded, or solid color glazed china made by Homer Laughlin with any backstamp, Sterling with the stylized "S" backstamp, or Hall with current rounded rectangle backstamp. The railroad topmark decals on china made by these companies were produced, applied, and fired by a decorator, not the manufacturer, except as follows:

Homer Laughlin —
• Central of Georgia "Macon" pattern
• Union Pacific "Winged Streamliner" pattern

Sterling China —
• Baltimore & Ohio "Capitol" pattern with gold logo
• Union Pacific "Winged Streamliner" pattern (1970s business car use; 1997+ gift catalog)
• Union Pacific "Corporate" pattern for business car use

Hall China —
• Union Pacific "Winged Streamliner" pattern (1997+ gift catalog)

Keep in mind, however, that recent patterns are not necessarily fakes or reproductions. American railroad china has been produced for use on Amtrak, business cars, short lines, luxury trains, and excursion trains since 1970. While some collectors prefer older ware, others find these pieces quite collectible. In addition, topmarked china continues to be used by several foreign railroads.

FAKE: Southern Pacific logo decal applied overglaze and fired on green underglaze lined creamer. Beware of this and other recent pieces decorated overglaze with railroad logos. For extensive information on fakes and reproductions, see *Dining on Rails* or any of the transportation china books by Richard W. Luckin.

Railroad Section Content

While the excellent railroad china books listed on the next page are currently available, a distinctly different approach is offered in this volume in an effort to supplement those works with:
◊ Quick reference identification aid: an alphabetical list of 325 railroad and railroad related china word and initial topmarks, along with a line art illustration or description of each including topmark color, if known
◊ A sampling of railroad and railroad related china photographs with value ranges
◊ Background information on dining car service

Railroad China References

The following are railroad china references written by Richard W. Luckin. Since 1980 Mr. Luckin has devoted a major portion of his life to the in-depth study of railroad china. His travels include visits to worldwide china manufacturers, railroad companies, museums, transportation libraries, and homes of ardent collectors. This research has resulted in the following works:

Dining on Rails—an Encyclopedia of Railroad China; 1st edition, © 1984, now considered a railroad collectible; 4th edition, © 1998, 488 pages (72 pages with 401 colored photographs were added in the 4th edition), currently available; with photographs and background information on 907 patterns including virtually all known American and Canadian railroad dining car patterns, as well as patterns used by traction lines, railroad station restaurants, and railroad operated hotels and ship lines. In addition there is an extensive section on reproductions and limited sections covering souvenirs, collector plates, and railroad china from around the world, plus a rarity guide. Related memorabilia, advertisements, and numerous dining car scenes are pictured throughout the book. Readers with a healthy imagination can ride or dine on all the roads, while paging through this book.

Teapot Treasury and Related Items; 1st edition, © 1987, 152 pages; presented in a similar format covering American and Canadian railroad china "beverage ware items" (i.e., teapots, creamers, and sugars).

Mimbres to Mimbreno, A Study of Santa Fe's Famous China Pattern; 1st edition, © 1992, 88 pages.

ButterPat World; 1st edition, © 1996, 256 pages; includes photographs and background information on 230 railroad patterns, as well as 127 ship and 217 airline patterns; also coverage of reproduction and fakes patterns.

To obtain information about these works write to:
RK Publishing
621 Cascade Ct.
Golden, CO 80403-1581

Railroad Section Bibliography

Many helpful books covering railroad history, as well as railroad flatware, hollow ware, and glassware are listed in the bibliography at the end of the railroad section.

Railroadiana Collectors Association

Railroadiana Collectors Association Inc. or RCAI, with a current membership of approximately 1300, publishes a quarterly magazine, *The Railroadiana Express*. Each issue has an article on railroad china by Richard Luckin. For membership information, write to:
Railroadiana Collectors Association Inc.
P.O. Box 8051
Rowland Hts., CA 91748

Railroadiana Collector Shows

Currently there are annual shows in the following cities:
Daytona Beach, Florida, in January and September
Dallas, Texas (Arlington or Irving, Texas), in March or April (transportation show)
Jacksonville, Florida, in February
Glen Ellyn, Illinois, in April and September
Helena, Montana, in April
Fort Worth, Texas, in May
Baltimore, Maryland (Timonium, Maryland), in May (transportation show)
Sacramento, California, in June
Little Rock, Arkansas, in June
St. Charles, Illinois, in June (transportation show)
Nashville, Tennessee, in June
Denver, Colorado, in July (transportation show)
Austintown, Ohio, in July
Atlanta, Georgia, in August
Sedalia, Missouri, in September
Gaithersburg, Maryland, in November (transportation show)

Dates and specifics, along with additional shows, are advertised in the *The Railroadiana Express*. Advertising flyers, some with admission discount coupons, may be available at your local antique shows and shops a month or two prior to a show.

Pullman

The first day coach converted by George M. Pullman, with hinged berths that folded up when not in use, rode the rails in 1859. The Pullman Palace Car Company was organized in 1867, and it wasn't long before it was operating first-class dining cars under contract on numerous railroad lines, some offering 12-course dinners. The company built, furnished, and operated sleeping, dining, and parlor cars. Although fares were more expensive, the high quality service and luxury cars, enhanced with a smoother ride, heightened Pullman's popularity. Nearly all American and Mexican railroads discontinued the use of their own sleeping and dining cars in favor of Pullman's. In 1944 Pullman was ordered to dissolve its monopoly and split into two companies. The split took place in 1947 when Pullman, Inc. became the manufacturer and Pullman Company, the operator. Eventually the Pullman Company was sold and came under joint ownership of the principal railroad companies. Forced into obsolescence by the competing airlines and interstate highway system, the company offered fine service until 1969, just prior to the advent of Amtrak.

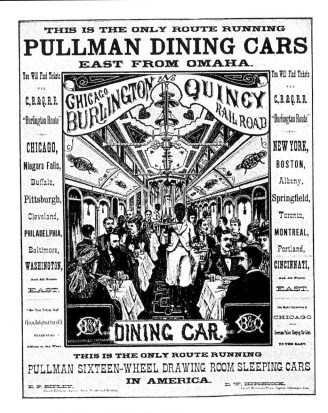

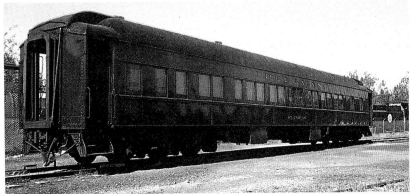

Pullman Dining Car

Richard Luckin Collection

Pullman dining car china and hollow ware service

"TRAIN OF TOMORROW"—ON THE RAILS TODAY

Every car ... observation lounge, sleeper, diner, chair car ... has glass-enclosed Astra Dome rising from the roof of the car. The Astra Dome dining compartment is pictured below.

General Motors SELECTED *Pullman-Standard*

TO BUILD THE "TRAIN OF TOMORROW"

Teamwork between industrial leaders has turned a "dream" train into practical reality. It began in General Motors' Electro-Motive Division, with sketches of an idea to give passengers a "sky-view" room and other innovations for all-over travel enjoyment. They chose Pullman-Standard for cooperation—to develop designs based on safe, sound car-building principles; to work out complete, detailed engineering plans; to execute the idea and to build

Observation Car ... "Train of Tomorrow"

a train of Pullman-Standard quality. The result— an innovation in car architecture—is the product of this cooperation.

Whenever a new streamliner takes the rails you have growing evidence of the progressiveness of American railroads. The mark of quality on deluxe new cars is the Pullman-Standard nameplate.

© 1947 P.-S. C. M. CO.

PULLMAN - STANDARD CAR MANUFACTURING COMPANY

Chicago, Illinois. Offices in six cities from coast to coast. Manufacturing plants at six strategic points

PULLMAN-STANDARD *... World's largest builders of streamlined railroad cars*

1947 advertisement

Fred Harvey

Not everyone traveled first class. In the early days, those who did not were forced to eat at railroad stations along the way. Meals were repetitious with the same foods being served morning, noon, and night and the time allowed to eat was very limited; often only 10 minutes. This began to change in 1876 when Fred Harvey, at the age of 41, took over the management of Santa Fe Railroad's Topeka depot restaurant. He was soon contracted to operate and supply food to all stations on the Santa Fe route. Later he became the concessionaire for all of Santa Fe's dining cars, depot restaurants, and hotels. He maintained high standards at his so-called "Harvey Houses," where even cowboys were not served without the proper attire. For this purpose, Mr. Harvey kept a number of jackets on hand. Meticulously prepared quality food was served

expeditiously by waitresses "of good character, young, and intelligent," better known as Harvey Girls, wearing black dresses and full-length white aprons. Considerably more time was allowed to

enjoy the sumptuous meals. Tables were covered with white table-cloths and set with silver-plated flatware and attractive china. All of this at a reasonable price! When Fred Harvey died in 1901 his sons, Ford and Byron Harvey, took over the business. The company incorporated in 1906 and continued to grow. Most of the Harvey restaurants closed in the 1920s and 1930s, but dining car service continued to increase. Millions of meals were served to military personnel during WWII, and some of the restaurants reopened for a time. Byron's sons took over the company after the war and there was more expansion including non-railroad affiliated restaurants. The Santa Fe Railroad sold all Grand Canyon hotels and restaurants to the National Park Service in 1954, who in turn gave the Fred Harvey Company a 20 year concession contract. In the 1960s additional non-railroad restaurants and catering operations were opened in various locations across the country, while nearly all of the original "Harvey Houses" had been closed. One-hundred forty Santa Fe dining and lounge cars were still being operated by the Harvey company at that time.

Wagon-Lits

Compagnie Internationale des Wagon-Lits, generally referred to as Wagon-Lits or CIWL, began operating railroad sleeping cars in Europe in 1876. Shortly thereafter dining, buffet, and salon cars were added. While most Wagon-Lits cars are contracted by European railroads, some are operated in the Middle East and Africa. With headquarters in Paris, the company also operates railroad station and airport restaurants, as well as river steamer dining rooms.

DINNER IS SERVED IN THE DINING CAR

In the early days of railway travel, trains which ran long distances stopped at certain stations to enable the passengers who did not carry their lunches to obtain meals at nearby hotels or restaurants. When the train came to a halt and the conductor shouted "Twenty minutes for refreshments," there was frequently a "mad scramble," every passenger seeming to be bent upon getting out of the train and into the restaurant ahead of the others. Plates of food were on the tables or counters in readiness. The first-comers fared pretty well, but those who came in last sometimes had to hurry back to the train before they had finished their meals.

In 1863, trains running between Philadelphia and Baltimore introduced a car fitted with an "eating bar"-something new in railroading. These cars had no kitchens, the food being cooked in restaurants in Philadelphia and Baltimore and placed in "steam boxes" in the cars just before the train's departure.

A few years later, George M. Pullman, who had won fame as a builder of sleeping cars, introduced what he called a "hotel car," equipped with a kitchen for preparing meals, with tables for serving meals, and with berths for sleeping, so that passengers could actually live in the car as they could in a home or a hotel.

Then, in 1868, Mr. Pullman introduced a dining car, equipped with a kitchen-the first passenger car designed exclusively for cooking and serving meals. This car was very popular, and before many years had passed dining cars were in use on many railroads.

Today, hundreds of passenger trains in the United States carry dining cars, providing travelers with a variety of foods and as excellent service as may be obtained in a first-class hotel or restaurant.

The interiors of modern dining cars are decorated in attractive style, many of them in gay pastel shades. Some have novel seating and table arrangements, including built-in lounge seats. Diffused lighting, colorful window drapes, and soft carpets suggest the friendly atmosphere of a neighborhood club or a home dining room. Tables prepared with snow-white linen, gleaming silverware and sparkling glasses, give promise of an appetizing meal to come. Air conditioning has made dining on the train a greater pleasure than ever before.

The dining car steward greets his guests at the door and ushers them to their tables. The white-coated waiters help them in the selection of their meals from the menu, place their orders with the chef, serve the dishes in proper style, and attend to the patrons' every want.

On some trains buffet cars are operated. There are also lunch counter cars which specialize in light lunches or meals at popular prices. Some trains include grill cars, a combination of cafeteria and soda fountain. These cars are especially popular on overnight trains. On many trains, tray service is provided, from the dining car direct to the passengers' seats. Pullman passengers frequently have tables put up in their rooms or compartments and have dining car meals served to them there.

When the passenger has finished his meal, the waiter brings the order blank (or check) on which the steward has written the amount of the meal. The passenger pays the waiter, and the waiter turns the order blank and money over to the steward. At the end of the run, the steward turns all order blanks and money over to the superintendent of dining car service or his assistant for forwarding to the treasurer.

In a year the railroads of the United States serve around 80,000,000 meals to their patrons.

Dining car crews-stewards, chefs, cooks, and waiters-are carefully selected. Each man must undergo a thorough physical examination before entering the service and at frequent intervals thereafter.

Newly employed cooks and waiters usually attend a school for dining car employees conducted by the railway company before they are allowed to go on the road. The school teaches them their duties and responsibilities. They are instructed in such matters as courtesy and deportment. Only in this way are the railroads able to maintain their high standard of service.

Reprinted from *A Study of Railway Transportation*, published by the Association of American Railroads in 195

The stairway in background leads to the upper dome level where you can dine under the open sky.

An Invitation to Dine in Luxury

This Astra Dome dining room has a rare charm revealed in soft, pleasing colors and textures...in exquisite table ware. Guests enjoy truly marvelous meals prepared from the finest of fresh foods, graciously served.

The Astra Dome dining cars are in service between Chicago and the Pacific Coast on the "CITY OF LOS ANGELES" and "CITY OF PORTLAND" Domeliners. These luxurious dome dining cars are an exclusive Union Pacific feature.

When arranging your next trip through the West, we suggest you ask to be routed on a Union Pacific Domeliner.
There is no extra charge — just extra pleasure.

UNION PACIFIC RAILROAD, Omaha 2, Nebraska

UNION PACIFIC RAILROAD

1955 advertisement

PREPARING DINNER IN THE DINING CAR KITCHEN

Many persons have wondered how it is possible for the railroad to prepare excellent meals for a train-load of passengers in a dining car kitchen smaller even than the kitchen of the average home. The secret is that the dining car kitchen has been designed with great care so as to get the maximum use out of every foot of space. There is a place for everything, and everything must be in its place.

The kitchen takes up a little less than one-fourth of the dining car. It is fitted with a large cooking range, a steam table to keep the food hot until served, electric mixers, refrigerators for meats and dairy products, coffee urns, cabinets, cupboards and shelves for dishes, silverware, and kitchen utensils. Overhead electric exhaust fans keep the kitchen ventilated.

At one end of the kitchen are drainboards, service tables, and an electric dishwasher. At the other end of the kitchen, nearest the dining room, is the pantry. Here are refrigerators and chill boxes for salad materials, cold dishes, ices, ice cream, and other foods which must be kept cold-all ready to be tastily arranged in dishes and served by the waiters.

The dining car steward is in charge of the entire dining car, including the kitchen. Directly in charge of the kitchen is the chef, who is a master of the culinary art, familiar with the preparation of all sorts of dishes. Nothing leaves the kitchen which fails to meet his discriminating approval. On an important run, where many meals are served, the chef usually has three assistants to help prepare the food. One man cooks the meats, another prepares the vegetables, and a third man makes up the salads, desserts, and cold plates. Within the broad range of their larder, these men can prepare almost any desired dish on short order. They are always glad to prepare special dishes for patrons who are "on a diet," or for the sick, or for infants and small children who cannot eat the regularly prepared dishes listed on the dining car menu.

When meals are being served, waiters are constantly coming and going, placing orders with the chef, and carrying away trays of dishes as rapidly as they are made ready for serving. At such times, the dining car kitchen presents a busy scene.

Careful study and planning are required to keep a railroad's fleet of dining cars fully equipped at all times. The railroads maintain commissaries at important terminals, stocked with provisions of all kinds, and equipped with refrigerators for the storage of meats, eggs, fish, butter, cheese, and other articles which must be kept cold. Expert buyers are employed by the railroads to purchase meats, fish, poultry, dairy products, fruits, vegetables, and other provisions.

Products from nearly every state in the Union are purchased by the railroads for use in dining cars.

The average dining car carries approximately 1,7oo pieces of tableware and kitchenware must be restocked frequently. The linen is laundered many times each year.

Before a dining car starts on a trip, its kitchen must be stocked with sufficient supplies to provide for any reasonable number of meals which it might be called upon to serve until it reaches another supply terminal. This calls for careful and intelligent planning to avoid wastage and unnecessary cost and also to avoid shortages.

Railway dining cars, lunch-counter cars, and buffet cars, as well as many railroad restaurants, are operated under the direction of a dining car superintendent.

Reprinted from *A Study of Railway Transportation*, published by the Association of American Railroads in 1951

Railroad China Advertisements

On the *Great Northern's* crack flyer
SYRACUSE CHINA

Jack Holt and Billie Dove on the Oriental Limited

OUTSIDE, the scene laid by Nature at her mightiest. Gigantic cliffs and snowy peaks. Gorges of dizzy depths. Rushing, roaring, writhing streams. Beauty! Incredibly awesome beauty. The Oriental Limited glides smoothly onward.

Inside, the scene reveals that man can triumph in his way as perfectly as Nature. Appetites made keen by mountain air are made more eager by the tempting menu. And eyes that have feasted on marvelous views are delighted with the exquisite beauty of Syracuse China.

Syracuse service is notably long wearing. Concealed in each graceful piece is strength to resist the shocks and strains which china inevitably meets under the extraordinary conditions encountered in dining-cars.

It is China to gratify the pride of the most exacting; to satisfy the strictest rules of economy. The Syracuse dealer near you will be glad to demonstrate this ware which bears the overwhelming preference of America's hotels, railroads, restaurants and steamship lines. Added to a great variety of ready-made patterns, is the privilege of ordering special designs with your own crest or monogram. Thus making the china service exclusively yours. Onondaga Pottery Co., Syracuse, N.Y.; 58 East Washington Street, Chicago; 342 Madison Avenue, New York.

RESTAURANT NEWS AND MANAGEMENT for June, 1927

A Pleasing Introduction
to a Meal *Well-served*

THIS brightly colored service plate greets all patrons of the Missouri Pacific's dining cars—a plate specially designed to symbolize the Road itself, and also to depict the floral beauty of the eleven states served by the Missouri Pacific.

Like many another great railroad system, and like hundreds of prominent restaurants, hotels and other institutions, the Missouri Pacific has long used Syracuse China exclusively. This is the natural result of our long experience in expressing tastefully in china the character and personality of any institution. It is prompted also by the reputation for long wear and low breakage enjoyed by this "home-like" institutional china; and finally by the fact

that the extraordinarily small breakage that does occur inevitably can always be replaced quickly and economically.

Syracuse China is made by the Onondaga Pottery Company, the world's largest maker of institutional ware. It is carried by institutional supply houses in every large city in America. You can examine stock patterns at your favorite supply house. Or, if you prefer your own pattern, monogram or coat of arms, your supply dealer will gladly submit suggested color patterns for the design you have in mind. ONONDAGA POTTERY COMPANY, Syracuse, New York. *New York Offices:* 551 Fifth Avenue. *Chicago Offices:* 58 East Washington Street.

SYRACUSE CHINA
A PRODUCT OF ONONDAGA POTTERIES
"Potters to the American People Since 1870"

Reprinted from *Dining on Rails* by Richard Luckin

THE MOST FAMOUS TRAIN IN THE WORLD IS EQUIPPED WITH *SYRACUSE CHINA*

© 1925 N. Y. Central R. R. Co.

LIKE a comet she bursts through the night, with her dazzling tail of glittering cars. A brighter flash—you glimpse the diner's wider windows. Then dark—the Century has passed.

In that diner the nation's elect are served. Here, indeed, is a need for the beauty of Syracuse China. And for its astounding wearability.

For dining-car service demands the practical as well as the beautiful. Strength to resist the chance of breakage that lurks in each tortuous curve—in each rapid stop.

To stand the unexpected shocks that crack and chip less sturdy ware.

Under almost incredibly difficult circumstances Syracuse China serves with distinction and economy. Certainly you can demand no more of the china you use than the Century does. Ask the Syracuse dealer near you to show you the many beautiful standard patterns, and examples of made-to-order work.

ONONDAGA POTTERY COMPANY
Syracuse, New York

58 E. Washington St.   342 Madison Ave.
Chicago, Ill.   New York City

SYRACUSE CHINA

1831

RESTAURANT NEWS AND MANAGEMENT for June, 1926

Reprinted from *Dining on Rails* by Richard Luckin

Speeding along the Hudson River . . .
the New York Central's famed 20th CENTURY LIMITED

Syracuse China

has been used since 1925 on the

New York Central

Beauty, wearability, long-term economy . . . plus the complete service of America's top-flight organization of china distributors!

Small wonder that Syracuse China is used by more leading dining cars, restaurants, hotels, clubs, schools, hospitals and steamship lines than any other table ware!

SYRACUSE
SINCE
1871
China
SYRACUSE, NEW YORK

Reprinted from *Dining on Rails* by Richard Luckin

"Old Ivory" Goes Traveling . . .

THEY call it "the Most Beautiful Train on Wheels." Its name, adopted from the official flower of Colorado, is The Columbine, and it speeds between Chicago and Denver on the Chicago and North Western Railway and the Union Pacific System.   The Columbine does not merely "carry passengers." It transports guests; and the two railroads see to it that service and appointments are in keeping with this ideal.   Hence it is that the dining cars of this crack flier are equipped with Syracuse "Old Ivory" in the specially created Columbine pattern shown here.   Dainty and appropriate as is its decoration, however, Syracuse China was chosen by the Chicago and North Western and Union Pacific for practical as well as aesthetic reasons. Exhaustive study persuaded the roads' officials that Syracuse China possesses, to an unusual degree for institutional ware, a distinctively home-like and attractive appearance.   This has likewise been the experience of other railroads, countless clubs, hotels and various prominent institutions, which have found Syracuse China—produced by the world's largest makers of institutional china—low in breakage, prompt and economical in replacement.   Nearly all institutional dealers are showing Syracuse China in scores of patterns and color harmonies. Or you may communicate direct with the Onondaga Pottery Company, Syracuse, New York. *New York Offices:* 551 Fifth Avenue—*Chicago Offices:* 58 East Washington Street.

Old Jvory
SYRACUSE CHINA

SYRACUSE CHINA
A PRODUCT OF ONONDAGA POTTERIES

DENVER   CHICAGO

Interior of one of The Columbine's commodious diners, giving a hint of the luxury it affords—including its Syracuse China Service.

Reprinted from *Dining on Rails* by Richard Luckin

DINING CAR, THE HIAWATHA OF THE CHICAGO, MILWAUKEE,
ST. PAUL AND PACIFIC R. R.

DINING CAR, LOUISVILLE & NASHVILLE R. R., LOUISVILLE, KENTUCKY

Reprinted from Syracuse China 75th Anniversary brochure

Railroad China and Value Ranges

Pattern Names and Codes

Pattern names and codes (railroad reporting mark and dash number) as listed in *Dining on Rails*, *Teapot Treasury*, and *ButterPat World* by Richard W. Luckin are used here to promote continuity in the hobby.

Manufacturers

Although many patterns were produced by several manufacturers, in most cases only those backstamped on illustrated pieces are noted.

China Backstamps

The manufacturer's name (usually shortened to one word) and manufacturer's trade name (if any; e.g. Old Ivory) are listed preceding the acronym "b/s" for backstamp. If the piece is also bottom marked with the railroad name, initials or logo, that information follows the manufacturer's name or tradename. "No b/s" indicates that the illustrated piece has neither a manufacturer nor a railroad backstamp.

Railroad Usage of Stock Patterns

While railroad usage of all illustrated stock patterns has been verified, each was undoubtedly used in at least some and possibly many restaurants, hotels, and other foodservice concerns. Proof that individual stock pattern pieces were actually produced for railroad use is impossible to establish unless ware is backstamped with a railroad name, initials, or logo. Without proof, value is reduced considerably. However, due to increased demand as ware representative of a particular line, the value is slightly higher than non-railroad related stock patterns.

Dates

Decades and date ranges refer to period in which the pattern was used by the railroad, unless otherwise indicated. Date codes are those marked on illustrated pieces.

Value Ranges

Each value range reflects the *illustrated piece only*: pattern, item, and size. Any variance can change the value considerably. "RR b/s" following a value range indicates the value of a railroad backstamped piece. Conversely, "not RR b/s" designates the value of a non-railroad back stamped piece. Pieces are assumed to be in good condition without cracks, chips, or excessive wear.

Because the asking price of railroad china varies to such an extreme from source to source, it is virtually impossible to offer accurate values. However, in an attempt to be as realistic as possible, prices gathered from collector shops, railroad, and transportation shows and mail order lists, along with estimates offered by experts from various regions of the United States were combined and averaged. Final figures were reverified by additional railroad china specialists. Again, please keep in mind that prices vary a great deal and that actual selling prices are ultimately determined by the requirements of the seller, along with the desire and willingness of the buyer. *Also see Value of Railroad China in the railroad section introduction and Factors in Determining Values in the Introduction.*

Comments on individual values would be welcomed for value range listings in future editions.

Photograph Order

Photographs are in alphabetical order by railroad name, then pattern name. Ware used in railroad related foodservice establishments appears at the end of the railroad china photograph segment.

Endnotes

Superscript numbers in photograph captions represent endnotes containing supplemental information. Endnotes immediately follow railroad related china photograph pages.

Larry Paul Collection

Amtrak "National" pattern 8¾" plate (AMTK-1a); gray line inside custom colored blue band is barely visible; Homer Laughlin b/s; 1979 date code; $18.00 – 22.00 not RR b/s.

American European Express "A-E Express" pattern cup and saucer (AEE-1); Rego b/s; circa 1990; train operated between Washington DC, White Sulphur Springs, WV, and Chicago in early 1990s; $40.00 – 50.00, not RR b/s.

Amtrak "National" pattern cream pitcher (AMTK-1b); custom glaze color; Hall b/s; 1970s – circa 1980s; $10.00 – 15.00 not RR b/s.

Atchison, Topeka & Santa Fe "California Poppy" exclusive pattern (ATSF-6); Bauscher, Hutschenreuther, O.P.CO. or Syracuse b/s; 1909 – 1971. 7¼" plate, $40.00 – 50.00 RR b/s, $30.00 – 40.00 not RR b/s; cup, $30.00 – 40.00 RR b/s, $24.00 – 30.00 not RR b/s.

Atchison, Topeka & Santa Fe "California Poppy" exclusive pattern (ATSF-6); Bauscher, Hutschenreuther, O.P.CO. or Syracuse b/s; 1909 – 1971; Bauscher pieces have highest value. Butter, $60.00 – 80.00 RR b/s, $30.00 – 40.00 not RR b/s; cocoa pot, $250.00 – 275.00 RR b/s, $200.00 – 225.00 not RR b/s.

Atchison, Topeka & Santa Fe "Griffon" exclusive pattern 7¾" plate (ATSF-8); O.P.CO. and Santa Fe Dining Car Service b/s; 1931 date code; $150.00 – 175.00 RR b/s.

Atchison, Topeka & Santa Fe "Mimbreno" pattern[1] (ATSF-9); Syracuse Old Ivory and Santa Fe b/s; produced in ivory body 1937 – 1959 and white body 1959 – 1971. Butter, $85.00 – 100.00 RR b/s original; sugar, $175.00 – 200.00 RR b/s original with cover (not shown).

Atlanta and West Point "Montgomery" pattern (A&WP-2); stock pattern; McNicol and The West Point Route b/s; produced for railroad in 1949. Cup & saucer, $275.00 – 350.00 RR b/s, $15.00 – 20.00 not RR b/s; 7¼" plate, $150.00 – 175.00 RR b/s, $9.00 – 12.00 not RR b/s.

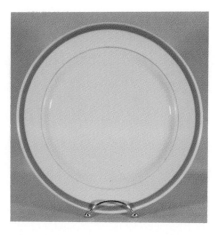

Atlantic Coast Line "Carolina" pattern 9" plate (ACL-1); stock pattern; Atlantic Coast Line Railroad and Sterling b/s; ordered 1940 – 1962 (1955 date code); also used by the Florida East Coast and the Southern Ry., each b/s accordingly; $50.00 – 65.00 RR b/s, $4.00 – 6.00 not RR b/s.

Larry Paul Collection

Atlantic Coast Line "Palmetto" pattern 10" long platter (ACL-3); Buffalo, GDA, McNicol, Shenango, or Warwick b/s; circa 1920s; $150.00 – 175.00 RR b/s, $95.00 – 110.00 not RR b/s.

Baltimore & Ohio "Centenary" pattern[2] 6¾" plate (B&O-4); border includes Diesel Electric "51"; Shenango and Baltimore & Ohio Railroad 1827 – 1927 b/s; made from 1949 – 1968; $90.00 – 115.00 RR b/s original.

Larry Paul Collection

Atlantic Coast Line "Flora of the South" pattern 7¼" plate (ACL-2); Buffalo Old Ivory and Atlantic Coast Line Railroad b/s; circa 1930s; $125.00 – 175.00 RR b/s.

Baltimore & Ohio "Centenary" pattern[2] 6¾" plate (B&O-4); border includes "Lord Baltimore"; Buffalo and Baltimore & Ohio Railroad 1827 – 1927 b/s; produced in 1938; $125.00 – 150.00 RR b/s.

Larry Paul Collection

Boston and Albany "Berkshire" pattern 5" high pitcher (B&A-1); O.P.CO. and B & A RR b/s; ordered 1913 – 1929; $175.00 – 225.00 RR b/s.

Larry Paul Collection

Buffalo, Rochester, and Pittsburgh "Safety Slogan" pattern 10½" long platter (BR&P-4a); Mayer b/s; circa 1920s; $250.00 – 300.00 not RR b/s.

Burlington Northern "Gold Key" pattern (BN-1); stock pattern; Jackson b/s; 1981 date code; used on business car. 7" plate, $8.00 – 10.00 not RR b/s; cup & saucer, $15.00 – 20.00 not RR b/s.

Larry Paul Collection

Canadian National "Bonaventure" pattern crescent salad (CN-3a); Grindley Duraline Hotelware b/s; 1960s – 1970s; $40.00 – 55.00 not RR b/s.

Canadian National System "Queen Elizabeth" pattern soup (CN-17); Royal Doulton b/s; 1923 – 1927; $60.00 – 75.00+ not RR b/s.

Canadian National System "Rupert" pattern saucer (CN-20); Sovereign Potters b/s; 1923 – 1954. Saucer, $12.00 – 15.00 not RR b/s; cup & saucer, $30.00 – 40.00 not RR b/s.

Larry Paul Collection

Canadian National "Toronto" pattern celery (CN-21); Sovereign Potters b/s; circa 1950s; $50.00 – 65.00 not RR b/s.

Canadian National "Transcontinental-CN" pattern saucer (CN-21.2) shown with plain cup; mustard and black lines on saucer; Vandesca-Syracuse and CN b/s; 1975 date code; patterned cup & saucer, $18.00 – 25.00 RR b/s.

Chesapeake & Ohio "Chessie" pattern ashtray (C&O-2); Syracuse b/s; 1955 – 1962 (1956 date code); $85.00 – 100.00 not RR b/s. Note: only ashtray, cup, and 9¾" plate in this pattern are decorated with the Chessie logo.

Chesapeake and Ohio "Staffordshire" pattern[4] fruit (C&O-9); stock pattern; Shenango Staffordshire and Chesapeake b/s; late 1940s; $75.00 – 90.00 RR b/s, $3.00 – 4.00 not RR b/s.

Canadian Pacific "Foliage" pattern crescent salad (CP-13); Ridgway Potteries and Canadian Pacific b/s; post-1955; $40.00 – 50.00 RR b/s.

Chesapeake and Ohio "George Washington" pattern (C&O-4a); Buffalo Old Ivory and C & O b/s.[3] Teapot, $450.00 – 600.00+; mustard, $100.00 – 125.00; cream pitcher, $80.00 – 100.00; sauceboat, $90.00 – 115.00; plate, $200.00 – 250.00+; each with RR b/s.

Chicago, Burlington & Quincy "Aristocrat" pattern A.D. cup & saucer (CB&Q-1a); Syracuse b/s; 1946 date code; $1,000.00 – 1,200.00 not RR b/s[5].

Larry Paul Collection

Chicago, Burlington & Quincy "Chuck Wagon" pattern 6¼"
plate (CB&Q-5); Trend shape; Syracuse and Vista Dome Denver Zephyr b/s; 1956 – 1968 (1967 date code); $125.00 –
175.00 RR b/s.

Larry Paul Collection

Chicago, Burlington & Quincy "Dubuque" pattern tan body
oatmeal (CB&Q-7); Buffalo Cafe au Lait b/s; circa 1930s;
$175.00 – 225.00 not RR b/s.

Chicago, Burlington & Quincy "Violets and Daisies" pattern
½" plate (CB&Q-13); O.P.CO. and C.B. & Q Railroad b/s;
1919 – 1971; pieces produced in latter years not RR b/s; $60.00
– 75.00 RR b/s, $24.00 – 30.00 not RR b/s.

Larry Paul Collection

Chicago, Burlington & Quincy "Cobalt" pattern coffee pot
(CB&Q-6); Hall b/s; circa 1930s; $150.00 – 175.00 not RR b/s.

Chicago, Burlington & Quincy "Violets and Daisies" pattern
(CB&Q-13); O.P.CO. and C.B. & Q Railroad b/s; 1919 – 1971;
pieces produced in latter years not RR b/s. Butter, $80.00 –
95.00 RR b/s, $30.00 – 40.00 not RR b/s; bouillon, $60.00 –
75.00 RR b/s, $24.00 – 30.00 not RR b/s.

Larry Paul Collection

Chicago, Indianapolis & Louisville "Monon" pattern 7¼" platter (Mon-1); Shenango b/s; 1951 – circa 1967; $85.00 – 100.00
not RR b/s.

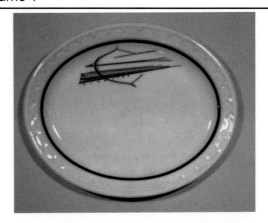

Chicago, Milwaukee, St. Paul, and Pacific "Hiawatha" pattern 7¼" platter (MILW-3); Syracuse Econo-Rim and Hiawatha b/s; ordered 1936 – 1937; $200.00 – 250.00+ RR b/s.

Chicago, Milwaukee, St. Paul, and Pacific "Galatea" pattern 9" soup (MILW-2); stock pattern; Syracuse Old Ivory and C.M. & ST.P. & P.R.R. b/s; ordered 1926 – 1944; $175.00 – 200.00 RR b/s, $20.00 – 25.00 not RR b/s.

Chicago, Milwaukee, St. Paul, and Pacific "Traveler" exclusive pattern (MILW-11); Syracuse Econo-Rim or Syracuse b/s on platter; produced 1937 – 1969. 7" long platter, $65.00 – 80.00 not RR b/s; cake cover, $125.00 – 150.00+ not RR b/s.

Chicago, Milwaukee, St. Paul, and Pacific "Peacock" pattern[6] 8" long platter (MILW-7); Syracuse Econo-Rim b/s; 1935 – 1969; $45.00 – 60.00 not RR b/s.

Chicago, Rock Island, and Pacific "El Reno" pattern 9" platter (CRI&P-1); Shenango b/s; circa 1950s; $150.00 – 200.00 not RR b/s.

Chicago, Rock Island, and Pacific "Golden Rocket" pattern grapefruit (CRI&P-3); Shenango Ivory b/s; circa late 1940s; $140.00 – 180.00 not RR b/s.

Larry Paul Collection

Chicago, Rock Island, and Pacific "Princeton" pattern 10" long celery (CRI&P-6); O.P.CO. b/s; circa 1912 – circa 1919; $150.00 – 200.00+ not RR b/s.

Larry Paul Collection

Cincinnati, Hamilton, and Dayton "Cincinnati" patter 8¼" long platter (CH&D-1); Maddock M-L b/s; early 1900s; do not confuse with electric line which operated 1926 – 1929; $300.00 – 350.00+ not RR b/s.

Larry Paul Collection

Delaware and Hudson "Adirondack" pattern 10½" service plate (D&H-1); Syracuse b/s; 1973 date code; $175.00 – 200.00 not RR b/s.

Larry Paul Collection

Delaware and Hudson "Canterbury" pattern fruit (D&H-2a); O.P.CO. b/s; ordered 1926 – 1946 (1927 date code); $75.00 – 100.00 not RR b/s.

Larry Paul Collection

Delaware, Lackawanna & Western "St. Albans" pattern[7] fruit (DL&W-6); stock pattern; O.P.CO. St. Albans © 1915 and D.L. & W.R.R.CO. b/s; ordered circa 1915 – 1949; $125.00 – 150.00 RR b/s, $8.00 – 10.00 not RR b/s.

Larry Paul Collection

Denver and Rio Grande "Curecanti" pattern 6¼" handled soup (D&RG-2a); O.P.CO. b/s; ordered 1908 – 1927; $250.00 – 300.00 not RR b/s.

Deutsche Speisewagen Gesellschaft "Rheingold" pattern (DSG-2); Bauscher and DSG b/s; circa 1950s; Rheingold (1928+), a "Train de Deluxe," employeed DSG catering (1949+) and joined the Trans-Europe Express (TEE) in 1957; $65.00 – 80.00 RR b/s.

Larry Paul Collection

Erie "Gould" pattern 9¾" long celery (ERIE-4); Shenango b/s; circa 1920s; $100.00 – 125.00 not RR b/s.

Larry Paul Collection

Erie "Susquehanna" pattern 10" long celery (ERIE-9); Buffalo and Erie Railroad b/s; circa 1920s; $100.00 – 125.00 RR b/s.

Florida East Coast "Seahorse" pattern 8" plate (FEC-10); stock pattern; O.P.CO. and F.E.C.Ry. b/s; 1937 date code; $125.00 – 150.00 RR b/s, $8.00 – 10.00 not RR b/s.

Great Northern "Glory of the West" exclusive pattern 9" long platter (GN-6); Onondaga Pottery and Great Northern Railway b/s; ordered 1940 – 1957 (1950 date code); $125.00 – 160.00 RR b/s.

Great Northern "Hill" pattern 12" platter (GN-7a); Greenwood b/s; circa 1890s; $200.00 – 250.00+ not RR b/s.

Larry Paul Collection

Great Northern "Mountains and Flowers" exclusive pattern 10" long celery (GN-8); Syracuse and Great Northern Railway b/s; circa 1940s – 1969 (1950 date code); $130.00 – 170.00+ RR b/s.

Great Northern "Mountains and Flowers" exclusive pattern ash-tray (GN-8); Syracuse and Great Northern Railway b/s; circa 1940s – 1969; $75.00 – 85.00 RR b/s.

Illinois Central "Coral" exclusive pattern fruit (IC-1); Syracuse b/s; 1935 – 1970; $30.00 – 40.00 not RR b/s.

Kansas City Southern "Roxbury" pattern (KCS-2); Syracuse Econo-Rim b/s; very prevalent stock pattern produced 1934 – 1980s; used on KCS 1934 – 1969. A.D. cup & saucer; $18.00 – 25.00 not RR b/s; 5½" plate, $5.00 – 7.00 not RR b/s.

Kansas City Southern "Roxbury" pattern (KCS-2); made by Syracuse, though not b/s; stock pattern; 1934 – 1969. Butter, $12.00 – 15.00 not RR b/s; creamer, $10.00 – 12.50 not RR b/s.

Louisville & Nashville "Regent" pattern butter (L&R-3); stock pattern; Syracuse Old Ivory Regent b/s; circa 1940s – 1960s; $30.00 – 40.00 not RR b/s.

Richard W. Luckin Collection

Minneapolis, St. Paul & Sault Ste. Marie "Snowflake" pattern baker (SOO-3); Knowles, Taylor, & Knowles b/s; $400.00 – 450.00 not RR b/s.

Larry Paul Collection

Missouri Pacific "State Flowers" pattern 10½" service plate (MP-11); O.P.CO. b/s; ordered 1929 – late 1940s; $275.00 – 350.00+ RR b/s, $250.00 – 325.00+ not RR b/s.

Larry Paul Collection

New York Central "Depew" pattern celery (NYC-5); stock pattern; Haviland and The New York Central Line b/s; 1893 – 1919; $125.00 – 150.00+ RR b/s.

Larry Paul Collection

New York Central "Dewitt Clinton" exclusive pattern 9½" long celery (NYC-6); Buffalo China and New York Central Lines b/s; 1925 – 1951; $80.00 – 100.00 RR b/s, $65.00 – 80.00 not RR b/s.

New York Central "Dewitt Clinton" exclusive pattern cup (NYC-6); O.P.CO. b/s; 1925 – 1951 (1944 date code); $35.00 – 40.00 RR b/s, $30.00 – 35.00 not RR b/s.

New York Central "Doric Black" pattern (NYC-6.1); stock pattern; recessed O.P.CO b/s (early 1940s); ordered 1939 – 1964. Cream pitcher; $12.00 – 15.00 not RR b/s. Teapot, $20.00 – 25.00 not RR b/s; sugar, $9.00 – 12.00 not RR b/s.

New York Central "Mercury" pattern bouillon (NYC-9); Syracuse b/s; ordered 1938 – 1967; $45.00 – 55.00 not RR b/s.

Larry Paul Collection

New York Central "Mohawk" pattern 10¼" plate (NYC-10); pattern produced on 10¼" plates only; O.P.CO. b/s; ordered 1938 – 1943; $125.00 – 150.00 not RR b/s.

New York, Chicago, and St. Louis "Fort Wayne" pattern 9" long platter[8] (NKP-3); platinum nickel plate road logo on rim; Shenango b/s; circa late 1940s; $250.00 – 300.00+ not RR b/s.

New York, New Haven & Hartford "Indian Tree-NH" pattern cup (NH-3) ; stock pattern; Buffalo and N-Y-N-H & H R-R CO. b/s; $30.00 – 40.00 RR b/s, $5.00 – 7.00 not RR b/s.

Larry Paul Collection

New York, New Haven & Hartford "Merchants" pattern 8½" plate (NH-5); Buffalo and N-Y-N-H & H R-R CO. b/s; circa 1930s; $140.00 – 165.00+ RR b/s.

Larry Paul Collection

New York, New Haven & Hartford "Old Saybrook" pattern oatmeal (NH-9a); decoration in well of oatmeal; McNicol b/s; circa 1950s; $50.00 – 60.00 not RR b/s.

Larry Paul Collection

Norfolk and Western "Bristol" pattern 11¾" long platter (N&W-1a); O.P.CO. b/s; 1918 date code; $100.00 – 125.00+ not RR b/s.

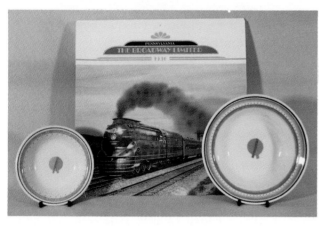

Pennsylvania "Broadway" pattern (PRR-3); 1935 – 1950s. Fruit; Mayer and Broadway Limited / PRR logo b/s; $25.00 – 35.00 RR b/s. Grapefruit; Scammell's Trenton China and PRR logo b/s; $30.00 – 40.00 RR b/s.

Pennsylvania "Purple Laurel" pattern bouillon (PRR-21); Scammell's Trenton and PRR logo b/s; 1920s – 1950s; $20.00 – 25.00 RR b/s.

Larry Paul Collection

Pullman "Verde Green" pattern cocoa pot (PUL-6); PULL-MAN, lettered in gold, is barely visible in photograph; Hall b/s; circa 1930s; $200.00 – 225.00 not Pullman b/s.

Pullman "Indian Tree-PUL" pattern 7½" plate (PUL-3); Syracuse b/s; circa 1930s – circa 1950s; $70.00 – 85.00 not Pullman b/s.

August M. Riccono Collection

Richmond, Fredericksburg & Potomac "Tri-Link" pattern egg cup (RF&P-2); O.P.CO. b/s; 1927 date code; $400.00 – 500.00 not RR b/s.

August M. Riccono Collection

Seaboard Air Line Railway "Miami" pattern butter (SAL-8); made by Onondaga Pottery; circa 1920s; $100.00 – 125.00 not RR b/s.

Southern Pacific "Prairie-Mountain Wildflowers" exclusive pattern (SP-11); Syracuse Econo-Rim and Southern Pacific Lines b/s; mid-1930s – 1950s. Cup & saucer, $90.00 – 110.00 RR b/s; 5½" plate, $50.00 – 60.00 RR b/s.

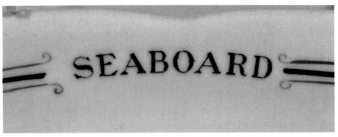

Larry Paul Collection

Seaboard Air Line Railway "Miami" pattern ll" long celery (SAL-8); O.P.CO. b/s; circa 1920s; $150.00 – 175.00 not RR b/s.

Richard W. Luckin Collection

Southern Pacific "Daylight" pattern cup & saucer (SP-2); pale orange (peach) glaze[9]; Franciscan Ware and Southern Pacific Lines or S.P.Co. b/s; 1939 – early 1940s on SP's Daylights; $400.00 – 500.00+ RR b/s, $15.00 – 20.00 not RR b/s.

Southern Pacific "Prairie-Mountain Wildflowers" exclusive pattern 7¼" plate (SP-11); Syracuse Econo-Rim and Southern Pacific Lines b/s; 1930s – 1950s (1940 date code); $60.00 – 75.00 RR b/s.

Southern Pacific "Sunset" pattern 9¼" long platter (SP-14); small SP logo[10]; O.P.CO. and Southern Pacific b/s; 1926 date code; $125.00 – 150.00 RR b/s.

Southern Pacific "Sunset" pattern 8" long baker (SP-14); large SP logo[10]; Buffalo and Southern Pacific b/s; circa 1920s; $145.00 – 175.00 RR b/s.

Spokane, Portland & Seattle "Red Leaves" 6¼" plate (SP&S-2); stock pattern; Shenango b/s; $8.00 – 10.00 not RR b/s.

Spokane, Portland & Seattle "American" pattern 8" plate (SP&S-1); stock pattern originally designed and produced for American Hotels Corp.; O.P.CO. b/s; 1930s and early 1940s (1930 date code); $10.00 – 15.00 not RR b/s.

August M. Riccono Collection

Texas and Pacific "T&P Arrow" pattern celery (T&P-6); O.P.CO. b/s; 1929 – late 1930s (1929 date code); $500.00 – 600.00 not RR b/s.

Union Pacific "Blue and Gold" 8" plate (UP-1); cobalt band flanked by gold lines on white body; stock pattern; Syracuse b/s; ordered 1942 – 1953 for use on The 49er; $9.00 – 12.00 not RR b/s.

Union Pacific "Challenger" pattern 6½" plate (UP-2); Syracuse Econo-Rim b/s; ordered 1937 – 1954; $55.00 – 65.00 RR b/s, $45.00 – 55.00 not RR b/s.

Union Pacific "Cheyenne" pattern tan body covered sugar (UP-3); stock pattern; Syracuse Adobe Ware and Union Pacific R.R. b/s; 1939 date code; $150.00 – 175.00 RR b/s, $6.00 – 8.00 not RR b/s.

Larry Paul Collection

Union Pacific "Columbine" pattern 9¾" plate (UP-4); O.P.CO. Old Ivory and Columbine b/s; ordered 1930 – 1941; $200.00 – 225.00+ RR b/s.

Union Pacific "Corporate" pattern cup & saucer (UP-4.1a); Sterling b/s; ordered 300 ten-piece place settings in 1990; $45.00 – 60.00 not RR b/s.

Union Pacific "Desert Flower" exclusive (after UP's initial purchase) pattern 8" long platter (UP-6); Syracuse and Union Pacific R.R. b/s; mid-1950s – mid-1960s; $35.00 – 45.00 RR b/s.

Union Pacific "Desert Flower" exclusive (after UP's initial purchase) pattern (UP-6); Syracuse and Union Pacific R.R. b/s; mid-1950s – mid-1960s. Grapefruit, $ 30.00 – 40.00 RR b/s; 7½" plate, $30.00 – 40.00 RR b/s.

Union Pacific "Harriman Blue" pattern (UP-8a); John Maddock & Sons and U.P.R.R. b/s on butter; impressed Scammell's Trenton and Union Pacific Overland shield logo b/s on plate; circa 1905 – circa 1950. Butter, $30.00 – 40.00 RR b/s; 7" plate, $40.00 – 45.00 RR b/s.

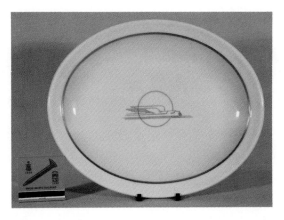

Union Pacific "Winged Streamliner" exclusive pattern 9½" long platter (UP-20); O.P.CO. or Syracuse[11] and Union Pacific R.R. b/s; ordered from Syracuse, 1936 – 1955; $50.00 – 65.00 RR b/s.

United States Bureau of Fisheries "Bureau of Fisheries" pattern 9¾" plate (USBF-1); Buffalo b/s; circa 1920s; said to be used at U. S. Bureau of Fisheries headquarters, as well as on their train cars; $75.00 – 100.00.

Union Pacific "Historical" pattern pickle (UP-9); Shenango and Union Pacific R.R. b/s; ordered 1927 – 1949; $200.00 – 225.00 RR b/s.

Union Pacific "Winged Streamliner" exclusive pattern sherbet (UP-20); Scammell's Trenton b/s; pre-1955; $50.00 – 65.00 not RR b/s. Note: 1997+ "Winged Streamliner" by Sterling and "Winged Streamliner" teapots by Hall made for gift shop, not dining car use.

Wabash "Banner" pattern 5½" plate (WAB-1); Syracuse b/s; circa 1947 – mid-1960s; $80.00 – 100.00 not RR b/s.

Wagon-Lits (European dining car operator). "Brussel's" pattern (W-L-1) gray-blue glazed 7" plate; Gien Porcelaine b/s; 1928+; $40.00 – 50.00. "Paris" pattern (W-L-2) light blue glazed A.D. cup; Richard Ginori b/s; circa 1960s – circa 1970s; $15.00 – 20.00.

Larry Paul Collection

Wagon-Lits (European dining car operator) "Internationale" pattern mustard (W-L-3); Hutschenreuther and Wagon-Lits b/s; circa 1980s; $20.00 – 25.00.

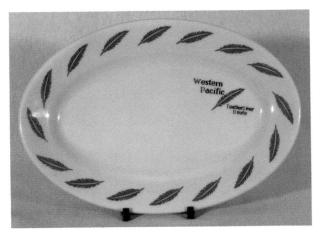

Western Pacific "Feather River" pattern 7½" long platter (WP-2); Shenango Incaware b/s; late 1940s – circa 1950s; $75.00 – 90.00 not RR b/s.

Railroad Associated
Foodservice Establishments

Canadian National System's Hotel Vancouver "Vancouver" pattern (CN-23); Royal Doulton b/s; early 1950s – late 1960s. 6¼" plate, $24.00 – 30.00; sauceboat, $30.00 – 40.00.

Canadian Pacific's Empress Hotel (Victoria, B.C.) "Empress Hotel" pattern cream pitcher (CP-11.1); Steelite tradename b/s; made by Ridgway; mid-1970s; $15.00 – 20.00.

Canadian Pacific Hotels "Floral" pattern cream pitcher (CP-12); Sovereign Potters and Canadian Pacific Hotels b/s; $50.00 – 65.00.

Chicago & Northwestern's Chicago station restaurant china, "Depot Ornaments" pattern 9¾" long platter (C&NW-3); stock pattern; Buffalo b/s; circa 1930s; $15.00 – 20.00.

Richard W. Luckin Collection

Grand Trunk Pacific's "Fort Garry Floral" hotel pattern platter (GTP-5); Guerin-Pouyat-Elite b/s; 1920s; $90.00 – 120.00.

Larry Paul Collection

The Greenbrier Hotel[12] (White Sulphur Springs, WV) "White Sulphur Springs" pattern match stand (C&O-12); O.P.CO. and Greenbrier b/s; 1941 date code; $60.00 – 80.00.

Larry Paul Collection

The Greenbrier Hotel[12] (White Sulphur Springs, WV) "Greenbrier" exclusive pattern 10½" plate (C&O-5b); Shenango b/s; 1971 date code; $25.00 – 35.00 (high end: earlier dates with Greeenbrier b/s).

Fred Harvey's "Encanto" pattern sugar (FH-5); usually has orange line near edge; stock pattern; O.P.CO. b/s; 1944 date code; pattern used at La Fonda hotel in Santa Fe, NM; $14.00 – 18.00.

Larry Paul Collection

Fred Harvey's "Gold Lion" pattern 11¼" service plate (FH-7); Syracuse b/s; 1968 date code; used at Gold Lion restaurant in Chicago's Union Station; $175.00 – 200.00.

Richard W. Luckin Collection

Fred Harvey's "Harvey Girl" pattern 9" plate (FH-8); Walker b/s; $150.00 – 175.00.

Richard W. Luckin Collection

Fred Harvey "Harvey Girl" pattern mug (FH-8a); Jackson b/s; dated October 1956; $125.00 – 150.00.

Fred Harvey "Trend" pattern saucer (FH-13); Syracuse China's *Berkeley* stock pattern on *Trend* shape; Syracuse *Trend* b/s; post-1955 (1962 date code); used at hotels on Santa Fe routes. Saucer, $5.00 – 7.00; 6" plate (not shown), $9.00 – 12.00.

Fred Harvey's "Webster" pattern 7¼" plate (FH-14); stock pattern; Syracuse b/s; 1951 date code; used El Tovar Hotel in the Grand Canyon; postcard of El Tovar shown at left; $9.00 – 12.00.

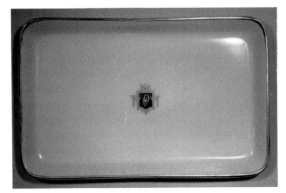

Larry Paul Collection

Hotel Pennsylvania (New York City; owned by PRR, 1919 – 1948) "Hotel Pennsylvania" pattern 10¾" long dresser tray (PRR-12c); matte yellow glaze; O.P.CO b/s; circa 1919 – early 1920s; $40.00 – 50.00+.

Larry Paul Collection

Hotel Roanoke (Roanoke, VA; owned by the Norfolk and Western 1882+) "Roanoke" pattern 10½" service plate (N&W-8a); O.P.CO. Old Ivory b/s; circa 1930s; $75.00 – 100.00.

Larry Paul Collection

John H. Murphy System (operated Erie and B & O station dining rooms, circa 1912 – circa 1941) "Egyptian Scarab" pattern creamer (MUR-l); Maddock's American b/s; circa 1912; $50.00 – 65.00.

Larry Paul Collection

New South Wales Railways Railroad Refreshment Room (Australia) "Sydney" pattern bowl (NSW-1); Grindley Duraline b/s; 1957 date code; $18.00 – 22.00.

Larry Paul Collection

"Reading YMCA" pattern 5¼" plate (RDG-5); Scammell's Trenton b/s; circa 1930s; the Reading operated nine YMCAs for their crews; $25.00 – 35.00.

Larry Paul Collection

Union News Co. 13 "Detroit Terminal" pattern 10¾" service plate; Maddock Lamberton China b/s; circa 1910s; $200.00 – 225.00+.

Larry Paul Collection

The White Hotel (White Sulphur Springs, WV; 1858 – 1922; owned by C&O Railroad 1910+) "The White" pattern 6¼" plate (C&O-9.1); Maddock England b/s; circa 1910 – circa 1922; $28.00 – 35.00.

Endnotes

[1] Pattern was reproduced and marked accordingly by Sterling China and on Buffalo China blanks in overglaze decoration; for a thorough study of this pattern refer to *Mimbres to Mimbreno* by Richard W. Luckin.

[2] Also made by Scammell and Sterling in the Lamberton body. Pieces with a Shenango and Interpace b/s, produced 1968 – 1977, or a Shenango 1827 – 1978 b/s, produced in 1978, are reproductions and were ordered by and initially sold at the B & O Museum, Baltimore, MD.

[3] Full backstamp: Made Expressly for Chesapeake & Ohio R.R. 1732 Bi-centennial 1932.

[4] Ashtray in this pattern is customized with a bold "C and O" topmark with train passing through bottom of the "O"; see logo on railroad china topmarks list.

[5] High value is due to rarity of piece; other pieces in pattern are valued at considerably less; for example, a bouillon has a value range of $150.00 – 175.00 not RR b/s.

[6] An exclusive railroad pattern with decorated embossed narrow rim ("Econo-Rim," as shown) and a non-railroad stock pattern with plain narrow rim or decorated non-embossed wide rim.

[7] Pattern also used by Missouri Pacific and backstamped accordingly.

[8] Platinum Nickel Plate Road logo at 12 o'clock position on cobalt band is barely visible in photograph; see railroad china topmark list for clear view of logo.

[9] Gladding, McBean and Co. also produced this Franciscan Ware pattern for Southern Pacific with fairly dark blue glaze (SP-2b).

[10] Produced by a number of manufacturers with variations in logo size and color of flowers; notice the differences in the two versions illustrated.

[11] Also manufactured by Scammell before 1955, Homer Laughlin after 1960, Sterling through the early 1990s for business cars, and teapots recently by Hall for gift shop.

[12] Owned by C & O Railroad, 1910+; currently operated by CSX Corporation.

[13] The Union News Company operated lunch counters and full scale restaurants at small and large railroad stations in the mid-western and eastern states.

Railroad and Railroad Associated China Topmarks

Use this list of word, letter, and number topmarks to identify railroad and railroad associated china. This is believed to be a complete list of all currently known American railroad china topmarks, except those that have the full name of a railroad including the word "Railroad" or "Railway" or the initials "RR" or "RY." In addition there are a number of Canadian and other foreign railroad china topmarks, along with many railroad associated topmarks.

For alphabetical purposes, the word "the" is disregarded. Initials precede full words, except the word "and." Where possible words and initials are shown in a style and layout similar to that of the actual topmark. "Stylized initials" or "stylized type" in the Description column indicates an unusual or ornate type design that is not as shown here. Topmark colors are specified in the Railroad and Comments column, if known.

Note: if letters are superimposed, it may be necessary to search for each letter alphabetically. Because a stylized "C" is easily mistaken for a "G," it is wise to search for both.

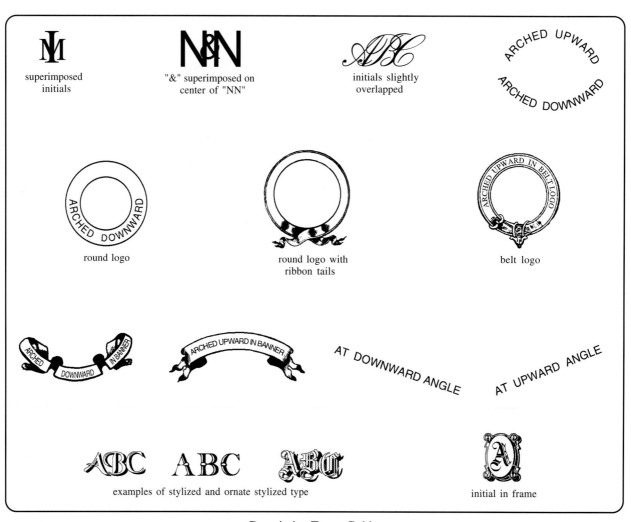

Descriptive Terms Guide

Initials and Words	Description or Illustration	Railroad and Comments
20 ᴛʜ <u>C E N T U R Y</u> <u>L I M I T E D</u>	similar to layout at left with variations in lines and vertical spacing	New York Central System • gray topmark • white on gray topmark
THE **4 0 0**	below train on service plate	Chicago & North Western System • dark red type

999	stylized embossed numbers fitted to shape of surrounding diamond	Used on a private car, the 999, purchased by the Rochester, Syracuse & Eastern, an electric railway, in 1910; the RS & E became the Empire United Railway in 1913 • gold topmark
1831		New York Central System; steam-powered locomotive, the Dewitt Clinton, built in 1831, illustrated on pattern • multicolored topmark
A&WPRR	stylized script initials	Atlanta and West Point Railroad • brown outlined blue topmark
AEE	overlapped stylized script initials	American European Express; luxury train operated between Washington DC, White Sulphure Springs, WV, Chicago, and New York in the early 1990s • gold initials on cobalt blue oval
THE AK·SAR·BEN	"Ak·sar·ben" arched upward above knight on horse with Burlington Route logo superimposed on train below	Chicago, Burlington & Quincy Railroad • blue-green type with multicolored graphics topmark
The Alton Route	arched slightly upward	Chicago & Alton Railroad • orange topmark
Amtrak		Amtrak; on samples made by Jackson China in the 1970s • blue and red topmark
Atlantic Coast Line		Atlantic Coast Line Railroad; state names are in different order on actual topmark • brown and orange topmark • green and red-orange topmark • variation: orange logo with "Y.M.C.A." arched upward above and "Waycross, GA." arched downward below
B	stylized script "B" and dolphin inside diamond shape	Used in Hotel Breakers, operated by Florida East Coast Hotel Company, Flagler System (Florida East Coast Railway) • gold topmark
B & O	B & O	Baltimore & Ohio Railroad • maroon topmark
B and O		Baltimore & Ohio Railroad • blue initials and black train topmark
B&O		Baltimore & Ohio Railroad • dull blue topmark • dark red topmark

B&O		Baltimore & Ohio Railroad • white topmark on cobalt blue glaze on ashtray only
B & O R.R.	round logo with domed building in center; "B & O" in left side and "R.R." in right side of banner which goes through logo and behind domed building	Baltimore & Ohio Railroad • gold topmark
B&O.S.W.	stylized script initials	Baltimore & Ohio Southwestern Railroad • blue initials
B&O ALL THE TRAINS RUN VIA WASHINGTON	"All The Trains Run Via Washington" arched upward in round logo superimpised on diamond shape; "B&O" in center of logo; "&" intertwined with "B" and "O"	Baltimore & Ohio Railroad • rust topmark
& B O SYSTEM	"B & O" arched upward above winged crest; "System" arched downward below; see *"JHM System" topmark for illustration of crest*	Used in dining rooms along the Baltimore & Ohio Railroad's route, operated for the railroad by John H. Murphy • turquoise, black, and rust topmark
BC&A		Baltimore, Chesapeake & Atlantic Railroad • green topmark
COURTEOUS *B.C.Electric* SERVICE	"B.C. Electric" at upward angle	British Columbia Electric Railroad • green topmark
B. R & P.	stylized initials	Buffalo, Rochester & Pittsburgh Railway • blue topmark
B. R & P.		Buffalo, Rochester & Pittsburgh Railway • blue topmark
B. R & P. RY	stylized initials; "B.R. & P." arched upward above "Ry."	Buffalo, Rochester & Pittsburgh Railway • blue topmark
BLACKHAWK	below large full-color decal of an American Indian	Chicago, Burlington & Quincy Railroad
BLUE COMET	white type on blue band	Central Railroad of New Jersey
Burlington Route	type identical to the following topmark; no background or frame	Chicago, Burlington & Quincy Railroad • black topmark
Burlington Route		Chicago, Burlington & Quincy Railroad • red topmark • gold type with black background and red frame topmark • gold topmark on green or colbalt blue glaze

C&A	ornate stylized initials; "C" and "A" superimposed; "&" inside top portion of "A"	Chicago & Alton Railroad • purple topmark with gold accents
C & E I		Chicago & Eastern Illinois Railway • topmark: orange initials and lines on blue background
C&LC		Cadillac & Lake City Railway; operated tourist and freight trains until 1971 and tourist excursions until 1989 • green topmark • green topmark surrounded by gold scrolls
C & M ELECTRIC RAIL ROAD RAVINIA PARK	"Electric Rail Road" in banner; banner superimposed on and intertwined in stylized "C & M"; "Ravinia Park" arched slightly downward	Used in Chicago & Milwaukee Electric Railroad operated restaurant, Ravena Park, circa 1904 – circa 1909 • brown, green, and orange topmark
C & O	C & O	Chesapeake & Ohio Railway • blue topmark
C&O	barely overlapped ornate stylized initials	Chesapeake & Ohio Railway • blue topmark
C&O		Chesapeake & Ohio Railway • topmark: brown outlined orange "C" and "O" with black "&"
C AND O		Chesapeake & Ohio Railway • gold topmark on ashtray only
C & s		Colorado & Southern Railway • orange topmark • green topmark • blue topmark
CB Q		Chicago, Burlington & Quincy Railroad • dark red topmark on tan body
CFE		Used in the Hotel Breakers in Palm Beach, FL, owned by Florida East Coast Hotel Company, Flagler System (Florida East Coast Railway) • gold topmark
CGR		Canadian Government Railways • green topmark
CH&D		Cincinnati, Hamilton & Dayton Railroad; became part of Baltimore & Ohio Railroad in 1917; do not confuse with the Cincinnati, Hamilton & Dayton electric railway which operated 1926 – 1929 • topmark: black outlined red initials surrounded by black and red oval

C H P	layout as shown at left, except "C" slightly overlaps upper left of "H"; running Indian at right of "H"; train engine at right of "P"	Chihuahua Pacific Railroad of Mexico (Ferrocarril de Chihuahua al Pacifico), 1955 – 1987 • brown topmark
CM&PSRY.	stylized initials; "&" inside lower portion of "M"; "RY" inside top portion of "S"	Topmark inside Chicago, Milwaukee & Puget Sound Railway's cups; matching saucer topmarked "The Olympian" • gold topmark
C.M.& St.P.	arched upward	Chicago, Milwaukee & St. Paul Railway • dark red topmark
CM&SᵀP	stylized initials; "&" inside lower portion of "M"; "T" inside top portion of "S"	Topmark inside Chicago, Milwaukee & St. Paul Railroad's cups; matching saucer topmarked "The Olympian" • gold topmark
C<small>MPS</small>		Chicago, Milwaukee & Puget Sound Railway • dark green topmark
CN		Canadian National Railways, 1961+ • brown topmark
CNR		Canadian Northern Railway, pre-1919, or Canadian National Railways, post-1918 • brown topmark • rust-brown topmark • green topmark
CNR	stylized initials	Canadian National Railways • topmark: white embossed initials on brown glaze
CNR PRINCE ARTHUR HOTEL	"CNR" in stylized ornate script above shield; crowned lion standing on another crown inside shield; "Prince Arthur Hotel" at upward angle in banner below	Used in Prince Arthur Hotel, Port Arthur, Ontario, operated by Canadian National Railways • gold topmark
CNR PRINCE EDWARD HOTEL	"N" inside "C"; "CNR" on maple leaf above shield; crown above winged lion in shield; shield surrounded by maple leaves; "Prince Edward Hotel" in banner below shield	Used in Prince Edward Hotel, Brandon, Manitoba, operated by Canadian Northern Railway • gold topmark
C.N.RYS. BOARDING CAR DEPT	"C.N.Rys." and "Boarding Car" arched upward	Canadian National Railways • green topmark
C P R	initials inside shield with beaver on top	Canadian Pacific Railways • blue topmark
CPR		Canadian Pacific Railway • green topmark • blue topmark
CPR	superimposed ornate stylized initials	Canadian Pacific Railway • green topmark

CVR	superimposed ornate stylized initials	Central Vermont Railway • green topmark
CANADA RAILWAY NEWS Co.	arched upward in belt logo with maple leaf in center	Used in railroad station dining facilities operated by the Canada Railway News Company • teal topmark
CANADA RAILWAY NEWS CoLIMITED	arched upward in belt logo with maple leaf in center	Used in railroad station dining facilities operated by the Canada Railway News Company • teal topmark • green topmark
CANADIAN NATIONAL		Canadian National Railways, to 1961 • brown topmark: brown type on white rectangle or white type on brown rectangle • gold topmark on green glaze • gold, orange & rust topmark
CANADIAN NATIONAL HOTELS LIMITED	inside rectangle; rectangle on maple leaf	Used in hotels owned and operated by the Canadian National Railways, to 1961 • rust and mustard topmark
Canadian National System	mustard type on solid rust semi-circle; semi-circle on maple leaf; maple leaf on outlined blue background	Canadian National Railways, to 1961 • mustard, rust, brown, and blue topmark
CANADIAN NORTHERN		Canadian Northern Railway; became Canadian National Railways in 1918 • blue topmark
CANADIAN PACIFIC	CANADIAN PACIFIC	Canadian Pacific Railway • blue type
Canadian Pacific Pavilion EXPO 86	"Canadian Pacific Pavilion" arched upward at 12 o'clock position; "Expo 86" arched downward at 6 o'clock position	Used in Canadian Pacific Railway's pavilion at the 1986 Exposition • blue topmark
CARITAS	stylized type enclosed in rounded rectangle	Used on a private car, the Caritas, based in Denver, Colorado; recent pattern • purple overglaze topmark
CENTRAL of GEORGIA "THE RIGHT WAY"	 surrounded by scroll work with "The Right Way" arched downward below	Central of Georgia Railway • red-orange topmark
CENTRAL of GEORGIA hospital	"Central of Georgia" arched upward above "hospital"	Used in hospital in Savannah, Georgia, operated by Central of Georgia Railway, 1927 – circa 1958 • blue topmark
The Challenger	stylized type	Union Pacific Railroad • yellow outlined rust topmark on tan body

CHATEAU LAURIER GRAND TRUNK	"Chateau Laurier" in banner above shield; "Grand Trunk" arched downward below	Used at Chateau Laurier, Ottawa, Ontario; owned and operated by Grand Trunk Western Railway • maroon, blue, and tan topmark • gold topmark
Chessie "Chessie" below the famous Cat		Chesapeake & Ohio Railway • black topmark • topmark variation: similar cat in gray with pink nose and ears; without the word "Chessie"
CHICAGO AND NORTHWESTERN LINE OCCIDENTAL		Used at Chicago & North Western Railway's hotel and depot in Eagle Grove, Iowa • white type on rust and black topmark
CHICAGO MILWAUKEE ST. PAUL AND PACIFIC	"Chicago" arched upward; "Milwaukee" and "And" on upward angle; "St. Paul" arched downward; "Pacific" straight	Chicago, Milwaukee, St. Paul & Pacific Railroad • gold topmark with white type
CHICAGO ST. LOUIS "THE ONLY WAY" KANSAS CITY		Chicago and Alton Railroad • green topmark with serif type • green and rust topmark with sans-serif type • gold and black topmark with serif type
THE CHUCK WAGON		Chicago, Burlington & Quincy Railroad • brown and gray topmark
Colorado & Southern	Colorado & Southern	Colorado & Southern Railway • orange topmark
The COMMODORE	"Commodore" arched downward in banner below "The" and clipper ship	On service plate used in hotel connected to the Grand Central Terminal and owned by the New York Central System • maroon topmark
CORNWALLIS INN	in banner below shield	Used at inn operated by Canadian Pacific Railway • blue topmark
COURTEOUS *B. C. Electric* SERVICE	"B.C. Electric" at upward angle	British Columbia Electric Railroad • green topmark
DAR	barely overlapped stylized script initials above shield	Dominion Atlantic Railway • blue topmark
"The D & H"		Delaware and Hudson Railroad • blue letters • brown outlined green letters • white letters on rust shield

D & I R		Duluth & Iron Range Railroad • black outlined orange topmark
D.&.R.G.	stylized initials	Denver & Rio Grande Railroad • teal topmark
D S G		Deutsche Speisewagon Gesellschaft (German Dining Car Company) • black topmark
Daylight		Southern Pacific Railroad Company • black topmark • silver topmark on black glaze
THE DELAWARE AND HUDSON COMPANY	"The Delaware and Hudson Company" in banner below complex graphic: crane above shield flanked by two uniformed men, with on shield	Delaware and Hudson Railroad • topmark: multicolored including yellow "D&H" on red shield
DENVER & RIO GRANDE	stylized type	Denver & Rio Grande Railroad • teal topmark
DINING INTER-STATE SERVICE	"Dining" arched upward and "Service" arched downward in round logo with across "Interstate" in center	Used in railroad station dining facilities operated by Interstate News Co. • green and orange topmark
DINING THE INTER-STATE NEWS Co SERVICE	"Dining" arched upward and "Service" arched downward in round logo; "Inter-state" across center, below "The" and above "News"; "Co." below "News"	Used in railroad station dining facilities operated by Interstate News Co. • green and brown topmark
Dixie	stylized script type	St. Louis Southwestern Railway • gold topmark
"THE DIXIELAND"	"THE DIXIELAND"	Chicago & Eastern Illinois Railway • orange topmark
DULUTH MISSABE & NORTHERN		Duluth, Missabe & Northern Railway • topmark: black outlined gold type on orange background
E	"E" above crown; crown and "E" inside maple leaf outline	Used in Queen Elizabeth Hotel of Montreal, operated by Canadian National Railways System • dull blue topmark

THE EAGLE	THE EAGLE	Texas & Pacific Railway and Missouri Pacific Railroad • black topmark
Electroliners	stylized script type	Chicago, North Shore & Milwaukee Railroad, a traction line • brown topmark on tan body • gold topmark on brown glaze
Erie	*Erie*	Erie Railroad • dark pink and light green topmark • variation: "Erie" straight, rather than at an upward angle
ERIE		Erie Railroad • black diamond and solid black circle with white letters (as shown) • cobalt diamond and solid cobalt circle with white letters • cobalt diamond and hollow cobalt circle with cobalt letters • black diamond and hollow black circle with black plain or outlined letters • cobalt diamond and cobalt outlined solid orange circle with cobalt outlined letters • solid pink diamond and solid red circle with white letters
ERIE SYSTEM	"Erie" inside diamond shape above winged crest; "System" arched downward below crest; see *JHM System" topmark for illustration of crest*	Used in dining rooms located on the Erie Railroad routes, operated for the railroad by John H. Murphy • turquoise, black, and rust topmark
F.E. & M.V.R.R.	arched upward in banner	Fremont, Elkhorn & Missouri Valley Railroad • rust topmark
FEC		Used in hotel owned by Florida East Coast Hotel Company, Flagler System (Florida East Coast Railway) • yellow green topmark
FEC		Used in Hotel Alcazar in St. Augustine, FL, owned by Florida East Coast Hotel Company, Flagler System (Florida East Coast Railway) • yellow green topmark
F.E.C.Ry.	stylized script initials	Florida East Coast Railway (Flagler System) • dull blue topmark
FH		Used in Harvey Houses at Santa Fe railroad stations, Fred Harvey hotels or resorts, or on Santa Fe dining cars • gold outlined black topmark
FH		Used in Harvey Houses at Santa Fe railroad stations, Fred Harvey hotels or resorts, or on Santa Fe dining cars • black outlined gold topmark

F H		Used in Harvey Houses at Santa Fe railroad stations, Fred Harvey hotels or resorts, or on Santa Fe dining cars • orange topmark
FORT GARRY GRAND TRUNK PACIFIC	"Fort Garry" in banner above shield; "Grand Trunk Pacific" arched downward below shield	Used at the Fort Garry in Winnipeg, Manitoba, owned and operated by Grand Trunk Pacific Railway • gold topmark
THE FORT GARRY GRAND TRUNK PACIFIC	"The Fort Garry" in banner above shield; "Grand Trunk Pacific" arched downward below shield	Used at the Fort Garry in Winnipeg, Manitoba, owned and operated by Grand Trunk Pacific Railway • green and pink topmark
Fred Harvey		Used at a Harvey Houses or on Santa Fe dining cars • gold topmark on black
Fred Harvey		Used in Fred Harvey restaurant in Chicago's Dearborn Station • reddish-brown topmark on tan body
FRED HARVEY SANTA FE ROUTE		Used in Harvey House at Santa Fe railroad station or on Santa Fe dining cars • dark red topmark
Fred Harvey SINCE 1876	"Fred Harvey" on solid gray oval; "Since 1876" below in mustard banner	Used in Chicago's Union Station Gold Lion restaurant and perhaps other Fred Harvey dining facilities • gray and mustard topmark
FRISCO SYSTEM		St. Louis-San Francisco Railway • black topmark
G	*G*	Used in Greenbrier Hotel, White Sulphur Springs, WV; operated by Chesapeake & Ohio Railway and taken over by CSX • gold topmark on cobalt blue band, in center of gold lined plate, or superimposed on gazebo on service plate
G_CT	superimposed stylized initials inside oval on shield, shield inside wreath	Used in dining facilities operated by the Union News Company at New York Grand Central Terminal • gold and blue topmark • red and blue topmark
GH	superimposed stylized initials in ornate frame	Used in Greenbrier Hotel, White Sulphur Springs, WV; operated by Chesapeake & Ohio Railway • multicolored topmark
GM&O		Gulf, Mobile & Ohio Railroad • pink topmark

G N		Great Northern Railway • rust outlined yellow topmark
GNR	stylized initials	Great Northern Railway • white embossed topmark on brown glaze
GNR		Great Northern Railway • rust outlined yellow topmark
G.T.P.	stylized script identical to type style of the following topmark	Grand Trunk Pacific Railway used this china pattern on trains in early 1900s; the G.T.P. was taken over by Canadian National Railways in 1923; note – also reportedly used on Canadian National's trainferry, S.S. *City of Grand Rapids* in circa 1970 • green topmark
G.T.R.		Grand Trunk Railway • green topmark
G O L D E N ROCKET		Chicago, Rock Island & Pacific Railway • red-orange topmark
GOLDEN STATE	oranges above, below or between "Golden State"	Chicago, Rock Island & Pacific Railway and Southern Pacific Railroad Company joint operation • orange and green topmark
GRAND TRUNK PACIFIC	in banner above shield	Grand Trunk Pacific Railway • gold topmark
GREAT NORTHERN		Great Northern Railway • blue topmark on two patterns which also include children's characters • gold topmark cobalt blue, black, green, or violet glaze; on ashtray only
The Greenbrier	below illustration of gazebo	Used in Greenbrier Hotel, White Sulphur Springs, WV; operated by Chesapeake & Ohio Railway and taken over by CSX • green topmark
GULF COAST LINES	triple underline below "Gulf Coast Lines"	Gulf Coast Lines, a group of railroads operating between Brownsville, TX, and New Orleans, LA • cobalt blue topmark
H	steepled building in lower portion of "H"	Used in Homestead Hotel, Allegheny Mountains of VA; operated by Chesapeake & Ohio Railway • green topmark
HP	intertwined stylized initials in ornate frame; frame topped with urn and swag ties	Used in Hotel Pennsylvania, Manhattan, NYC, owned by the Pennsylvania Railroad, 1919–1948 • gold and blue topmark
HR	overlapped stylized initials inside ornate frame	Used in the Hotel Roanoke, Roanoke, VA, owned and operated by the Norfolk and Western Railway • orange and green topmark • gold topmark on rust band on service plate

HIAWATHA	HIAWATHA	Chicago, Milwaukee, St. Paul & Pacific Railroad • topmark: blue letters below train
Hampton E.H.&A. ST. RY. CO. Casino		Used in dining room operated by Exeter, Hampton & Amesbury Street Railway, a traction line • blue topmark
THE HOOSIER	stylized type surrounded by ornate frame	Chicago, Indianapolis & Louisville Railway • green topmark
The Hoosier Limited	stylized type; "Hoosier Limited" arched upward	Chicago, Indianapolis & Louisville Railway • green topmark
HOTEL ALCAZAR ST AUGUSTINE, FLA	shield inside wreath with crown above; "Hotel Alcazar" arched downward below wreath; "St. Augustine, Fla" below "Hotel Alcazar"	Used in Hotel Alcazar in St. Augustine, FL; owned by Florida East Coast Hotel Company, Flagler System (FEC Railway) • blue and brown topmark
HOTEL CNR SYSTEM	"Hotel" arched upward and "System" arched downward in round logo with maple leaves on left and right; slightly overlapped "CNR" initials in center of logo	Used at hotel operated by Canadian National Railway, pre-1919; Canadian National Railways, post-1918 • gold topmark
HOTEL CHAMPLAIN	"Hotel Champlain" arched downward in banner below complex graphic including shield below ship, flanked by an American Indian and an explorer	Hotel owned and operated by the Delaware and Hudson Railroad • multicolored topmark
HOTEL DEL MONTE	"Hotel Del Monte" in banner below ornately framed crest; crown above crest	Hotel Del Monte, Monterey, California, opened in 1880, was associated with the Southern Pacific • black topmark
THE HOTEL GRUNEWALD CATERING NEW ORLEANS	"The Hotel Grunewald Catering" inside wreath; "New Orleans" below	Hotel Grunewald Catering of New Orleans, LA, provided food service for two Gulf Coast Lines trains • teal topmark
HOTEL PENNSYLVANIA	embossed block type	Used in Hotel Pennsylvania, Manhattan, NYC, owned by the Pennsylvania Railroad, 1919–1948 • embossed topmark on teal glaze on match stand only
HOTEL ROANOKE ROANOKE, VA. THE HOUSE BY THE SIDE OF THE ROAD	"Hotel Roanoke" above "Roanoke, Va." arched upward at 12 o'clock position; "The House By The Side Of The Road" arched downward at 6 o'clock position	Used in the Hotel Roanoke, owned and operated by the Norfolk and Western Railway; pattern used until early 1990s • gold topmark
HOTEL ROYAL PALM	arched downward in banner below palm tree	Used in Hotel Hotel Royal Palm, Miami Beach, Florida, owned by Florida East Coast Hotel Company, Flagler System (Florida East Coast Railway) • green topmark

HOTEL ROYAL PALM MIAMI FLORIDA	"Hotel" and "Royal" on left side of palm tree; "Palm," "Miami," and "Florida" on right side	Used in Hotel Hotel Royal Palm, Miami Beach, Florida, owned by Florida East Coast Hotel Company, Flagler System (Florida East Coast Railway) • rust and green topmark
HOTEL VANCOUVER	"Hotel" and "Vancouver" on maple leaf with "Vancouver" arched downward; maple leaf on gray outlined blue background	Used ar Hotel Vancouver, Vancouver, B.C., owned and operated by the Canadian National System • brown, mustard, blue, and gray topmark
IC		Illinois Central Railroad • topmark: gold initials and wreath with cobalt blue center • black topmark on white body • black topmark on blue body
IC_{RR}		Illinois Central Railroad • black topmark
ILLINOIS CENTRAL	 ILLINOIS CENTRAL	Illinois Central Railroad • cobalt blue topmark
INDIANAPOLIS **INTERSTATE** THE ELECTRIC WAY LOUISVILLE	"Indianapolis" arched upward and "Louisville" arched downward in round logo; vertical stripes in center of logo; "The Electric Way" superimposed over "Interstate" across center of logo	Used on Interstate Public Service Company dining cars running between Indianapolis and Louisville • deep orange topmark
INTERNATIONAL AND GREAT NORTHERN	"International and" arched upward; "Great Northern" arched downward below	International and Great Northern Railroad • black topmark
INTER STATE	"Inter" arched upward on left and "State" arched upward on right in banner; banner below spread-winged eagle superimposed on sun	Used in railroad station dining facilities operated by Interstate News Co. • blue, rust, and brown topmark
JHM SYSTEM		Used in railroad station dining rooms operated by John H. Murphy • turquoise, black, and rust topmark
K.C.F.S. & G.	initials arched slightly upward	Kansas City, Fort Scott & Gulf Railroad • blue and gold topmark • dark red topmark
KANSAS CITY SOUTHERN	arched upward in round logo with black crow flying over field in center	Kansas City Southern Railroad • gold, deep orange, and black topmark
KEY ROUTE I N N	on key shaped logo; "Key Route" arched upward and "Inn" arched downward in oval on key stem; black train on length of key stem	Used at inn operated by Key System, an Oakland-San Francisco traction line • green and black topmark

Kᴇʏ Rᴏᴜᴛᴇ Iɴɴ	"Key Route" arched upward above "Inn"	Used at inn operated by Key System, a traction line • teal topmark
L.& D.H.R.R.	**L.& D.H.R.R.**	Used in dining room operated by Lowell & Duquette Horse Railroad, a horsedrawn railroad which operated until 1891 • dark red or black topmark
L&HR		Lehigh & Hudson River Railway • blue topmark • red topmark
L M S	L M S	London, Midland and Scottish Railway of Great Britain
LNER		London North Eastern Railway of Great Britain • black topmark • gold topmark
LʀV		Lehigh Valley Railroad • topmark: gold initials on aqua diamond
L.V.	"L.V." in black diamond on red swallowtail flag	Lehigh Valley Railroad • topmark: white type, black diamond and red flag
L.V.		Lehigh Valley Railroad • topmark: white type, black diamond, dark red flag and green wreath • topmark: white type, gold diamond, dark red flag and gold wreath; recent pattern • gold topmark on cobalt blue glaze
Lackawanna Railroad	in rectangle	Delaware, Lackawanna & Western Railroad • topmark: gray type inside gray rectangle • topmark: white type on outlined solid teal rectangle
LAKESIDE INN C.N.E.R. PORT D HOUSIE	"Lakeside Inn" arched upward and "Port d Housie" arched downward in round logo; "C.N.E.R" across center of logo	Canadian National Electric Railway • deep pink and gold topmark
LIBERTY BELL ROUTE		Used in Lehigh Valley Transit's station, Philadelphia, Pennsylvania, or on their buffet car, 999; note: originally made by Maddock; watch for recent reproductions made by other manufacturers • brown, rust, and mustard topmark
Lone Star	*Lone★Star*	St. Louis Southwestern Railway • gold topmark

LORADO TAFT'S COLOSSAL STATUE OF BLACKHAWK AT OREGON, ILL VISIBLE FROM THE BURLINGTON	"LORADO TAFT'S COLOSSAL STATUE OF BLACKHAWK AT OREGON, ILL VISIBLE FROM THE BURLINGTON" below Blackhawk statue decal	Chicago, Burlington and Quincy Railroad • topmark: dark red type under full-color decal of American Indian statue
M		Chicago, Indianapolis & Louisville Railway (Monon Route) • topmark: white initial on dull green circle
M E		Morristown and Erie Railroad; recently manufactured and used on parlor car • gray topmark
M^P	"P" superimposed at upper left of "M"	Missouri Pacific Railway; pre-1917 • green and pink topmark
M R Y	stylized initials fitted to shape of surrounding diamond	Munising, Marquette & Southeastern Railway • teal topmark
THE MACDONALD GRAND TRUNK PACIFIC	"The MacDonald" in banner above shield; "Grand Trunk Pacific" arched downward below shield	Used at hotel in Edmonton, owned and operated by Grand Trunk Pacific Railway • green and rose topmark
MAIN LINE *Rio Grande* THRU THE ROCKIES		Denver & Rio Grande Western Railroad; recent (1987+) business car pattern • topmark: red with gold outlines
MEMPHIS ROUTE	on red star	Kansas City, Fort Scott & Memphis Railroad, 1888 – 1901 • red topmark
MICHIGAN CENTRAL	MICHIGAN CENTRAL	Michigan Central Railroad • dark red topmark
Midland Route	arched slightly upward	Colorado Midland Railway • teal topmark
The *MILWAUKEE* ROAD	stylized type	Chicago, Milwaukee, St. Paul & Pacific Railroad • rust topmark
THE MINAKI INN GRAND TRUNK PACIFIC	"The Minaka Inn" in banner above shield; "Grand Trunk Pacific" arched downward below shield	Used at hotel, owned and operated by Grand Trunk Pacific Railway • green and beige topmark
Minerva	stylized script type arched downward	Used on Lehigh Valley Railroad's private car, *Minerva* • pink topmark
MISSOURI PACIFIC	**MISSOURI PACIFIC**	Missouri Pacific Railway; pre-1917 • black topmark
MISSOURI PACIFIC IRON MOUNTAIN	"Missouri Pacific" arched slightly upward; Iron Mountain" arched barely downward below	Missouri Pacific Railroad; the Iron Mountain Route became part of the Missouri Pacific in 1917 • black topmark

MISSOURI PACIFIC LINES		Missouri Pacific Railroad • gold topmark on cobalt blue glaze
MITROPA	MITROPA	Mitropa of Germany, 1916 – present • black topmark
Mitropa	stylized script type	Mitropa of Germany, 1916 – present • red topmark
N	*N*	Ontario Northland Railway; recent pattern • cobalt blue topmark
N A R		Northern Alberta Railways • black topmark
N & W	**N & W**	Norfolk & Western Railway • dark red topmark • topmark variation: full sized "&" replaced by underlined "&" over "RR"; also dark red
N&W	stylized initials inside wreath; "&" superimposed on center of "NW"	Norfolk & Western Railway • green, blue, and light brown topmark
N & W RY	initials fitted to shape of surrounding circle	Norfolk & Western Railway • white topmark on maroon glaze; on ashtray only
N&WRy	slightly overlapped stylized script initials	Norfolk & Western Railway • green and brown topmark
N. O. P. & L. Co.		Used on Northern Ohio Power & Light Company's business car, The Northern, or in the Akron, Ohio, station dining room, 1926 – 1931 • topmark: green initials with black oval
N P		Northern Pacific Railway • topmark: mustard "N" and rust "P"
N. S. W. G. R. R.R.R	"N. S. W. G. R." arched upward in belt logo; "R.R.R." in center of logo below crown	New South Wales Victorian Railways of Australia; used in "Railroad Refreshment Room" at depot • red topmark • green topmark
N Y C	N Y C	New York Central System • gray topmark
NYC		New York Central System • rust topmark ("Mercury" pattern) • rust topmark without vertical lines ("Mercury" pattern companion pieces)

NYC	≡NYC≡	New York Central System • black topmark on salmon glaze; 10⅛" plates only
N Y C	N Y C	New York Central System • red topmark
NYC AND *HRR*	*NYC&HRR*	New York Central & Hudson River Railroad • brown topmark
𝕹.𝖄.𝕮.& 𝕳.𝕽.𝕽.	𝕹.𝖄.𝕮.& 𝕳.𝕽.𝕽.	New York Central & Hudson River Railroad • maroon topmark
NYC STATION RESTAURANT UTICA, N.Y.	NYC STATION RESTAURANT UTICA, N.Y.	Used in New York Central Station's dining room in Utica, New York • green topmark
N.Y.C. STATION Utica, N.Y.	in banner above knight's helmet, flowers, and scrolls	Used in New York Central Station's dining room in Utica, New York • blue topmark
N.Y. P.& N.	N.Y. P.&N.	New York, Philadelphia & Norfolk Railroad • green topmark
𝕹.𝖄.𝕻.&𝕺.	stylized gothic initials	New York, Pennsylvania & Ohio Railroad • blue topmark
NEW YORK Cᴇɴᴛʀᴀʟ LINES	NEW YORK CENTRAL LINES	New York Central System • gold topmark • black topmark
New York New Haven and Hartford	New York New Haven and Hartford	New York, New Haven, and Hartford Railroad • green topmark • gold topmark • gold topmark with "The" at left of "New York"
Nɪᴄᴋᴇʟ Pʟᴀᴛᴇ Rᴏᴀᴅ	NICKEL PLATE ROAD	New York, Chicago & St. Louis Railroad • dark blue topmark • platinum words inside platinum rectangle on cobalt blue band
Nɪᴄᴋᴇʟ Pʟᴀᴛᴇ Rᴏᴀᴅ	stylized type inside wreath	New York, Chicago & St. Louis Railroad • green topmark
Nɪᴄᴋᴇʟ Pʟᴀᴛᴇ Rᴏᴀᴅ	stylized type on solid red circle	New York, Chicago & St. Louis Railroad • topmark: brown type on red circle
NORTH SHORE LINE *MCRRCo*	"North Shore Line" arched upward in oval belt logo; slightly overlapped stylized script initials in center of logo	Michigan Central Railroad Co. • dull blue topmark

THE **NORTHWESTERN** LINE		Chicago & North Western Railway • brown topmark
Northern Pacific	**Northern Pacific**	Northern Pacific Railway • maroon topmark
NORTHERN PACIFIC	"Northern" arched upward and "Pacific" arched downward in round logo	Northern Pacific Railway • red and dark blue topmark

NORTHERN
PACIFIC
YELLOWSTONE PARK LINE
		Northern Pacific Railway
		• red and black topmark, as shown
		• black topmark with "YELLOWSTONE PARK
		  LINE" inverted
		• gold topmark with "YELLOWSTONE PARK
		  LINE" inverted on green glaze

O.R.&N.	stylized script initials	Oregon Railway and Navigation Company • maroon topmark
O.R.& N.Co.	O.R.& N.Co.	Oregon Railway and Navigation Company; watch for reproductions without manufacturer backstamp • black topmark
OW		New York, Ontario & Western Railway • orange "O" and green "W" on topmark
OW & R R Co		Oregon-Washington Railroad & Navigation • teal topmark
THE OLYMPIAN	gold stylized type	On Chicago, Milwaukee & Puget Sound Railway and Chicago, Milwaukee, and St. Paul Railway saucers • gold topmark
OVERLAND ROUTE	"Route" arched upward below "Overland"	Union Pacific Railroad
"THE OVERLAND ROUTE"	"Overland" arched upward	Union Pacific Railroad • green topmark
P&WV		Pittsburgh and West Virginia Railway • rust topmark; on ashtray only
PCo		Pennsylvania Railroad; turn-of-the-century pattern by Knowles, Taylor, and Knowles • teal topmark

P&LErr		Pittsburgh & Lake Erie Railroad • blue-green topmark • dark green outlined green topmark • brown topmark • cobalt blue and gold topmark
PRR		Pennsylvania Railroad System • gold topmark • variation: brown topmark with slightly more detailed initials
PRR	PRR	Pennsylvania Railroad System • rust topmark
– PACIFIC – COMFORT SPEED SAFETY ELECTRIC	"– Pacific –" arched upward and "Electric" arched downward in round logo; "Comfort" and "Speed" arched upward and "Safety" arched downward in inner circle on logo; lightening bolt in center of logo	Used in Pacific Electric Railway's dining room at the Alpine Tavern, as well as station dining rooms in Southern California • dark orange topmark
Pacific Hotel Co	stylized script type	Used at Union Pacific Railroad's hotels operated by the Pacific Hotel Company, circa 1889+ • orange topmark
THE PARKER RY. NEWS CO.	"The Parker Ry. News Co." arched upward in belt logo; train behind right side of logo, through center and across left side	Used in railroad station dining facilities along Central of Georgia Railway route in Georgia, operated by Parker Railway News Co. • green topmark
PENNSYLVANIA SYSTEM		Pennsylvania Railroad System • red topmark
Pere Marquette System	inside rectangle	Pere Marquette Railway; also operated car ferries across Lake Michigan • teal topmark
PHOEBE SNOW	below decal of uniformed woman	Delaware, Lackawanna & Western Railroad; pattern may be sample only • green topmark
The Phoebe Snow	stylized script type on solid circle	Used on Phoebe Snow business car; ordered in 1989 • maroon topmark
Poland Spring ESTABLISHED 1794 SAPIENTIA DONUM DEI	ornate crest below "Established 1794" and above "Sapientia Donum Dei"	Used in the Poland Spring Hotel, partially owned by the Maine Central Railroad • green topmark
PUBLIC SERVICE	"Public" arched upward and "Service" arched downward in round logo; double triangle in center of logo	Used in Public Service of New Jersey electric railroad's private car and possibly the company dining room • gold topmark

PUEBLO UNION DEPOT HOTEL		Used in Pueblo, Colorado, railroad station dining room • red topmark
PULLMAN	PULLMAN	Used on Pullman dining cars • black topmark • gold topmark on green glaze
PULLMAN		Used on Pullman of Great Britain dining cars
Q&C		Queen & Crescent Route; *see next entry* • dark blue topmark
QUEEN & CRESCENT ROUTE	"Queen & Crescent Route" on solid rectangle alternates with "Q & C" inside irregular shape around rim	Queen & Crescent Route; consisted of five railroads running between "the Crescent City" (New Orleans) and "the Queen City" (Cincinnati); the route became part of Southern Railway System • mustard and black topmark
$_R A^R$		Alaska Railroad
RI		Chicago, Rock Island & Pacific Railway • dark green outlined sage green topmark • solid red topmark
RI		Chicago, Rock Island & Pacific Railway • red topmark
RI THE ROCKET	 THE ROCKET	Chicago, Rock Island & Pacific Railway • red topmark • topmark: red outlined gold "R" and red "I"
RPR		Pennsylvania Railroad System • rust topmark • gold topmark • red topmark • black topmark on teapot only • brown topmark on tan body • topmark: maroon with double shield outline • topmark: gold letters, turquoise shield, and gold shield outline

R T R		Used in Reading Terminal restaurant, Philadelphia, Pennsylvania • green and red topmark
R Y	crown above superimposed stylized initials	Used at the Royal York in Toronto, operated by Canadian Pacific Railway
Reading	**Reading**	Philadelphia & Reading Railway, Reading Company (railroad) operating company until 1924 • cobalt blue topmark
Reading Co. Y.M. C.A.	"Reading Co." in white type on solid diamond shape; "Y. M. C. A." below	The Reading Company (railroad) owned and operated several Y.M.C.A.s along its routes • cobalt blue topmark
Rheingold	Rheingold	Deutsche Speisewagen Gesellschaft (German dining Car Company); the Rheingold, a luxury train, employed DSG services in the 1950s; pattern is backstamped DSG • rust topmark
RICHMOND WASHINGTON LINE		Richmond, Fredericksburg & Potomac Railroad • orange and black topmark • black topmark with "Line" inside rounded rectangle, rather than inside banner as shown
Rio Grande	*Rio-Grande*	Denver & Rio Grande Western Railroad • cobalt blue topmark
RIO GRANDE HOTEL CO. SCENIC LINE OF THE WORLD	"Rio Grande Hotel Co." arched upward in round logo with scenic view in center; "Scenic Line Of The World" in banner superimposed on bottom of logo	Rio Grand Hotel Co., owned by Denver and Rio Grande Railroad, operated hotels along the railroad's routes • orange topmark
Rio Grande Hotel Co.	**Rio Grande Hotel Co.**	Rio Grand Hotel Co., owned by Denver and Rio Grande Railroad, operated hotels along the railroad's routes • maroon topmark
Rio Grande *Prospector*	*Rio-Grande* at 12 o'clock position and "Prospector" (in same type style) at 6 o'clock position; illustration of prospector and mule in center of 9" plate only	Denver and Rio Grande Western Railroad • cobalt blue topmark
Rio **Grande** *Zephyr*	stylized type as on preceding topmark	Denver & Rio Grande Western Railroad; used on the Zephyr's final run in 1983 and sold to passengers • black topmark
ROAD OF The *Streamliners*	**ROAD OF** The *Streamliners*	Union Pacific Railroad • black topmark
Rock Island	inside shield	Chicago, Rock Island & Pacific Railway • topmark: white logo on black glaze; on ashtray only
The Route of Phoebe Snow	"Phoebe Snow" on upward angle	Delaware, Lackawanna & Western Railroad; pattern ordered 1949 – 1959 • rust topmark

RUSSELL Y.M.C.A.	"Russel" above outlined triangle; "Y.M.C.A." on outlined rectangle superimposed on center of triangle	Chesapeake & Ohio Railway operated this YMCA in Russell, Kentucky • cobalt blue topmark
S	inside circle	New York, Susquehanna & Western Railroad; recent business and dining car #510 use; also supplied to the New York, Susquehanna & Western Technical and Historical Society • topmark: red "S" inside gold circle
SGRR	SGRR	Saudi Government Railway of Saudi Arabia • green topmark
SP	SP	Southern Pacific Railroad Company; pattern ordered for business cars in 1984 • gold topmark
SsG		Swiss Dining Car Company
SSG	stylized initials inside diamond shape	Swiss Dining Car Company
St.LSW	slightly overlapped stylized script initials	St. Louis Southwestern Railway • gold topmark
S T- Ry CO OP	slightly overlapped stylized script initials	Used in British Columbia Electric Street Railway employee's cafeteria until late 1970s • brown topmark
SALT LAKE ROUTE	"Salt Lake" arched upward and "Route" arched downward in round logo; arrowhead in center of logo	San Pedro, Los Angeles & Salt Lake Railroad • blue topmark • blue and green topmark
SANTA FE	SANTA FE	Atchison, Topeka & Santa Fe Railroad • blue topmark
Santa Fe	"Santa Fe" at upward angle; underline arched slightly upward	Atchison, Topeka & Santa Fe Railroad • gold topmark
SANTA FÉ	barely arched downward	Atchison, Topeka & Santa Fe Railroad • black topmark
SANTA FÉ ROUTE	"Santa Fé" barely arched downward; "Route" below	Atchison, Topeka & Santa Fe Railroad • black topmark
SANTA FÉ ROUTE	SANTA FÉ ROUTE	Atchison, Topeka & Santa Fe Railroad • green topmark
SANTA FÉ ROUTE	arched downward in banner below flowered scrolls	Atchison, Topeka & Santa Fe Railroad • blue topmark
SANTA FÉ ROUTE	arched downward in banner; banner draped on rod	Atchison, Topeka & Santa Fe Railroad • topmark: light and dark rose outlined in gold

SEABOARD	**SEABOARD**	Seaboard Air Line Railway • cobalt blue topmark • black topmark
S̲EABOAR̲D	S̲EABOAR̲D	Seaboard Air Line Railway • blue outlined orange topmark
𝕾𝖊𝖆𝖇𝖔𝖆𝖗𝖉	𝕾𝖊𝖆𝖇𝖔𝖆𝖗𝖉	Seaboard Air Line Railway • rust topmark
𝕾𝖔𝖔	stylized type	Minneapolis, St. Paul and Sault Ste. Marie Railroad, more commonly known as the "Soo Line" • blue topmark
SOO LINE		Minneapolis, St. Paul and Sault Ste. Marie Railroad • red topmark • straight (rather that tilted as shown) black topmark with white type
THE *SOUTH* *SHORE*		Duluth, South Shore & Atlantic Railway • rust topmark • inverted black topmark
SOUTHERN	**SOUTHERN**	Southern Railway System • black topmark
THE SOUTHERN **SR** SERVES THE SOUTH		Southern Railway System • brown, orange, and white topmark • tan, orange, and white topmark
Southern Pᴀᴄɪғɪᴄ	stylized type	Southern Pacific Railroad Company • topmark: raised white type on green glaze; on teapot only
SOUTHERN PACIFIC Hᴏsᴘɪᴛᴀʟ	"Southern Pacific" arched upward in belt logo; "Hospital" in center	Employee hospitals were operated by the Southern Pacific Company in San Francisco, Sacramento, and a number of other locations • teal topmark
SOUTHERN LINES PACIFIC		Southern Pacific Railroad Company • blue topmark • green, orange, and brown topmark • green, orange, rust brown topmark • gold topmark on cobalt blue glaze • gold topmark on green glaze
SOUTHERN PACIFIC SUNSET OGDEN & SHASTA ROUTES COMPANY	"Southern Pacific" arched upward and "Company" arched downward in round logo; "Sunset Ogden & Shasta Routes" with sun above and rail below in center	Southern Pacific Railroad Company • teal topmark • blue topmark • green topmark • maroon topmark
SOUTHERN SUNSET OGDEN & SHASTA ROUTES PACIFIC	"Southern" arched upward and "Pacific" arched downward in round logo; "Sunset Ogden & Shasta Routes" with sun above and rail below in center	Southern Pacific Railroad Company • rust and black topmark

SUNSET EXCURSIONS *Washington* *San Francisco* LINE	1) stylized type in center of piece; sun above "Sunset"; "Excursions," "Washington and "San Francisco" arched downward and "Line" arched upward 2) stylized type near edge; sun above "Sunset"; "Excursions" and "Washington" arched downward and "San Francisco" arched upward	Southern Pacific Railroad Company • blue topmarks
THE **SUNSHINE SPECIAL**	slightly arched upward	Missouri Pacific Railroad; may be backstamped Iron Mountain Route, which became part of the Missouri Pacific in 1917 • outlined mustard topmark
T AND **P**		Texas & Pacific Railway • deep orange topmark with railroad name replaced by scrolls and without locations as shown: • brown topmark • orange, rust, white, and black topmark • gold topmark • gold topmark on cobalt blue
T E E		Trans-Europ Express, 1957 – early 1990s • gold topmark
TAHOE •TAVERN•	below pine tree; pine tree and "Tahoe" in rectangle; "•Tavern•" in attached rectangle below	Tavern operated by Lake Tahoe Railway • green topmark
TEXAS & PACIFIC	**TEXAS & PACIFIC**	Texas & Pacific Railway • black topmark
TEXAS *AND* **PACIFIC.**	**TEXAS** *AND* **PACIFIC.**	Texas & Pacific Railway • green topmark
TORONTO TERMINALS RAILWAY	TORONTO TERMINALS RAILWAY	Though the name indicates it, this is not a railway; the company built (circa 1915) and operated the Union Passenger Station and Terminal in Toronto for CNR and CPR • green topmark
TRURO N.S. I.C.R. DINING HALL		Used at Intercolonial Railway's dining hall in Truro, Nova Scotia; the Intercolonial, 1876+, was taken over by the Canadian Government Railways in 1913 • green topmark
The *Turquoise Room*	stylized script type	Atchison, Topeka & Santa Fe Railroad; used on the Super Chief's Pleasure Dome Lounge car in the Turquoise Room; ordered 1950 – 1969 • aqua topmark
UN **Co**	initials in an oval, on a shield and inside a wreath; "U" and "N" slightly overlapped; "O" inside "C"	Union News Company operated lunch counters and full scale restaurants at large and small railroad stations in the mid-western and eastern states; had 450+ concessions in 1945 • blue & mustard topmark • green topmark

UNC		Union News Company (*see information in previous entry*) • red and blue topmark • orange and green topmark
U.P.H MAIN DINING ROOM	U.P.H MAIN DINING ROOM	Used in the Union Pacific Hotel, operated by Union Pacific Hotel Co. for Union Pacific Railroad • green topmark
U.S.B.F.	fish on diamond in the center of flag; "U.S.B.F." below flag	United States Bureau of Fisheries; USA; 1903 – 1940; consolidated with the Bureau of Biological Survey to form the Fish and Wildlife Service in 1940; china reportedly used on the Bureau's train cars, at well as at headquarters • red, white, and blue topmark
UNION PACIFIC	on upper portion of standard Union Pacific shield logo	Union Pacific Railroad; very limited quantity ordered in 1986 • gold topmark on cobalt blue band
UNION PACIFIC	same as Union Pacific Shoshone topmark without "Shoshone"; *see Union Pacific Shoshone below*	Union Pacific Railroad; ordered in 1990 for business cars • red, blue, and white topmark with gold filigree
UNION PACIFIC ARDEN	same as Union Pacific Shoshone topmark with "Shoshone" replaced with "Arden"; *see Union Pacific Shoshone below*	Union Pacific Railroad; used on business car, *Arden* • red, blue, and white topmark with gold filigree
UNION PACIFIC THE OVERLAND ROUTE		Union Pacific Railroad • red, blue, and white topmark • red, blue, and white topmark without "The Route" • blue partially inverted topmark • orange topmark with "Overland" on upward angle, rather than downward angle as shown
UNION PACIFIC SHOSHONE		Union Pacific Railroad; used on business car, *Shoshone* • red, blue, and white topmark with gold filigree
V^R& T.R.R.	V^R& T.R.R.	Virginia & Tennessee Railroad; 1856+; consolidated with two other railroads to become the Atlantic, Mississippi & Ohio Railroad in 1870 • dark red topmark
VICKSBURG ROUTE	on outlined solid rectangular	Yazoo and Mississippi Valley Railroad, leased the Vicksburg, Shreveport & Pacific Railroad, 1926 – 1953 • deep orange topmark
VICTORIAN RAILWAYS	arched downward in banner below crown	Victorian Railways of Australia • red topmark

VIRGINIAN	VIRGINIAN	Virginian Railway • deep orange topmark
WL		Wagon-Lits, European sleeping and dining car operator; china used on the luxury trains, *Fleche d'Or and Blue Train*, in the late 1920s • gold topmark
WL		Wagon-Lits, European sleeping and dining car operator • cobalt blue topmark, circa 1920s – circa 1930s
WL		Wagon-Lits, European sleeping and dining car operator • cobalt blue topmark, circa 1960s – circa 1970s • maroon topmark, circa 1980s
W M		Western Maryland Railway • green topmark
WT		Used in the Washington Terminal, built in 1907 by the B & O and Pennsylvania railroads; the main dining area was known as The Gateway Restaurant • blue topmark • gold topmark • green outlined topmark • gold outlined blue topmark
WABASH		Wabash Railroad • red and blue topmark • blue-green topmark without "Follow the Flag" • blue topmark inside wreath without "Follow the Flag"
THE WEST POINT ROUTE	THE WEST POINT ROUTE	Atlanta and West Point Railroad • orange topmark
THE **West Point** **ROUTE**		Atlanta & West Point Railroad • rust topmark • orange topmark variation: • gray topmark with Gothic type and title case
Western **Pacific** **Feather River Route**	type layout as shown at left with maroon feather between "Pacific" and "Feather"	Western Pacific Railroad • red, black, and maroon topmark
WESTERN **FEATHER RIVER ROUTE** **PACIFIC**		Western Pacific Railroad • green topmark • gold topmark on cobalt blue glaze • white type, blue background, gold circle and rectangle and brown feather

THE WHEELING WAY		Wheeling and Lake Erie Railway • green topmark
The White	at upward angle	Used at The White Hotel, White Sulphur Springs, WV, operated by the Chesapeake & Ohio Railway, 1910 – 1922 • green topmark
WHITE SULPHUR SPRINGS W. VA.	gazebo above "White Sulphur Springs," arched downward; "W.VA" below	Greenbrier Resort, White Sulphur Springs, WV; operated by Chesapeake & Ohio • green topmark
THE WISCONSIN CENTRAL LINE		Wisconsin Central Railroad, operated by the Minneapolis, St. Paul and Sault Ste. Marie Railroad since 1909, became part of the Soo Line Railroad in 1961 and Wisconsin Central Ltd. in 1987 • purple topmark

Railroad Section Bibliography

ButterPat World
by Richard W. Luckin
© 1996
RK Publishing Company

Canadian Pacific
by Jim Lotz
© 1985
Bonanza Books

A Century of Trains
by Basil Cooper
© 1988
Gallery Books

The Collector's Book of Railroadiana
by Stanley L. Baker and
    Virginia Brainard Kunz
© 1976
Castle Books

*Dining on Rails – an Encyclopedia
    of Railroad China*
by Richard W. Luckin
© 1984, 1990, 1994, 1998
RK Publishing Company

The Great Trains
edited by Bryan Morgan
© 1973
Bonanza Books

*Historical Guide to North American
    Railroads*
compiled by George H. Drury
edited by Bob Hayden
first printing 1985, fourth printing 1992
Kalmbach Publishing Co.

*The History of the Atchison, Topeka &
    Santa Fe*
edited by Pamela Berkman
© 1988
Bonanza Books

The History of the Canadian National
edited by Keith MacKenzie
© 1988
Bonanza Books

*The History of the New York Central
    System*
by Aaron E. Klein
© 1985
Bonanza Books

The History of the Pennsylvania Railroad
by Timothy Jacobs
© 1988
Bonanza Books

The History of the Southern Pacific
by Bill Yenne
© 1985
Bonanza Books

*The History of Trains – From the Orient
    Express to the Bullet Trains*
by Massimo Ferrari and Emanuele Lazzati
© 1989
Crescent Books

Interurban Railways of the Bay Area
by Paul C. Trimble
© 1977
Valley Publishers

The Lost Pleasures of the Great Trains
by Martin Page
© 1975
William Morrow and Company, Inc.

*Luxury Trains – From the Orient Express to
    the TGV*
by George Behrend
© 1982
The Vendome Press

Meals by Fred Harvey
by James David Henderson
first printing 1969, revised printing 1985
Omni Publications

*Mimbres to Mimbreno, A Study of
    Santa Fe's Famous China Pattern*
by Richard W. Luckin
© 1992
RK Publishing Company

Mr. Pullman's Elegant Palace Car
by Lucius Beebe
© 1961
Doubleday & Company, New York

North American's Great Railroads
by Thomas York
© 1987, reprinted 1994
Barnes and Noble Books

North American Locomotives
by Brian Hollingsworth
© 1984, Salamander Book Ltd.
Crescent Books, New York

The Official Guide of the Railways
© 1965
National Railway Publication Co.

RailRoad Collectibles
by Stanley Baker
1985 (Third Edition)
Collectors Books

RailRoad Collectibles
by Stanley Baker
1990 (Fourth Edition)
Collectors Books

The Railroader's
text by Keith Wheeler
© 1973, reprinted 1975
Time Life Books

Railways Past, Present, and Future
by G. Freeman Allen
© 1982
Portland House

*Silver at your Service – A Collector's Guide to
    Railroad Dining Car Flatware Patterns*
by Arthur L. Dominy and
Rudolph A. Morgenfruh
© 1987
D & M Publishing

*Silver Banquet II – A Compendium on
    Railroad Dining Car Silver Pieces*
by Everett L. Maffett
© 1990
Silver Press

*Sparkling Glass – A Collector's Guide
    to Railroad Glassware*
by Larry R. Paul
© 1991
Railroad Collectors Association, Inc.
(currently available from RCAI – *see page 202*)

Supertrains
by Aaron K.Klein
© 1985
Exeter Books

Teapot Treasury and Related Items
by Richard W. Luckin
© 1987
RK Publishing Company

*The Train Watcher's Guide to North
    American Railroads*
compiled by George H. Drury
© 1984
Kalmbach Publishing Co.

The Trains We Rode
by Lucius Beebe and Charles Clegg
© 1965/1966
1993 reprint of two volume book
Promontory Press

Through by Rail
by Charles Gilbert Hall
© 1938

Miscellaneous Transportation China

Greyhound depot, 1952 advertisement.

Greyhound Post House "Stagecoach" pattern cup & saucer; Syracuse b/s; 1963 date code; $40.00 – 50.00.

Greyhound Post Houses

In 1939 Greyhound lunchrooms at rest stops, depots, and terminals were operated by independent concessionaires and the food and service was unacceptable to Greyhound executives. Because of this, the decision was made to begin operating their own restaurants. At the same time several new terminals were being built in Atlanta, Georgia, and Dayton, Ohio, and other large cities. These were the locations of the first Post Houses. Eight, offering high quality food, were operating by 1940. By 1947, 98 Greyhound Post Houses were serving meals in 24 states and Canada and in 1950 the number totaled 139. Growth continued with an additional 10 restaurants by 1955. The restaurant business accounted for approximately 10 percent of Greyhound's income. Between 1978 and 1982 most Post Houses were converted to Burger King fast-food operations.

Greyhound Post House "Stagecoach" pattern 6¼" plate; Syracuse b/s; 1959 date code; $28.00 – 35.00.

London Transport Catering saucer; J.E. Heath b/s, 1978 date code. Saucer, $10.00 – 12.50; cup & saucer, $24.00 – 30.00.

Military China ~ On Land and Sea

Walter Reed Hospital, Washington D.C. United States Army Medical Department china is used here and at U. S. military medical facilities around the world.

Camp Blanding Hospital in Florida. Over 200 buildings were connected with covered walkways. This hospital had beds for over 2,000 patients during World War II.

War and Navy Building, Washington, D. C. Department of the Navy china is used here.

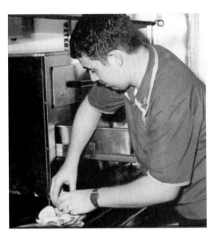

Photographs and caption from USS *Enterprise* CVN-65 yearbook

"The wardroom division is composed of many talented individuals who's main goal is to provide the officers of the 'Big E' the finest meal services and stateroom accommodations possible. S-5 (wardroom division) also hosted elaborate luncheons and receptions for numerous distinguished visitors that embarked the *Enterprise*. Moreover, special events such as candlelight dinners, pie and ice cream parties, and pizza nights were hosted to boost the morale of the officers onboard the 'Carrier With Class'."

1899 *Harper's Weekly* photograph of enlisted personnel mess aboard the *Olympia*. While officers are served on topmarked china, enlisted men use enameled metal ware in this early photograph, later metal trays with plain white vitrified china bowls and mugs and currently plastic trays, mugs, and bowls.

Manufacturers of American Military China

During World War II all American commercial china manufacturers produced ware for the United States military. Apparently it was considered a part of the war effort. Even Royal China and Taylor, Smith and Taylor, which ordinarily made only non-vitrified household china at that time, manufactured medium-heavy gauge vitrified china for the United States Medical Department. Since the 1970s Jackson, Shenango, Mayer, and Homer Laughlin have been the primary manufacturers.

U.S. Navy China Topmarks

Admiral's Mess

Vice Admiral's Mess

Rear Admiral's Mess

Captain's Mess

Wardroom Officer's Mess

Junior Officer's Mess

Warrant Officer's Mess

U. S. Army Branch Insignia
(1941)

Engineers
Corps *

Air Corps

Signal Corps

Medical
Corps *

Quartermaster
Corps *

Ordnance
Department

Finance
Department

National
Guard Bureau

Military
Intelligence
Division

U.S. Military
Academy *

* logo topmarks military china

United States Army Medical Department 9½" high pitcher (USAMD-1); Greenwood b/s; 1900 – 1910; $110.00 – 140.00.

United States Army Medical Department egg cup (USAMD-1); Sterling b/s; circa early 1940s; $11.00 – 14.00.

United States Army Medical Department (USAMD-1); Carr b/s; dated 1943. Butter, $20.00 – 25.00; mustard, $20.00 – 25.00.

United States Army Medical Department (USAMD-1); McNicol b/s; circa early 1940s. 4" high pitcher, $22.00 – 28.00; 7" plate, $10.00 – 12.50.

United States Army Medical Department 10¼" grill plate (USAMD-1); Shenango b/s; 1950 date code; $20.00 – 25.00.

United States Army Medical Department 8½" long sauceboat (USAMD-1a); Shenango b/s; circa early 1940s; $24.00 – 30.00.

United States Army Medical Department (USAMD-1b); unusual rust-brown decoration; Shenango b/s; circa 1930s. Cream pitcher, $18.00 – 24.00; 9" plate, $15.00 – 20.00.

United States Army Medical Department (USAMD-2); Shenango b/s, 1956 date code (left); Sterling b/s, 1962 date code (right). Cup, $8.00 – 10.00; 9" plate, $15.00 – 20.00.

United States Army Medical Department (USAMD-2); Sterling b/s, 1951 date code (left); Wallace b/s (right). Creamer, $12.00 – 16.00; egg cup, $9.00 – 12.00.

United States Army Medical Department 9" long sauceboat (USAMD-2); Caribe b/s; early 1950s; $22.00 – 28.00.

United States Army Medical Department (USAMD-2); Sterling b/s, 1952 date code (left); Iroquois b/s, 1951 date code (right). Mustard, $18.00 – 22.00; 4½" high pitcher, $22.00 – 28.00.

United States Army Medical Department (USAMD-3); Buffalo By Oneida b/s (left); Homer Laughlin b/s (right); late 1980s – early 1990s. Mug, $12.00 – 16.00; 6¼" plate, $8.00 – 10.00.

U.S. Navy Rear Admiral's mess handled bouillon (USN-3); O.P.CO. b/s; 1942 date code; $18.00 – 22.00.

U. S. Navy Captain's mess 6½" plate (USN-4); Buffalo b/s; circa early 1940s; $11.00 – 14.00.

U. S. Navy Wardroom Officer's mess A.D. cup (handle behind cup) & saucer (USN-5); O.P.CO. b/s; 1942 date code; $24.00 – 30.00.

U. S. Navy Wardroom Officer's mess cup & saucer (USN-5); Shenango b/s; 1950 date code; $20.00 – 25.00.

U. S. Navy; Shenango b/s. Wardroom Officer's mess 9" plate (USN-5), 1978 date code, $14.00 – 18.00. Junior Officer's mess 10" plate (USN-6), circa 1940s, $18.00 – 22.00.

U. S. Navy; Tepco b/s; circa early 1940s. Warrant Officer's mess 7" plate (USN-7), $12.00 – 16.00; Junior Officer's mess cup (handle behind cup; USN-6), $9.00 – 12.00.

Department of the Navy (USN-8); McNicol-Martin b/s, 1960s
(left); Walker b/s, 1959 date code (right). Handled bouillon,
$10.00 – 12.50; egg cup, $9.00 – 12.00.

Department of the Navy cup & saucer (USN-8); Jackson b/s;
1982 date code; $18.00 – 24.00.

Department of the Navy 10" plate (USN-8); Shenango b/s; 1978
date code; $15.00 – 20.00.

United States Coast Guard oatmeal (USCG-1); 13 stars on
shield; Shenango b/s; early 1940s; $20.00 – 25.00.

United States Coast Guard cup & saucer (USCG-2); Mayer b/s;
1973 and 1974 date codes; $22.00 – 28.00.

United States Coast Guard 6¼" plate (USCG-2); Mayer b/s;
1974 date code; $12.00 – 15.00.

United States Army Transport (USAT-1); Syracuse Old Ivory b/s; early 1940s; the Transportation Corps, a branch of the U. S. Army, was created in 1942 "to bring together in one agency the many transportation functions then scattered throughout the army." Handled bouillon, $15.00 – 20.00; sauceboat; $20.00 – 25.00.

U. S. Quartermasters Corps 9½" long sauceboat (USQMC-1); embossed logo near handle; Shenango and U.S.Q.M.C. b/s; circa early 1940s; $22.00 – 28.00.

U. S. M. Commissary 7" long platter (MCOM-1); Wallace and U.S.M. COM. b/s; early 1940s; $12.00 – 15.00.

United States Strike Command 3½" tray; Thos. D. Murphy Co. b/s; $5.00 – 6.50.

Marines Memorial Association saucer (USMC-1); Jackson b/s; 1969 date code. Saucer; $11.00 – 14.00. Cup & saucer; $24.00 – 30.00.

Naval Air Training Center (Corpus Christi, TX) cadet mess 9" long sauceboat (USN-9); no b/s; $30.00 – 40.00.

West Point Military Academy double egg cup (USARMY-1); no b/s; circa 1930s; $40.00 – 50.00.

U. S. Hotel Thayer (West Point, N.Y.) cream pitcher (USARMY-2); West Point Academy logo in center; Shenango b/s; circa 1940s; $30.00 – 40.00.

West Point Military Academy ashtray (USARMY-3); Shenango Incaware b/s; 1940s; $28.00 – 35.00.

Annapolis U. S. Naval Academy egg cup (USN-10); Mayer b/s; circa 1930s; $30.00 – 40.00.

Royal Military College of Canada butter (RCM-1); Dunn, Bennett & Co. b/s; 1930s; $24.00 – 30.00.

Canadian Royal Air Force cup (RCAF-1); Grindley Duraline b/s; 1966 date code; $10.00 – 12.50.

Fort Shafter Officers' Mess (Hawaii) 10" plate (USARMY-4); Shenango b/s; dated 1949; $35.00 – 42.00.

Fort Ord (Seaside, California) cup (handle behind cup; USARMY-5); Tepco b/s; circa 1950s. Cup, $18.00 – 24.00; cup & saucer, $40.00 – 50.00.

Air Force Plant 78 10½" plate (USAF-1); Wallace b/s; 1950s; $28.00 – 35.00.

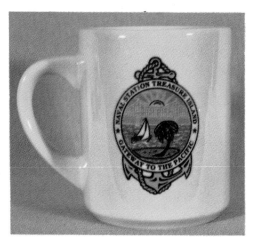

Treasure Island Naval Station mug; Crestor, Inc. b/s; 1970s; $15.00 – 20.00.

USS *Kitty Hawk* (aircraft carrier) mug; Ultima b/s; circa 1980s; $10.00 – 12.50.

Larry Paul Collection

Student Officers Open Mess; Shenango b/s; 1958 date code. Cup, $18.00 – 24.00; cup & saucer, $40.00 – 50.00.

Government China

China used in any government (city, county, state, country, or the like) owned dining area including on an official yacht or aircraft. Such dining facilities may be operated in conjunction with any government agency (e.g., CIA), bureau (e.g., FBI), department (e.g., Treasury Department), service (e.g., U. S. Forest Service), governing body (e.g., Senate, House of Representatives, or parliament), embassy (U. S. or foreign), and so forth. Commercial government china does not include ware used strictly by residents in the private living quarters of a government owned building, but rather that used in an official capacity, such as entertaining foreign dignitaries. Military china is covered in its own section.

Courtesy of ABCO International

Air Force One china

Courtesy of Royal Doulton

Australian Parliament, Canberra, Australia

White House China

While the chances of running across a piece of White House china are perhaps slim-to-none, assuming it would find a home in a museum rather than at an antique show if ever discarded, such china does merit coverage. These patterns have been reproduced in the form of collector plates for those who are interested. Several originals are shown on the following page which is reprinted from *The White House*, © 1962 by the White House Historical Association, "a non-profit organization, chartered in 1961, to enhance understanding, appreciation and enjoyment of the Executive Mansion." Should you ever tour the White House, the china is on display in the ground floor China Room.

CHINA COLLECTION

MONROE *dinner plate by Dagoty of Paris, about 1817 (top left). Plate from the Haviland state service made in Limoges, France, used in the Lincoln administration, 1861-1865 (upper right). Left, a plate from Grant's Haviland service with a small U. S. Seal in the border decoration, 1869-1877. Right, a plate from the Harrison administration, 1889-1893, made in Limoges. These four 19th-century examples have a definite similarity in form and in the delicacy of the painted decoration.*

WEDGWOOD *(England) plate from the Theodore Roosevelt administration, 1901-1909, at upper left of lower group. Upper right, a service plate from the Lenox china purchased during the term of Woodrow Wilson, 1913-1921. Below left, a plate from the Lenox service ordered during the Truman administration, 1945-1953. Below right, one of the Castleton dinner service plates ordered during the Eisenhower administration, 1953-1961.*

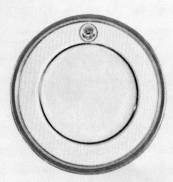

Larry Paul Collection

United States Senate saucer; Scammell's Trenton b/s; circa 1920s. Saucer, $30.00 – 40.00; cup & saucer, $65.00 – 85.00+.

American Embassy (Paris, France) 4½" long tray; Haviland b/s; circa 1920s; $18.00 – 22.00.

Veterans Administration 4½" high pitcher; Shenango b/s; 1930s; $20.00 – 25.00.

Statue of Liberty ashtray; Carr Glo-Tan b/s; 1940s; $22.00 – 28.00.

National Home for Disabled Volunteer Soldiers 9¾" salad; backstamp only, as shown; made by Glasgow Pottery; March 3, 1865 on backstamp refers to the date the home was established; produced in 1899; $50.00 – 65.00.

Larry Paul Collection

United States Bureau of Fisheries "Bureau of Fisheries" pattern 9¾" plate (USBF-1); Buffalo b/s; circa 1920s; said to be used at U. S. Bureau of Fisheries headquarters, as well as on their train cars; $75.00 – 100.00.

Courtesy of China Concepts

Peru's "Presidential" pattern presidential aircraft butter
(PER-1); gold line and decal on white body; China Concepts
b/s; dated 1996; $25.00 – 32.00.

Courtesy of Pickard

The U.S. Department of State has selected Pickard to
supply the official china used in American Embassies
around the world. When our ambassadors entertain
emporers, presidents, and queens, in Tokyo, Cairo and
Madrid, they set the table with our country's
finest...Pickard

Courtesy of Pickard

United Nations china

Western and Southwestern Theme Restaurant China

"BOOTS 'N SADDLE"

Western and southwestern theme restaurant china is primarily a product of the 1940s – early 1960s. While many American commercial china companies produced this "all-American" restaurant china at some point during that period, two California firms stand out in particular: Tepco China and Wallace China.

Tepco produced the following patterns: "Western Traveler" in brown transfer print on a tan body and occasionally dark red transfer print on a white body, "Broken Wagon Wheel" in stencil airbrushed brown on a tan body, "Early California" in brown transfer print on a tan body, as well as dark red, green, or cobalt blue transfer print on a white body, "Ox Head" in stencil airbrushed maroon on a white body, and "Branding Iron" in brown transfer print on a tan body (branding irons on border spell-out Tepco).

Wallace's Westward Ho patterns were designed by Till Goodan and originally produced for the Wentz Company. These include "Rodeo" and "Little Buckaroo" (a child's pattern), each in multicolor transfer print (brown, rust, green, and yellow) on a tan body with brown border, "Boots 'n Saddle" in multicolor transfer print on a tan body (illustrated on poster at left), "Longhorn" in brown and rust transfer print on a white body with brown border, and "Pioneer Trails" in rust transfer print on a tan body. Other Wallace western patterns include, "49er" in rust transfer print on a white body and "Chuckwagon" in rust transfer print on a tan body.

Two of Wallace's Westward Ho patterns, "Little Buckaroo" (a child's cup, 9½" plate and oatmeal) and "Rodeo" (7½", 9½", 11", and 14" plates, 16" platter, 12½" long baker, oatmeal, cup & saucer plus larger cup, salt & pepper, cream pitcher, covered sugar, coffee pot, and water pitcher), have been recently reproduced. "Texas-based True West has faithfully re-created the original heavy roll rim design and colors so accurately, you can mix it with your old china" according to the True West brochure. The ware is backstamped with the Westward Ho mark, but "Wallace China, Made in California...U.S.A" is replaced by "True West, Comanche, Texas, 1991" (and perhaps other years).

Though flaws such as foreign particle specks and pre-glaze chips are common on both Wallace and Tepco china (particularly Tepco), they seem to have little effect on its value.

Tepco China's very popular "Western Traveler" pattern

Sterling China reintroduced the "Bunk House" pattern on the left and the "El Rancho" pattern on the right in 1993. Originally a tan body, it is now produced in an ivory body.

Photographs are in alphabetical order by pattern name. Patterns named by the manufacturer are in standard type and those named by the author are in italics. Photographs of western restaurant name or logo topmarked china follow.

"Branding Iron – *Border*" pattern sugar and cup (WST-1); branding irons spell out "TEPCO"; Tepco b/s. Sugar, $20.00 – 25.00; sugar with lid, $38.00 – 45.00; cup, $15.00 – 20.00; cup & saucer, $35.00 – 45.00.

"Branding Iron* – *Bronco*" pattern 7" plate (WST-1a); branding irons spell out "TEPCO"; Blue Ridge China b/s (made by Tepco); $28.00 – 35.00.

"Branding Iron* – *Lasso*" pattern 9½" plate (WST-1b); branding irons spell out "TEPCO"; Tepco b/s; $32.00 – 40.00.

"Branding Iron* – *Saddle*" pattern 9½" plate (WST-1c); branding irons spell out "TEPCO"; Tepco b/s; $32.00 – 40.00.

"Broken Wagon Wheel" pattern (WST-2); Tepco b/s. 7¼" plate, $22.00 – 28.00; cream pitcher, $35.00 – 42.00.

"Broken Wagon Wheel" pattern cup & saucer (WST-2); Tepco b/s; $35.00 – 45.00.

* The "Western Traveler" pattern, with a Pony Express theme, and the "Branding Iron" pattern, with branding irons which spell out TEPCO on the border, are two distinct patterns according to Tepco's catalog. "Branding Iron" pieces backstamped Western Traveler should not be considered "Western Traveler" pattern.

"Bunk House – *Tan Body*" pattern cup (WST-3); Caribe b/s; 1969 date code; "Bunk House – Ivory Body" currently produced by Sterling China (WST-3a). Cup, $14.00 – 18.00; cup & saucer, $30.00 – 40.00.

"*Cartoon Cowboy*" pattern 10¼" plate (WST-4); Shenango of California b/s; 1962 date code; $25.00 – 32.00.

"*Cartoon Cowboy*" pattern (WST-4); Shenango of California or Shenango b/s; 1962 and 1968 date codes. 6¼" plate, $14.00 – 18.00; saucer, $12.00 – 15.00; cup & saucer, $24.00 – 30.00.

"*Cattle Brands*" pattern (WST-5); Jackson b/s; 1967 date code. Saucer, $14.00 – 18.00; cup & saucer, $30.00 – 40.00.

"Chuck Wagon" pattern (WST-6); Wallace b/s; 1950s. Cream pitcher, $40.00 – 50.00; A.D. cup & saucer, $65.00 – 80.00.

"Early California – *Brown*" pattern mug (handle behind mug; WST-7); Tepco b/s; $40.00 – 50.00.

"Early California – *Green*" pattern 13¼" compartment plate (WST-7a); Mfg. Exclusively for National Restaurant System by Tepco China b/s; green print on white body are unusual colors in this pattern; $125.00 – 160.00.

"Early California – *Green*" pattern 7" soup (WST-7a); Tepco b/s; green print on white body are unusual colors in this pattern; $30.00 – 40.00.

"El Rancho – *Tan Body*" pattern (WST-8); handles behind cup & mug; Wallace b/s; 1940s–1950s; "El Rancho – Ivory Body" currently produced by Sterling China (WST-8a). Wallace cup, $15.00 – 20.00; Wallace mug, $18.00 – 24.00.

"49er" pattern fruit (WST-9); Wallace b/s; sometimes b/s "49er"; 1940s; pattern also made with a tan body (WST-9a); $22.00 – 28.00.

"*Gold Rush Gear*" pattern cream pitcher (WST-10); Harold's Club (Reno, NV) and other topmark restaurant companion piece; Russel Wright design; Sterling b/s; 1958 date code; $40.00 – 50.00.

"Longhorn" pattern (WST-11); Wallace Westward Ho Longhorn b/s; 1940s–1950s. 10½" plate, $38.00 – 45.00; mug, $20.00 – 25.00.

"*Ox Head – Rust*" pattern mug (WST-12); Syracuse Econo-Rim b/s; 1943 date code; $40.00 – 50.00.

"*Ox Head – Rust*" pattern 8¼" plate (WST-12); Syracuse Econo-Rim b/s; 1947 date code; $32.00 – 40.00.

"*Ox Head – Brown*" pattern (WST-12a); Homer Laughlin b/s; 1969 date code. Cup, $16.00 – 22.00; cup & saucer, $35.00 – 45.00.

"Ox Head – *Maroon*" pattern fruit (WST-12b); Tepco b/s; $20.00 – 25.00.

"*Ranch Hand*" pattern (Shenango's pattern name: "Roundup") 6¼" plate (WST-13); Shenango Incaware b/s; 1953 date code; $25.00 – 32.00.

"Rodeo" pattern cream pitcher (WST-14); Wallace b/s; 1950s; $50.00 – 65.00.

"Rodeo – *Border*" saucer (WST-14a); Wallace Westward Ho b/s; 1940s–1950s; identical border used on "Boots 'n Saddle" and "Little Buckaroo" patterns; $14.00 – 18.00.

"*Southwest Desert*" pattern cup (WST-15); Wallace b/s; circa 1940s. Cup, $20.00 – 25.00; cup & saucer, $35.00 – 42.00.

"*Steer and Cattleman*" pattern 5¾" saucer (WST-16); Walker b/s; 1967 date code. Saucer, $14.00 – 18.00; cup & saucer, $30.00 – 40.00.

"Sundown" pattern cup (WST-17); Syracuse b/s; 1954 date code. Cup, $20.00 – 25.00; cup & saucer, $35.00 – 42.00.

"Sundown" pattern (WST-17); Syracuse b/s; 1956 date code. Covered sugar, $45.00 – 60.00; cream pitcher, $24.00 – 30.00.

"*Thirst Quench*" pattern grapefruit (WST-18); Wellsville Swing Ware b/s; circa 1950s–1960s; $22.00 – 28.00.

"Thirst Quench" pattern cup (WST-18); Wellsville Swing Ware b/s; circa 1950s–1960s. Cup, $18.00 – 22.00; cup & saucer, $38.00 – 45.00.

"Weary Rider" pattern cup & saucer (WST-19); Shenango Incaware b/s; 1940s; $38.00 – 45.00.

"Western Traveler" pattern celery (WST-20); Tepco Western Traveler b/s; $28.00 – 35.00.

"Western Traveler" pattern 11" long platter (WST-20); Tepco Western Traveler b/s; $40.00 – 50.00.

"Western Traveler" pattern (WST-20); Tepco b/s. Cup, $16.00 – 22.00; cup & saucer, $35.00 – 45.00; 6¼" plate, $24.00 – 30.00.

"Western Traveler" pattern (WST-20); Tepco b/s. Oatmeal, $22.00 – 28.00; mug, $20.00 – 25.00.

"Western Traveler – *Red*" 6" plate (WST-20a); Tepco b/s; red print on white body are unusual colors in this pattern; $28.00 – 35.00.

Bonanza restaurant 9½" plate; Wallace Desert Ware b/s; late 1950s; $40.00 – 50.00.

Cattlemens Restaurant (West Coast & Southwestern chain) mug; no manufacturer b/s; circa 1980s; $14.00 – 18.00.

Chuck Wagon footed mug; Mayer b/s; pre-1950; $30.00 – 40.00.

Larry Paul Collection

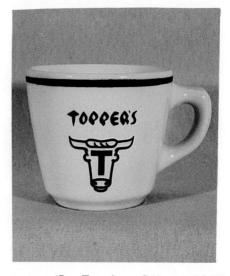

Rod's Steak House (Williams, AZ) salt; restaurant name on reverse side; no manufacturer b/s; made by Wallace China; circa 1950s. Salt, $22.00 – 28.00; salt & pepper, $45.00 – 60.00.

Topper's restaurant (San Francisco, CA) cup; McNicol-Martin b/s; 1960s. Cup, $16.00 – 22.00; cup & saucer, $32.00 – 40.00.

Western Sizzlin Steak House 6¼" plate; Homer Laughlin b/s; 1988 date code; chain restaurant located in central and southern states, east of the Great Divide; $20.00 – 25.00.

Southwestern design covered sugar; Syracuse Adobe Ware b/s; 1953 date code; may be a custom design or stock pattern; $50.00 – 65.00.

Sittin' pretty...

In addition to restaurants, western theme china was commonly used at dude ranches in the 1950s and 1960s.

Oriental Restaurant China

Bush Garden, Seattle, Washington

Joe Jung's 9¾" plate; Jackson b/s; 1974 date code; $20.00 – 25.00.

China Seas Restaurant (San Francisco, CA) fruit; Jackson b/s; 1978 date code; $12.00 – 15.00.

House of Wong (San Leandro, CA) jong; Jackson and Cook's Hotel & Restaurant Supply b/s; circa 1950s; $10.00 – 12.50.

The Stevens Hotel (Chicago, IL) 9½" plate; Scammell Lamberton b/s; circa 1930s; $24.00 – 30.00.

Dick's Dragon Restaurant 7½" plate; Wallace b/s; circa 1950s; $14.00 – 18.00.

Peking Gourmet Inn (small East Coast chain) Oriental cup; Homer Laughlin b/s; early 1990s; $5.00 – 6.00.

Ah Fong's compote; Jackson b/s; 1970s; $24.00 – 30.00.

Far East Cafe (San Francisco and other California locations) 7"
plate; Tepco b/s; circa 1950s–1960s; $15.00 – 20.00.

Kuo Wah (San Francisco, CA) 6¼" plate; Mayer b/s; circa
1940s; $12.00 – 15.00.

The China Rose; Tatung b/s. Teapot, $20.00 – 25.00; Oriental
cup, $5.00 – 6.00.

Colonel Lee's Mongolian Bar-B-Q (Mountain View, CA) 7"
chop suey; no manufacturer b/s; $12.00 – 15.00.

The China Rose; Tatung b/s. Ashtray or 6" plate, $6.00 – 8.00
each.

10½" diameter, 3½" deep custom crested salad; Jackson b/s;
1965 date code; $30.00 – 40.00.

"Blue Willow" pattern rice; Hall b/s; circa 1930s; $20.00 – 25.00.

"Red Willow" pattern fruit; McCobb shape; Jackson McCobb b/s; 1975 date code; $12.00 – 15.00.

"Mayfair" pattern 8" plate; O.P.CO. "Mayfair" b/s; 1931 date code; $16.00 – 22.00.

"Blue Willow" pattern 8" plate; Cook's Hotel & Restaurant Supply and Jackson b/s; circa 1940s; $16.00 – 22.00.

"Red Willow" pattern Oriental cup; Jackson b/s; 1981 date code; $10.00 – 12.50.

"Confucius" pattern 7" chop suey; Tepco b/s; circa 1950s–1960s; $20.00 – 25.00.

Transfer printed chow mein; Jackson b/s; 1962 date code; $14.00 – 18.00.

Transfer printed Oriental sauce; Jackson and Cook's Hotel & Restaurant Supply b/s; circa 1950s; $9.00 – 12.00.

Yet Wah (Larkspur, San Francisco, and other California locations) Oriental cup; Buffalo embossed b/s; circa 1970s; $6.00 – 8.00.

Transfer printed Oriental cup; Jackson and Cook's Hotel & Restaurant Supply b/s; circa 1940s; $7.00 – 9.00.

"Tien Hu Crimson" pattern; Buffalo b/s; early 1980s. 9½" platter; $8.00 – 10.00. Oriental cup; $3.00 – 4.50.

"Canton" pattern jong; H.F. Coors Alox b/s; 1980s; $3.00 – 4.00.

Sushi Sam's (San Mateo, CA) pale blue tumbler; Sai Japan b/s; circa 1980s; $10.00 – 12.50.

Snopy 6" plate; Golden China b/s; circa 1970s; $125.00 – 15.00.

Chinese Village (Portland, OR) 7½" plate; no manufacturer b/s; $5.00 – 7.00.

Overglaze lined and decaled Oriental sauce. At left, Cathay b/s. At right, Tatung b/s. $4.00 – 5.00 each.

Oriental cups. At left, no manufacturer b/s. At right, Jackson b/s, 1983 date code. $4.00 – 6.00 each.

Oriental cups. At left, China Castle (Torrance, CA), T.T.C. China b/s. At right, Chef Chu's (Los Altos, CA), Jackson b/s, 1982 date code, $6.00 – 8.00 each.

奇ㄑ 怪《ㄨㄞˋ*

Oriental Tabletop Ideas from Hall

*Marvellous!

Japanese–style A La Carte Plates

This unique blend of Eastern and Western influences sets off any meal, from Oriental to Occidental.

50920/8-896

9930/8-891

9930/5210

19810/5204-1

Noritake Chinese Service

The spark of this service reflects the gaiety of Chinese cuisine. The dignity and presence of Noritake dinnerware combine with the exuberance of a Chinese banquet to create a unique adventure for your honoured guests.

This full line of colorful utensils makes possible Chinese dining in its fullest.

大觀苑

50116/7-402

50116/7-404

50116/7-406

50116/7-408

50116/7-410

The Show Plate

50116/7-412

50116/7-409

Sports Related Restaurant China

China used at a foodservice establishment in or associated with a sports stadium, ski resort, bowling alley, race track, or any sports facility. This ware is quite scarce and sought by both restaurant china and sports memorabilia collectors.

San Francisco Giants' stadium restaurant (San Francisco, CA) 7¼" plate; Syracuse b/s; 1961 date code; $75.00 – 100.00.

San Francisco Giants' stadium restaurant (San Francisco, CA) 6½" plate; Jackson b/s; 1981 date code; $60.00 – 80.00.

Larry Paul Collection

New York Coliseum; Sterling Lamberton b/s; circa 1960s. Cup, $45.00 – 60.00; cup & saucer, $100.00 – 125.00.

Squaw Valley (Squaw Valley, CA, site of the 1960 Winter Olympics); Tepco b/s; circa 1950s – early 1960s. 5½" plate, $20.00 – 25.00; cup & saucer, $30.00 – 40.00.

Casino Restaurant China

Demand for casino memorabilia including gaming chips, dice, playing cards, swizzle sticks, ashtrays, and china is at an all-time high. China is by far the most difficult to locate.

Casino reference

Casinos and Their Ashtrays
by Art Anderson
© 1994
This work offers a capsule history of a 100+ casinos and contains photographs of nearly 800 ashtrays. Both the histories and the pictures aid in the identification and dating of casino china.
For ordering information write to:
    Art Anderson
    P.O. Box 4103
    Flint, MI 48504-0103

China pattern codes
    To promote continuity in the area of casino collectibles, casino codes as designated in *Casinos and Their Ashtrays* by Art Anderson are listed in photograph captions. Each is followed by "-CH" (to differentiate between china in the generic sense and ashtrays) and a sequential dash number. While the majority of the ashtrays in Mr. Anderson's book are glass, a few are medium-to-heavy gauge commercial china, such as the Cal-Neva Biltmore ashtray. In that case, the addition of "-CH" was unnecessary.

Photographs
    Photographs are in alphabetical order by casino name. Casino location and years of operation are included in photograph caption.

Trader Dick's (Sparks, Nevada)

Bonanza Hotel (Las Vegas, NV; 1967–1970; after demolition the property became the site of the MGM Grand Hotel) 10½" plate (BON-CH-01); Syracuse b/s; 1967 date code; $30.00 – 40.00.

Cal-Neva Biltmore (Lake Tahoe, NV; 1951–1952; name changed to Tahoe Biltmore Hotel and Casino, 1952–1958) ashtray (CNB-02); Wallace b/s; 1951; $75.00 – 100.00.

Desert Inn (Las Vegas, NV; 1950–present; originally Wilbur Clark's Desert Inn, the name changed to MGM Desert Inn in 1987 and later the Sheraton Desert Inn) (DIC-CH-01); Shenango b/s. 5" plate, 1969 date code, $24.00 – 30.00; cream pitcher, 1953 date code, $40.00 – 50.00.

El San Juan Hotel and Casino (San Juan, Puerto Rico; 1987–present) ashtray (ESJ-CH-01); Abco Trading b/s; late 1980s; $10.00 – 12.00.

George's Gateway Club (Lake Tahoe, NV; 1949–1959; name changed to Harvey's Wagon Wheel) 6" plate (GGW-CH-01); Tepco b/s; 1950s; $70.00 – 90.00.

Hacienda Hotel & Casino (Las Vegas, NV; 1957–present) cream pitcher (HAC-CH-01); McNicol b/s; late 1950s; $60.00 – 80.00.

Harold's Club (Reno, NV; 1935–1996) cream pitcher (HCR-CH-01); Sterling b/s; 1964 date code; $40.00 – 50.00.

Harvey's Wagon Wheel casino (Lake Tahoe, NV; 1944–1961; name changed to Harvey's Resort Hotel, however the wagon wheel logo continued in use for sometime) cream pitcher (HAV-CH-01); Shenango b/s; 1961 date code; $35.00 – 42.00.

The Holiday (Reno, NV; 1955–present) A.D. cup and saucer (HOL-CH-01); Syracuse b/s; 1966 date code; $50.00 – 65.00.

Keith's Model T Truck Stop (Winnemucca, NV; 1969–early 1970s; name changed to Model T Truck Stop) cup & saucer (MTT-CH-01); Shenango b/s; 1971 and 1973 date codes; $100.00 – 125.00.

Kings Castle Hotel and Casino (Incline Village, Lake Tahoe, NV; 1969 – 1974; became Hyatt Resort Hotel & Casino in 1975 and Hyatt Regency in 1990) pewter-like 11" service plate (KCC-CH-01); Wilton RWP b/s; $24.00 – 30.00.

Mapes Hotel & Casino (Reno, NV; 1947–1982) (MAP-CH-01); Tepco b/s; 1950s. 6¼" plate, $30.00 – 40.00; cream pitcher, $45.00 – 55.00.

Nevada Lodge casino (Lake Tahoe, NV; 1960–1988; name changed to Tahoe Biltmore Lodge, 1988+) fruit (NCL-CH-01); Shenango b/s; 1972 date code; $20.00 – 25.00.

Nevada Lodge casino (Lake Tahoe, NV; 1960–1988; name changed to Tahoe Biltmore Lodge) celery (NCL-CH-01); Mayer b/s; 1964 date code; $28.00 – 35.00.

Riviera Hotel and Casino (Las Vegas, NV; 1955–present) cream pitcher (RIV-CH-01); Wallace b/s; late 1950s; $40.00 – 50.00.

Showboat Hotel & Casino (Las Vegas, NV; 1954–present) bouillon (SHO-CH-01); Tepco b/s; circa 1950s–early 1960s; $35.00 – 42.00.

Trader Dick's Restaurant at John Ascuaga's Nugget Casino (Sparks, NV; 1960–present) tumbler (NJA-CH-01); no b/s; front and back views shown; $12.00 – 15.00.

Amusement Park and Fairground Restaurant China

There are hundreds, perhaps thousands of amusements parks and fairgrounds across America and around the world. Because most of the tableware is disposable, durable ware is all the more desirable.

Disneyland (Anaheim, CA) 6" melamine plate; Plastic Mfg. Co. Epicure b/s; circa 1980s; $12.00 – 15.00.

Disneyland (Anaheim, CA) 6½" plate; Homer Laughlin b/s; 1993 date code; $18.00 – 24.00.

Larry Paul Collection

Disney World (Lake Buena Vista, FL; 20 miles southwest of Orlando) mug; Mayer b/s; 1977 date code; $22.00 – 28.00.

Humboldt County Fairgrounds (Humboldt County, CA) fruit; Wallace b/s; 1950s; $14.00 – 18.00.

Marineland of the Pacific (Los Angeles, CA) 6¼" plate; Syracuse b/s; 1962 date code; $25.00 – 32.00.

Courtesy of Royal Doulton

Department and Drug Store Lunch Counter and Cafeteria China

Liggett's Drug Store (East Coast drug store chain) 7" plate; Warwick; dated 1945; $30.00 – 40.00.

Montgomery Ward (nationwide department store chain) 9" plate; Syracuse b/s; 1972 date code; $16.00 – 22.00.

Walgreens (nationwide variety store chain) grapefruit; O.P.CO. b/s; 1943 date code; $25.00 – 32.00. Walgreens cup; Syracuse b/s; 1946 date code. Cup, $18.00 – 22.00; cup & saucer, $40.00 – 50.00.

Montgomery Ward (nationwide department store chain) 5½" plate; Syracuse b/s; 1964 date code; $14.00 – 18.00.

Sears mug; Syracuse b/s; 1973 date code; $18.00 – 24.00.

Walgreens (nationwide variety store chain) 9½" compartment plate; Syracuse Econo-Rim b/s; 1946 date code; $40.00 – 50.00.

Walgreens (nationwide variety store chain) mug; Shenango b/s; 1975 date code; $20.00 – 25.00.

Woolworth's (nationwide variety store chain) 7¼" plate; O.P.CO. b/s; 1930 date code; $38.00 – 45.00.

Woolworth's in San Francisco, California, in 1953.

Company Cafeteria and Executive Dining Room China

Crocker Bank (California) 9" plate; Sterling Medallion b/s; 1977 date code; $15.00 – 20.00.

Edison Service oatmeal; O.P.CO. b/s; 1931 date code; $25.00 – 32.00.

Fireman's Fund Insurance Company 9" plate; Walker b/s; 1956 date code; $30.00 – 40.00.

Fireman's Fund Insurance Company cup & saucer; Syracuse b/s; 1974 date code; $20.00 – 25.00.

General Motors 9¼" plate; Sterling b/s; 1968 date code; $50.00 – 60.00.

Grumman Aircraft Engineering Corporation jam; Iroquois b/s; 1947 date code; $20.00 – 25.00 without lid; $30.00 – 40.00 with lid.

Mercedes Benz cup & saucer (handle behind cup); Bauscher b/s; $32.00 – 40.00.

Metropolitan Life Insurance Company cup & saucer; Syracuse b/s; 1964 date codes; $30.00 – 40.00.

Metropolitan Life Insurance Company; Syracuse Syralite b/s; 1971 date codes. 9" plate, $15.00 – 20.00; cup, $9.00 – 12.00; cup & saucer, $20.00 – 25.00.

Nabisco Brands Inc. 7" plate; Sterling Lamberton b/s; 1985 date code; $15.00 – 20.00.

Reddy Kilowatt 9" plate; pattern may have been used by any of 200+ utility companies that participated in the Reddy Kilowatt Program, 1934+; Syracuse b/s; 1953 date code; $80.00 – 100.00.

Safeway 7¼" plate; Homer Laughlin b/s; 1972 date code; $14.00 – 18.00.

Larry Paul Collection

Sun Papers (Baltimore, MD, newspaper) 6" plate; Shenango b/s; circa 1930s–1940s; $18.00 – 22.00.

20th Century Fox (Hollywood, CA) 10½" plate; Syracuse Syralite b/s; 1983 date code; $28.00 – 35.00.

Manufacturer Samples, Display and Test Pieces, Commemoratives, Souvenirs, and Employee Gifts

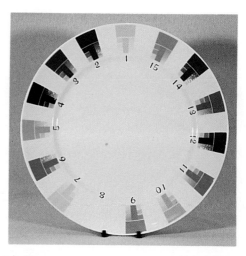

BIA Cordon Bleu 10" color sample plate; BIA Cordon Bleu b/s; $30.00 – 40.00.

BIA Cordon Bleu sample mug; BIA Cordon Bleu b/s; 1980s; $12.00 – 15.00.

Buffalo & Western New York Restaurant Association Show souvenir ashtray; Buffalo b/s; 1962 date code; $15.00 – 20.00.

Franmara in-glaze decal sample 7¾" plate; Franmara Spirito b/s; early 1990s; $24.00 – 30.00.

Larry Paul Collection

International Brotherhood Operative Potters AFL-CIO Union 5¾" piece; lists seven American restaurant china manufactures; no b/s; circa 1950s; $25.00 – 32.00.

Iroquois 9" topmark sample plate; Iroquois b/s; pre-1920; $125.00 – 150.00.

Jackson Vitrified China 3¾" advertising sample; Jackson b/s; 1930s; $45.00 – 60.00.

Homer Laughlin's Best China 11¾" foodservice distributor display plate; Homer Laughlin Seville b/s; early 1990s–present; $65.00 – 80.00+.

Homer Laughlin's Fiesta 11¾" foodservice distributor and retail store display plate; Homer Laughlin Fiesta b/s; late 1980s–present; $30.00 – 40.00.

Homer Laughlin China tour souvenir 5¾" plate; given during factory tours; no b/s or date code; recent; $6.00 – 8.00.

Mayer China topmark sample 9" plate; Mayer b/s; early 1900s; plate shows excessive wear; value given for good condition with clear decoration; $100.00 – 125.00+.

Larry Paul Collection

Mayer China advertising sample ashtray; Mayer b/s; 1930s; $40.00 – 50.00.

McNicol China 9" color sample plate; McNicol b/s; circa 1940s; $60.00 – 75.00.

Larry Paul Collection

McNicol China 3½" color trial piece; McNicol b/s; $30.00 – 40.00.

Noritake advertising 6½" sample ashtray; Noritake b/s; circa 1960s; $15.00 – 20.00.

Richard-Ginori 4" advertising sample; Richard Ginori b/s; $10.00 – 12.50.

Royal Doulton International Collectors Club 6½" plate; Royal Doulton b/s; recent; $10.00 – 12.50.

Scammell China advertising ashtray; Scammell Lamberton b/s; circa 1920s; $28.00 – 35.00.

Scammell China advertising piece; Scammell b/s; circa 1930s; $120.00 – 150.00.

Schmidt Porcelain advertising sample A.D. cup & saucer; Schmidt b/s; dated 1969; $15.00 – 18.00.

Shenango advertising sample match stand; no b/s; circa 1920s; $80.00 – 100.00.

Shenango China 1948 employee Christmas gift 10¾" plate; Shenango b/s; dated 1948; $50.00 – 60.00.

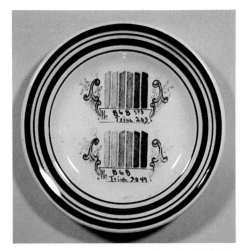

Shenango China 4½" color trial piece; no b/s; dated 1949; $30.00 – 40.00.

Larry Paul Collection

Shenango China 1978 employee Christmas gift 9" plate; letter to Shenango employees and Shenango logo in gold on the bottom; dated 1978; $20.00 – 25.00.

Larry Paul Collection

Shenango China 9¾" advertising plate; states Shenango's philosophy; Shenango b/s; 1984 date code; $40.00 – 50.00.

Larry Paul Collection

Sterling China 8" long display piece; Sterling b/s; circa 1950s; $30.00 – 40.00+.

Larry Paul Collection

Syracuse China (then Onongada Pottery) 9¾" topmark sample plate; O.P.CO. b/s; 1898 date code; $175.00 – 200.00+.

Syracuse China 3¾" 100-year commemorative; Syracuse b/s; dated 1971; $12.00 – 15.00+.

Larry Paul Collection

Syracuse China 7¾" 100-year commemorative ashtray; Syracuse b/s; dated 1971; $28.00 – 35.00.

Syracuse 1984 Distributor Meeting souvenir handled bouillon; Syracuse b/s; date 1984; $18.00 – 22.00.

Syracuse 1987 Distributor Conference souvenir custom decorated "Melrose" pattern 7¼" plate; Syracuse China Distributor Conference b/s; dated 1987; $22.00 – 28.00.

Tepco advertising ashtray; Tepco b/s; circa 1940s; $40.00 – 50.00+.

Larry Paul Collection

Walker China 4" sample ashtray; Walker Toltec b/s; 1940s; $35.00 – 42.00+.

Larry Paul Collection

Wellsville China 10" topmark sample plate; Wellsville b/s; 1950s; $75.00 – 100.00+.

Larry Paul Collection

Harold P. Zeissler Company (restaurant supplier) advertising ashtray; Scammell's Ivory Lamberton b/s; circa 1930s; $20.00 – 25.00.

Item Names

Although commercial china manufacturers have no truly standard terminology, the majority use the item names listed here.

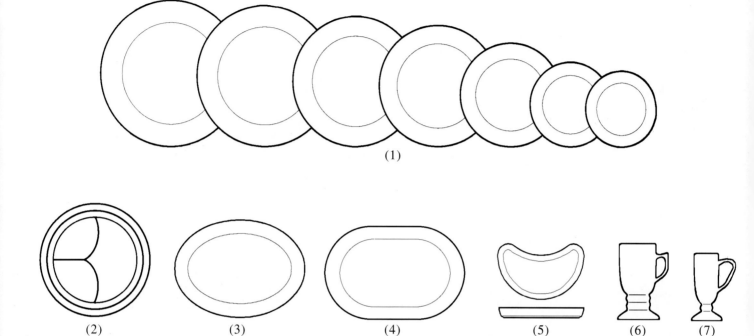

(1)

(2)   (3)   (4)   (5)   (6)   (7)

(8)   (9)   (10)   (11)   (12)   (13)   (14)   (15)   (16)

(1) Plates — commercial china manufacturers generally identify plates by size rather than type; exceptions include the chop, service, compartment, and bone plates.

> *Chop plate*: 11 inch plus diameter serving plate.
>
> *Service plate*: 10½" to 11½" in diameter, though sometimes slightly smaller; almost always custom decorated; it's on the table when the patron arrives and removed just before the meal is served; however, occasionally the appetizer, soup, or salad plate is placed on top of the service plate, which is then removed before the entree is served.

In general the sizes listed in catalogs are not the actual size; however, the size specified in photograph captions herein is the actual diameter to the nearest quarter inch.

(2) Compartment plate (or grille [also spelled grill] plate) — these became popular during the Great Depression of the 1930s.

(3) Platter — all oval or oblong "plates" are platters regardless of size; the length stated in photograph captions herein is the actual length to the nearest quarter inch.

(4) Platter

(5) Crescent salad (or bone plate)

(6) Irish coffee

(7) Café Brûlot

(8) Mug — a mug is placed directly on the table, rather than on a saucer.

(9) Mug, footed

(10) Cup and saucer

(11) A. D. (after dinner) cup and saucer

(12) Oriental cup (or Chinese tea cup)

(13) Egg stand

(14) Egg stand

(15) Egg cup, footed

(16) Double egg cup (combination of egg cup and egg stand)

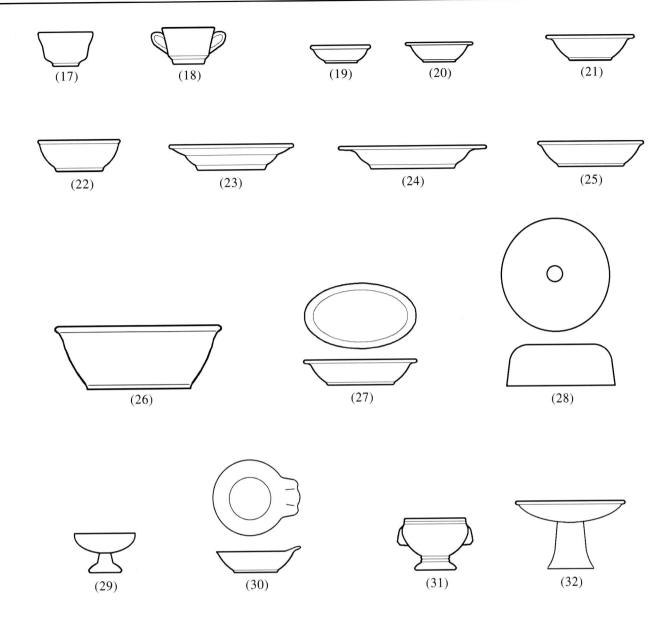

(17) Bouillon

(18) Bouillon, handled

(19) Fruit, coupe (rimless), RE[1]

(20) Fruit, narrow rim

(21) Grapefruit, narrow rim

(22) Oatmeal, RE[1] (or nappy)

(23) Soup, wide rim (or soup plate)

(24) Soup, wide rim (or soup plate)

(25) Soup, coupe (rimless), RE[1]

(26) Salad — also in smaller sizes, but proportionally deeper than a fruit, grapefruit, or soup.

(27) Baker, narrow rim — all oval bowls are bakers regardless of size.

(28) Cake cover (or toast cover)

(29) Sherbet (or footed egg cup)

(30) Ice cream shell

(31) Compote (or comport), lion head

(32) Compote (or comport), RE[1]

[1] rolled-edge

Note — with the exception of airline or Oriental pieces, a bowl is seldom called a bowl; rather it is referred to by the food it is most often used to serve.

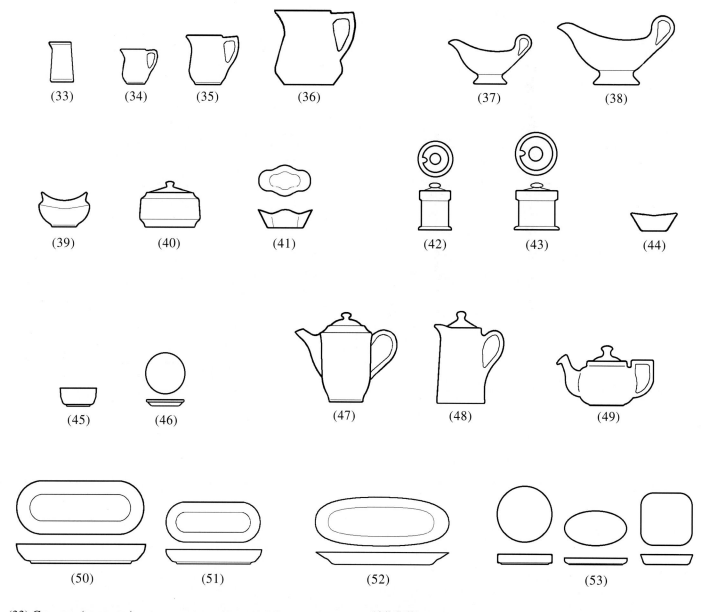

(33) Creamer (or cream)

(34) Cream pitcher, individual (or jug)

(35) Cream pitcher (or jug)

(36) Pitcher (or jug) — up to 109 oz. capacity and perhaps more; height of large pitchers is specified in photograph captions in these volumes.

(37) Sauceboat, individual

(38) Sauceboat

(39) Sugar, open (or sugar, room service)

(40) Covered sugar

Note: sugars and covers are individual items; as such, sugars were often supplied without covers.

(41) Sugar, open (or sugar, room service)

(42) Mustard

(43) Mustard (or jam)

(44) Jelly

(45) Butter pot, sauce, or nut

(46) Butter (or butter chip, butter pad, or butter pat)

(47) Coffee pot — produced in numerous shapes, but proportionally taller than a teapot.

(48) Cocoa pot

(49) Teapot (Boston teapot illustrated) — produced in numerous shapes, but proportionally shorter than a coffee pot.

(50) Celery

(51) Pickle (or small celery); a pickle is a shallow oval, oblong, elongated shell, or rounded diamond shaped piece, approximately 8 inches in length.

(52) Corn tray

(53) Tray — small custom decorated trays used to hold match books, mints, chocolates, or other small amenities.

Ultima China courtesy of World Tableware

Accessories and Oven-to-Table Pieces

(A) Baker — all oval "casseroles" are bakers regardless of size.

(B) Ramekin — may be round, square, fluted, or any shape; small square airline casseroles are also sometimes called ramekins.

(C) Shirred egg

(D) Pot pie

(E) Sugar, packet

(F) Salt

(G) Pepper

(H) Custard

(I) Casserole

(J) Marmite

(K) Fry pan server (or skillet)

(L) Casserole cover

(M) Marmite cover

(N) Rarebit

(O) Vase

Jackson China 1981 catalog

Oriental Items

(1) Chow mein, WE[1]
(2) Jong
(3) Chop suey, footed
(4) Chop suey, yecta mein
(5) Chop suey, chicken noodle

(6) Oriental cup (or Chinese tea cup)
(7) Oriental cup (or Chinese tea cup)
(8) Oriental cup (or Chinese tea cup)
(9) Oriental sauce, RE[2]

[1] welted-edge
[2] rolled-edge

Syracuse China 1937 catalog

(1) Dresser tray — approximately 10 inches long; similar to a pin tray, which is usually 5 to 6 inches long and proportionally narrower.

(2) Match stand

(3) Match stand

(4) Match stand

(5) Soap

(6) Candlestick, handled

(7) Candlestick

(8) Cuspidor

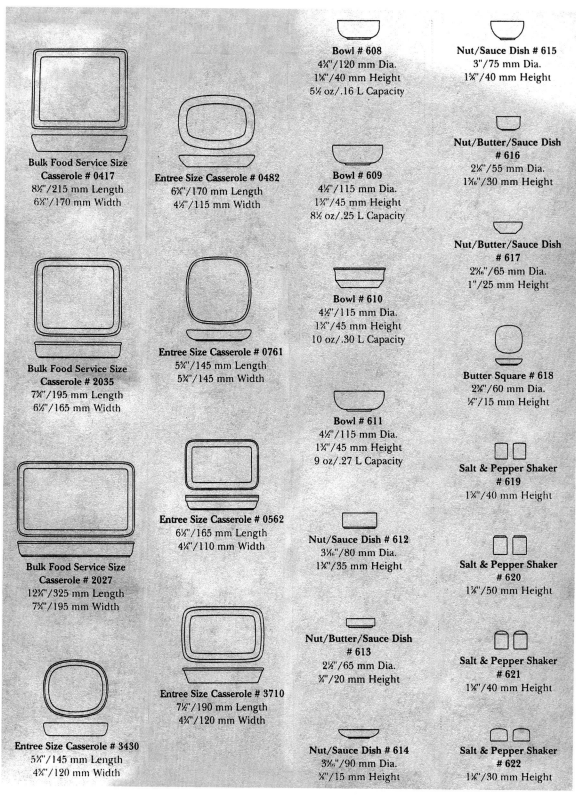

Bulk Food Service Size Casserole # 0417
8½"/215 mm Length
6¾"/170 mm Width

Bulk Food Service Size Casserole # 2035
7¾"/195 mm Length
6½"/165 mm Width

Bulk Food Service Size Casserole # 2027
12¾"/325 mm Length
7¾"/195 mm Width

Entree Size Casserole # 3430
5¾"/145 mm Length
4¾"/120 mm Width

Entree Size Casserole # 0482
6¾"/170 mm Length
4½"/115 mm Width

Entree Size Casserole # 0761
5¾"/145 mm Length
5¾"/145 mm Width

Entree Size Casserole # 0562
6½"/165 mm Length
4¼"/110 mm Width

Entree Size Casserole # 3710
7½"/190 mm Length
4¾"/120 mm Width

Bowl # 608
4¾"/120 mm Dia.
1¾"/40 mm Height
5½ oz/.16 L Capacity

Bowl # 609
4½"/115 mm Dia.
1¾"/45 mm Height
8½ oz/.25 L Capacity

Bowl # 610
4½"/115 mm Dia.
1¾"/45 mm Height
10 oz/.30 L Capacity

Bowl # 611
4½"/115 mm Dia.
1¾"/45 mm Height
9 oz/.27 L Capacity

Nut/Sauce Dish # 612
3⅛"/80 mm Dia.
1¾"/35 mm Height

Nut/Butter/Sauce Dish # 613
2½"/65 mm Dia.
¾"/20 mm Height

Nut/Sauce Dish # 614
3⅜"/90 mm Dia.
¾"/15 mm Height

Nut/Sauce Dish # 615
3"/75 mm Dia.
1¾"/40 mm Height

Nut/Butter/Sauce Dish # 616
2¼"/55 mm Dia.
1³⁄₁₆"/30 mm Height

Nut/Butter/Sauce Dish # 617
2⁹⁄₁₆"/65 mm Dia.
1"/25 mm Height

Butter Square # 618
2¾"/60 mm Dia.
½"/15 mm Height

Salt & Pepper Shaker # 619
1¾"/40 mm Height

Salt & Pepper Shaker # 620
1¾"/50 mm Height

Salt & Pepper Shaker # 621
1¾"/40 mm Height

Salt & Pepper Shaker # 622
1¼"/30 mm Height

Courtesy of ABCO International

Airline Ware

Commercial China Edges and Rims

Hotelware is often reinforced with a break and chip resistant rolled (below rim), welted (below rim), or beaded (above rim) edge for durability, though it is not necessary on the modern high-alumina bodies and frequently not used on fine gauge airline and upscale restaurant china. Such edges are, however, characteristic of American vitrified china made for the foodservice industry from the 1920s through the 1970s when today's most popular commercial china was produced. The rolled edge was introduced by the Onondaga Pottery Company (now known as Syracuse China) in 1896. It was the first American china created specifically to withstand the heavy usage of commercial dining establishments and became a worldwide hotelware standard.

Narrow rim commercial china was designed in the 1930s. The following is quoted from Syracuse China's company documented history: "No product made a more significant contribution to the company's ability to survive the Depression and provide employment for its workers than the 'Econo-Rim' shape. Introduced in the Adobe body in 1933, the new shape was developed and patented to meet specific needs of the railroad industry, which was entering the era of fast streamlined trains. With narrower longer cars, the dining cars of newer trains were fitted with smaller tabletops. The new shape was designed to provide space saving economies of a narrow rim without sacrificing any well space for foods. It was exactly what the railroads wanted."

Scalloped edge commercial china was produced on occasion as early as the late 1800s, before there was true differentiation between commercial and household china, but was not common until the 1950s and 1960s.

Various rounded rectangle or square shapes, such as Syracuse China's *Trend* shape, have been manufactured, some with a combination plain and scalloped edge.

Edge Shape and Rim Width

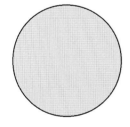

rimless (coupe), plain edge

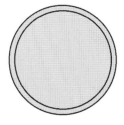

narrow rim, plain edge

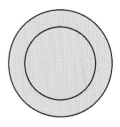

wide rim, plain edge

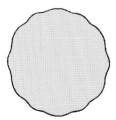

rimless (coupe), scalloped edge *

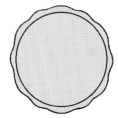

narrow rim, scalloped edge *

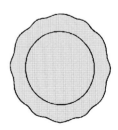

wide rim, scalloped edge *

* Representative of the many designs in which scallop shaped edges have been produced.

Plate

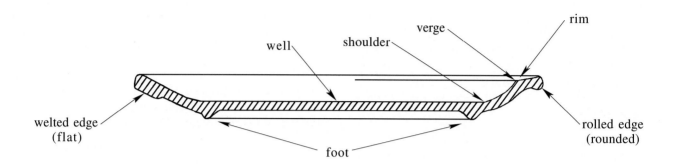

Coupe design (rimless) with welted edge is shown on the left. Rimmed design with rolled edge is illustrated on the right. Occasionally pieces have a rounded ridge above the edge (not shown), similar to the rolled edge, but smaller in radius. Manufacturers refer to this as cord or beaded edge. High-alumina vitrified china, bone china, and hard-paste porcelain ware frequently has no reinforcement above or below the edge.

Commercial China Body Material

Ceramic, a general term for any nonmetallic molded and fired object, comes from the Greek word "keramos," which translates to "potter's clay." Porcelain, though originally produced in China in circa 650 AD, comes from an Italian word, "porcella," a smooth white shell. Use of the word "china" began in English-speaking countries during the eighteenth century, relating its country of origin.

vitrified china (the word vitrified added to distinguish between true china and the generic term)

Composition: feldspar and quartz (percentages depend on other components) and 40% – 50% kaolin; sometimes flint, fritt (for glass-like appearance), ball clay, and alumina (for strength) in various combinations and amounts

Porosity and density: non-porous (less than 0.5 percent absorption of body weight per ASTM Standard C373); not quite as dense as hard paste porcelain

Firing: high temperature (2200°F – 2350°F) first (bisque) firing which vitrifies the ware; lower temperature (2000°F – 2200°F) second firing (glaze firing); — or single high temperature (2300°F – 2400°F) firing of glazed greenware

Translucence or opacity: generally fine gauge is quite translucent, medium gauge is slightly translucent, and heavy gauge is opaque; ball clay or addition of alumina tends to make ware opaque

Color: slightly off-white to ivory; addition of alumina or use of non-American clay produces whiter ware

Main area of manufacture: United States

Origin: Germany, 1794, and United States, late 1800s

bone china

Composition: 30 – 50% bone ash, 20 – 30% kaolin, 20 – 30% china stone, and sometimes additional alumina

Porosity and density: non-porous; very dense

Firing: high temperature (2200°F – 2300°F) first (bisque) firing which vitrifies the ware and lower temperature second firing (glaze firing)

Translucence or opacity: exceptionally translucent; added alumina produces a slightly less translucent body

Color: pure white to "warm white"

Main area of manufacture: England

Origin: England; perfected by Josiah Spode; introduced by Josiah Spode II soon after his father's death in 1797

stoneware (very few manufacturers have produced a stoneware body for the food-service industry)

Composition: 40 – 100% clay, 0 – 20% feldspar, and 0 – 40% quartz

Porosity: non-porous or extremely low porosity (1 to 3%)

Firing: depends on composition; lower temperature firing (1820°F – 1880°) may be followed by high temperature firing (2180°F – 2320°F) or the vice-versa; — or single high temperature (2180°F – 2320°F) firing of glazed greenware

Translucence or opacity: opaque

Color: off-white to brown

Origin: China, 100 BC

hard paste porcelain (commonly called true porcelain; cannot be cut with a file, thus said to be "harder than steel")

Composition: 40 – 60% kaolin, 20 – 30% feldspar, and 20 – 30% quartz

Porosity and density: non-porous; extremely dense

Firing: lower temperature (1470°F to 1740°F) first firing (bisque), leaves body porous; portion of glaze penetrates pours, forming a bond between body and glaze; very high temperature glaze firing (2515°F – 2590°F), far beyond point of vitrification; — or single very high temperature (2515°F – 2590°F) firing of glazed greenware

Translucence or opacity: usually quite translucent, however opaque if very thick

Color: pure white

Main area of manufacture: continental Europe, particularly Germany

Origin: Meissen, Germany, by Friedrich Bottger, 1709

soft paste porcelain

Composition: 30 – 55% kaolin, 20 – 40% feldspar, 25 – 40% quartz and sometimes additional alumina

Porosity and density: non-porous; not quite as dense as hard paste porcelain

Firing: lower temperature (1470°F to 1740°F) first firing (bisque), leaving body porous; portion of glaze penetrates pours, forming a bond between body and glaze; high temperature glaze firing (2200° to 2515°F); — or single high temperature (2300° to 2515°F) firing of glazed greenware

Translucence or opacity: usually quite translucent, however opaque if very heavy gauge

Color: white

Main areas of manufacture: Asia and South America

earthenware (seldom used for restaurant ware after 1920)

Composition: varies; may contain some or all of the following — clay, quartz, feldspar, flint, and china stone

Porosity: not vitrified; slightly to very porous

Firing: higher temperature (1910°F – 2100°F) first firing (bisque) and lower temperature (1820°F – 1880°) glaze firing

Translucence or opacity: opaque

Color: off-white to yellow-orange

Additional commercial tableware bodies:

glass-ceramic: *Pyroceram* by Corning

laminated glass: *Comcor* by Corning

white glass: by Anchor Hocking, Corning, and so forth

melamine: by National Plastics, Plastics Mfg., and others

pewter-like metal: by Wilton, Bon Chef, and others

Glossary of Body Material and Firing Terms

alumina: aluminum oxide (AlO_2). While present in all clay, an additional portion of this compound is sometimes added to hotelware paste. High alumina content generally produces a more dense, durable, shock resistant body which tends to be whiter in color and less translucent.

ball clay: has high degree of plasticity. Strengthens ware and increases density. Tends to make body opaque and off-white or ivory in color.

bisque (biscuit): unglazed fired clay body.

bone ash: calcium phosphate; burnt ground cattle bones. Acts as a flux in bone china and imparts translucence.

body: molded ceramic object, exclusive of glaze and added decoration.

china stone: a combination of feldspar, quartz, and mica. Acts as a flux. Also called Cornwall stone, as this combination of minerals is primarily found in Cornwall, England.

clay: finely ground minerals; decomposed rocks; plastic (see plasticity).

cordierite: a thermal shock resistant ceramic material developed in the USA in 1912. While it cannot be verified as formulas remain proprietary, cordierite may be a key component of such products as *Steelite* or Corning's *Pyroceram* and *Corningware*.

earthenware: any non-vitrified, and therefore porous, fired ceramic body; fired to a temperature below the point of vitrification. A sudden change in temperature frequently causes glaze crazing, i.e., a web of cracks in glaze only. Moisture discolors (stains) body when glaze is crazed, cracked, or chipped.

feldspar (or feldspath): crystalline (hard and glassy) minerals, mainly aluminum silicates. Acts as a flux in the vitrification process, fusing body materials together. Increases hardness and translucency of ware.

flint: very finely ground hard quartz; pure silica.

fritt: ground partially fused silica and flux.

glaze: finely ground glass suspended in water; actual formula generally contains kaolin, feldspar, quartz, and other minerals. Greenware or bisque is dipped in or sprayed with glaze, which transforms into a transparent or opaque glass-like finish when fired.

gloss: another word for glaze.

greenware: an unfired clay body.

ironstone: medium-heavy gauge off-white earthenware; also called white granite, semi-porcelain, or opaque china. Early ironstone (i.e., Mason's) is said to contain a high percentage of metallic oxide for durability. Marked on low porosity (fairly dense) ware in the late 1800s to mid-1900s. More recently backstamped on very porous household china. However, some ware marked ironstone is actually fully vitrified china, e.g. Dunn, Bennett & Co. Ltd.'s "Vitreous Ironstone," circa 1960s.

kaolin: *pronounced kay-o-lin*; fine-grained fairly pure, white clay. Comes from the word "Kao-ling," i.e., "high hills" in China; also called "china clay." Forms mullite needles to which feldspar bonds during firing; referred to as "the bones" of a porcelain or china body.

kiln: an enclosure in which ceramics are fired to a high temperature. Bottle and beehive kilns, so-named because of shape, were used in the early years. Most of these were replaced with tunnel kilns by the 1930s. Roller kilns were introduced in the 1960s and are used at modern factories today. Ware rolls slowly through these open-ended kilns on flatbed cars, as it did through the older tunnel kilns. However, tunnel kilns are tall enough to walk through, whereas the opening of the roller kiln resembles a large pizza oven. China can now be fired, cooled, and unloaded in an extremely short period of time.

non-porous: impermeable to liquids. Generally defined as less than two-percent body weight absorption. The more stringent ASTM Standard C373 allows absorption of less than 0.5 percent of body weight.

opaque: blocks passage of all light.

paste: body material; clay in the generic sense.

plasticity: a property of clay which allows its shape to be altered by pressure, yet retain its shape when pressure is removed. Degree of plasticity varies according to body material formula and amount of water added.

quartz: a hard glassy mineral known as crystalline silicon dioxide (SiO_2). Aids in shape retention during firing and contributes to body hardness.

semi-porcelain: a marketing term usually backstamped on off-white earthenware (whiteware) from circa 1885 to circa 1930. Some pieces so marked are quite porous and others are fairly dense.

semi-vitrified: ware was presumably fired to a point near vitrification. However, much of the ware so-marked was clearly fired to a considerably lower temperature, i.e., it is very porous. Some say the word is virtually a misnomer — ware is either vitrified or it is not.

translucent: diffuses light, but allows its passage; neither clear nor opaque. Body formula and firing temperature determine degree of translucency. To examine for translucency, hold piece up to bright light and move an object directly behind it. If movement is at all visible, the piece is somewhat translucent.

vitrification: conversion of body composition to a non-porous state by means of fusion (see feldspar) during a high temperature firing. The point of vitrification varies according to composition, but is around 2200°F. Vitrification is a primary requirement of hotelware for durability, as well as sanitary reasons.

vitreous or vitrified: fused body that is impermeable to liquids; i.e., non-porous. Fired to the point of vitrification. Vitrified bodies are fairly apparent; examine unglazed foot for smooth, non-porous (dense) surface.

Manufacturing Processes

Photographs and captions on the following pages are reprinted from *The Making of Baucsher Hard Porcelain* with Bauscher's permission. Although manufacturing and firing processes vary from company to company depending on equipment, technology, and body formula, many manufacturers now employ modern techniques similar to those described and illustrated.

The main variation is in firing. Both vitrified china and bone china are vitrified in the first (bisque) firing, then fired to a lower temperature in the second (glaze or gloss) firing, while porcelain (as described on the following pages) is vitrified in the second firing.

In addition, certain vitrified china manufacturers, notably the Hall and Homer Laughlin china companies, fire glazed greenware. In a single high temperature firing beyond the point of vitrification, the body and the glaze mature together, forming a chip and abrasion resistant product. It is also possible to single-fire porcelain.

Design and Production Moulds

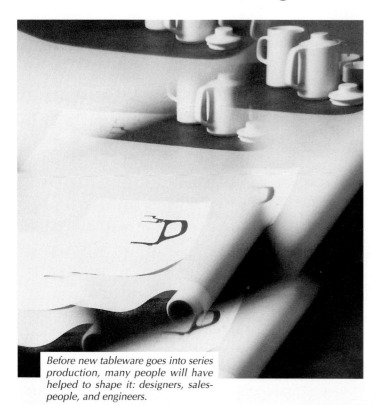

Before new tableware goes into series production, many people will have helped to shape it: designers, salespeople, and engineers.

Regardless of whether the material is turned, cast, or pressed, the mould must first be produced. What should it look like, what purpose should it serve? Various specialists ponder the matter and team work is required: salespeople, designers, and engineers work together.

Particularly in the hotel porcelain sector, good shape is a difficult matter. Because good shape must meet apparently contradictory requirements: functionality on the one hand and aestheticism on the other.

The gastronomy sector requires porcelain which is easy to handle during storage, serving, and cleaning. It must be stackable, and stable but not clumsy-looking. It can thus be seen that economical, efficient use is not the only consideration. Good shape is also part of the aesthetics stimulus. An attractive shape is essential for achieving a good atmosphere around the table.

The art of design lies in combining all these aspects. The object is not to produce a fashionable piece of frippery but a form that is "right." And when we are talking about a tableware system—as in the case of Bauscher—one article must match the other. Each piece a thing in itself but still part of the whole.

The first step is the drawing and the final stage the plastic form. Much has to be thought out before the detailed drawing is ready—as a basis for the manufacturing process.

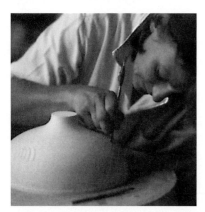

The plaster core of a cloche (Carat series)

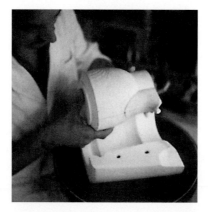

Plaster core and side part of the master mould

Plastic patterns determine the dimensions of the production moulds.

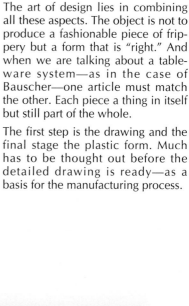

Production of a plaster production mould

Raw Material Preparation

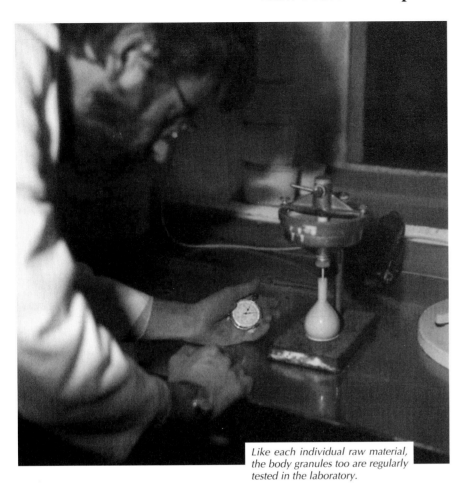

Like each individual raw material, the body granules too are regularly tested in the laboratory.

Kaolin, feldspar, and quartz: the materials from which porcelains are made. About 50% of kaolin, 25% of feldspar, and 25% of quartz—that is, very generally, the mixing ratio. The exact composition is a company secret. Each company does something a little different. The fact that Bauscher does something different to the rest is borne out by the internationally recognized quality of its hard porcelain. Special novel bodies were created through intense development work. The aim was to produce durable tableware capable of withstanding (almost) any stress during use in hotels and restaurants.

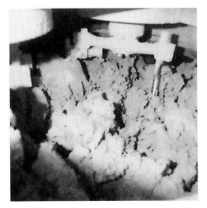

Good hotel porcelain can only be produced if the body is thoroughly mixed.

These strands will subsequently be converted into, for example, plates.

Rotary Moulding

In the rotary moulding shop, circular articles are shaped. Only everything that is rotationally symmetric can be made here.

Plates and cups, in particular, are rotationally symmetric.

Of course, rotary moulding is no longer done entirely by hand as in the past. The machine plays a decisive role here in ensuring that the correct shape is obtained. But rotary moulding is still carried out on a rotating disc, as in the past.

A great deal of manual skill is needed here, since precision is of primary importance.

A plate being "jiggered"

The plate edge (the technical term is "rim") is trimmed and sponged off.

The plaster mould and rotating mould operate in conjunction with one another. Together, they each shape one side of the article being moulded. A distinction is made between jolleying (in the plaster mould) and jiggering (on the plaster mould). The hollow articles, i.e. cups, etc., are jolleyed; jiggering gives plates and bowls.

The cup handles are cast separately—also in a plaster mould, of course.

Production of salad bowls on a conveyor line

A handle is stuck on. (Another technical term: "stuck up.")

Courtesy of Bauscher

Casting

In Bauscher pots, the spout and handle are not stuck on, but form part of the (cast) article. The cast pot is being removed from the plaster mould after shrinkage.

Pot casting on a conveyor belt

Casting also involves two processes. These are referred to as hollow casting and solid casting.

Pots are hollow-cast articles. Casting slip fills the production mould to the rims. Then, the plaster starts to work; slip is sucked up, water enters the mould, ceramic particles accumulate on the inside of the mould, and the body is formed.

Finding out when it has reached the correct thickness is a matter of fine instinct. The process of body formation must be stopped at the right moment. The still fluid slip is poured out, leaving what will become the pot. Since it shrinks slightly, it can soon be removed from the mould.

Casting porcelain slip on a "carousel"

Once the body has formed, the excess is poured out.

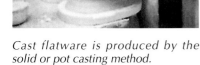

Cast flatware is produced by the solid or pot casting method.

All edges and mould seams are broken off and sponged off with a moist sponge.

Each piece of Bauscher porcelain is stamped with a brand, which represents the highest quality.

Courtesy of Bauscher

Dry Pressing and Bisque Firing

The most recent method of shaping porcelain tableware is isostatic pressing. This is a method with prospects, and specialists talk about a "revolution." In fact, pressing not only dispenses with the traditional operations, but is also more precise. One hundred percent dimensional accuracy ensures high, uniform quality. Plaster moulds are no longer used for this purpose. This very modern technique does not follow the conventional method of shaping ceramic body. Metal moulds in large presses shape the powder body under high pressure.

Until recently, only flat articles were produced in this manner. Now, hollow articles are also successfully pressed.

Only the pot, the traditional motif of all tableware, is still made by the old method. It has to be cast.

A fully loaded trolley from the tunnel furnace after bisque firing.

Porcelain has to be fired twice, and it is almost always fired three times. The third firing process is not obligatory, but is optional. It is used for making the article more attractive by adding decoration.

Bisque firing, the first of these stages, performs many functions: it cleans the body, compacts the porcelain, and makes it porous so that it can be glazed.

The tableware articles are conveyed into the tunnel furnace on firing trays. The furnace operates 24 hours a day. This is because the firing process takes a long time, 25 to 30 hours for bisque firing and over 40 hours for subsequent glaze firing.

The temperature during the first firing is 950 to 1000 degrees centigrade.

After the firing process, dust is removed—not in the manner of the housewife but quickly and easily with compressed air.

Glazing

As already mentioned, the porcelain is now porous. This ensures that the glaze is sucked in thoroughly and uniformly.

The process appears simple: immersion and rotation. The glaze in the vat is almost the same material as the porcelain body itself, except that it is thinner. Kaolin, feldspar, and quartz, as well as chalk, dolomite, and water.

Before glaze firing, the glaze has to be removed again form some areas. These are the areas where the porcelain articles stand. Otherwise they would stick on firing because the glaze becomes viscous in the furnace.

Thus, plate feet and cup rims usually have no glaze. However, Bauscher has nevertheless managed to develop a glazed cup rim which is convenient to drink from.

Ingenious solutions: results of an idea which now seems simple. Bauscher has found many such solutions: the non-dripping spout, the pot lid that doesn't fall off even when the last drop is being poured out, etc., etc., etc....

Machine glazing

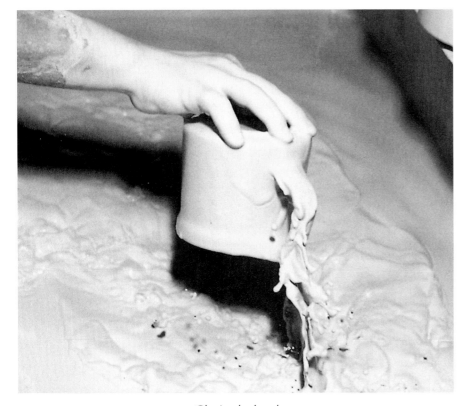

Glazing by hand

The base of each porcelain article is freed from glaze on a sponge belt.

Courtesy of Bauscher

Glaze Firing

It is this process in which porcelain is actually made. The glaze fuses with the body, which becomes compact and smooth. It acquires its white color, too, in the second firing—at final temperatures of about 1420 degrees centigrade.

At the same time, shrinkage occurs (with the loss of one-sixth of its volume, as already mentioned.) This is a side effect and, if anything, is undesirable. But it is taken into account and therefore causes no harm.

Not only does the second firing last longer than the first, but it also requires special preparation. Hollow articles are passed through the fire on special firing trolleys. Each flat article on the other hand must be placed in a special sagger. This is required for protection. Otherwise, it would be impossible to stack plates and dishes in the furnace: the glaze, which becomes viscous during firing would stick or fuse them to one another.

However, stacking is necessary since firing space is valuable and must be utilized optimally.

Is it necessary to carry out glaze firing for more than 40 hours? The specialists have long been asking. There is now a rapid firing process which reduces the firing time to about 3 hours—even for bisque firing. At present, however, it still plays a rather minor role. This will presumably change. Just as much has changed in the course of the 100 years or more during which Bauscher has been a specialist in hotel porcelain. And many changes and new developments carry a trademark: Bauscher Weiden.

The plates are automatically inserted into the saggers.

A modern rapid glaze firing furnace

A fully loaded tunnel furnace trolley in front of a furnace for glaze firing.

Fired hard porcelain emerges from the furnace.

Decorating Techniques

The Wedgwood hotelware
design team are available to
interpret your requirements
or advise on creating a
special decoration. Their
services are free of charge.

Create the Pattern

The Custom Collection is the perfect starting point for your chinaware, because it is the collection that needs you to complete it! Select your design. Design it yourself. Or let our Jackson designers create it for you. Choose the bands, borders, patterns and colors that suit your operation.

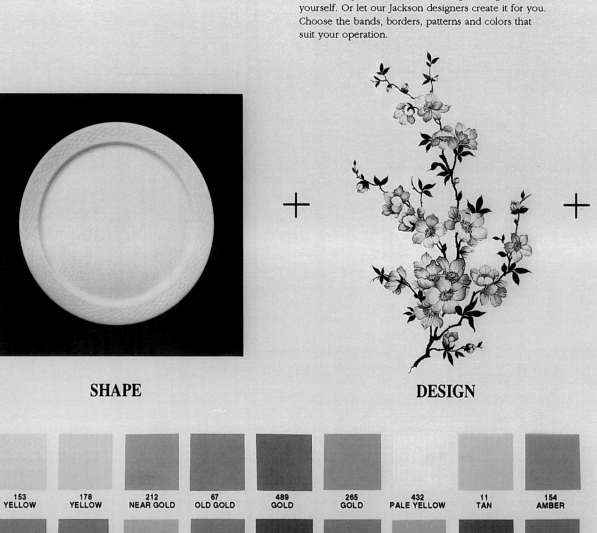

SHAPE + **DESIGN** +

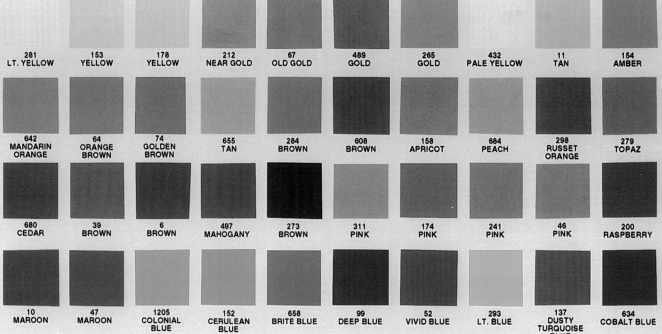

281 LT. YELLOW	153 YELLOW	178 YELLOW	212 NEAR GOLD	67 OLD GOLD	489 GOLD	265 GOLD	432 PALE YELLOW	11 TAN	154 AMBER
642 MANDARIN ORANGE	64 ORANGE BROWN	74 GOLDEN BROWN	655 TAN	284 BROWN	608 BROWN	158 APRICOT	684 PEACH	298 RUSSET ORANGE	279 TOPAZ
680 CEDAR	39 BROWN	6 BROWN	497 MAHOGANY	273 BROWN	311 PINK	174 PINK	241 PINK	46 PINK	200 RASPBERRY
10 MAROON	47 MAROON	1205 COLONIAL BLUE	152 CERULEAN BLUE	658 BRITE BLUE	99 DEEP BLUE	52 VIVID BLUE	293 LT. BLUE	137 DUSTY TURQUOISE BLUE	634 COBALT BLUE

that sets your style

Be creative with pastel tints or rich hues, simple or involved motifs. Add a crest or your own proud name. The result will be your Custom Collection. Unique, distinctive, and the perfect complement to the foods you serve ... to the decor of your foodservice operation.

COLOR = **YOUR DINING SERVICE**

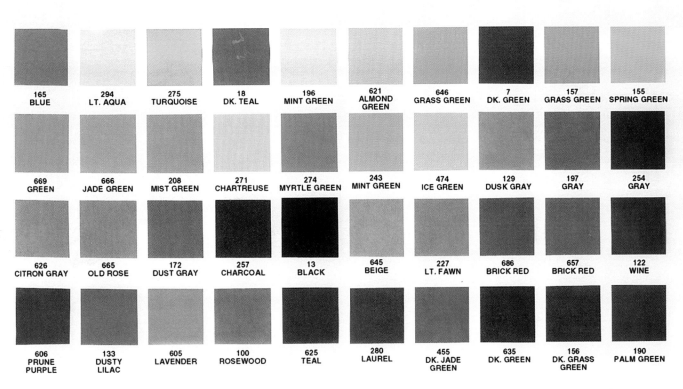

165 BLUE	294 LT. AQUA	275 TURQUOISE	18 DK. TEAL	196 MINT GREEN	621 ALMOND GREEN	646 GRASS GREEN	7 DK. GREEN	157 GRASS GREEN	155 SPRING GREEN
669 GREEN	666 JADE GREEN	208 MIST GREEN	271 CHARTREUSE	274 MYRTLE GREEN	243 MINT GREEN	474 ICE GREEN	129 DUSK GRAY	197 GRAY	254 GRAY
626 CITRON GRAY	665 OLD ROSE	172 DUST GRAY	257 CHARCOAL	13 BLACK	645 BEIGE	227 LT. FAWN	686 BRICK RED	657 BRICK RED	122 WINE
606 PRUNE PURPLE	133 DUSTY LILAC	605 LAVENDER	100 ROSEWOOD	625 TEAL	280 LAUREL	455 DK. JADE GREEN	635 DK. GREEN	156 DK. GRASS GREEN	190 PALM GREEN

by Jackson China

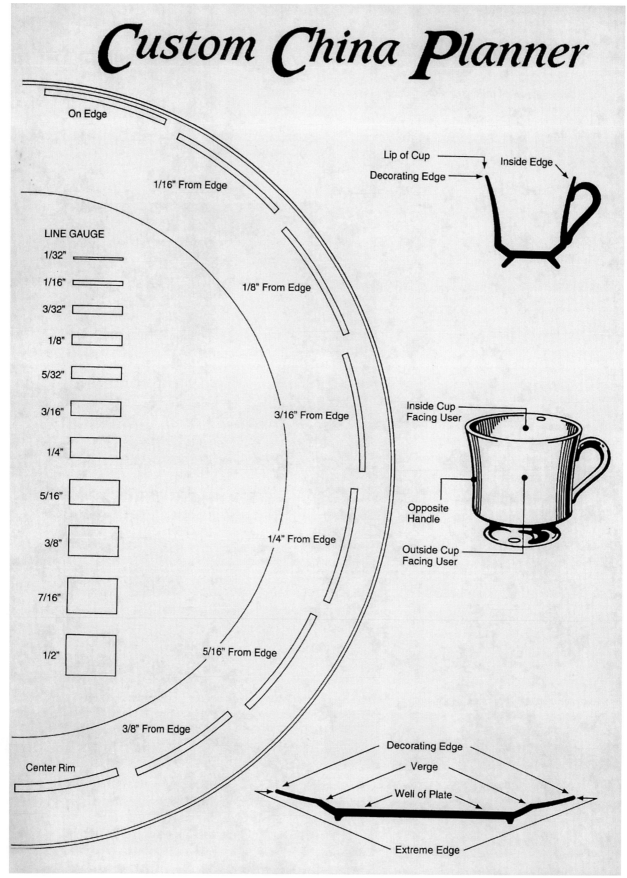

Custom China Planner

On Edge

1/16" From Edge

1/8" From Edge

3/16" From Edge

1/4" From Edge

5/16" From Edge

3/8" From Edge

Center Rim

LINE GAUGE

1/32"
1/16"
3/32"
1/8"
5/32"
3/16"
1/4"
5/16"
3/8"
7/16"
1/2"

Lip of Cup
Decorating Edge
Inside Edge

Inside Cup Facing User
Opposite Handle
Outside Cup Facing User

Decorating Edge
Verge
Well of Plate
Extreme Edge

Courtesy of H.F. Coors

Many manufacturers offer customers a selection of stock and custom decals, along with choice of color, width (gauge), and placement of lines and bands.

Private clubs are not the only establishments that see the necessity of custom design. Buckingham's, at the Conrad Hilton in Chicago, has its own special signature design. **Oskar Hrach**, director of food and beverages for the hotel, feels custom design gives his restaurant what he calls, "that special touch."

"Guests expect it. They realize it justifies the money they spend at the restaurant," Mr. Hrach said. "Our waiters tell us people do comment about the beautiful china. I feel, if you are going to establish your restaurant as a fine eating establishment, you need it," he stated. The black-and-gold custom design makes a striking accent to the plush red and wood decor of the elegant room.

Buckingham's capitalized on its custom design by giving miniatures of the pattern to customers on New Year's Eve. "It was something they could take home, put in their china cupboard and remember," Mr. Hrach said. "They will have it all year, and it will remind them of us, a constant reminder of where they have been - a personalization in a sense. It will make them want to come back to our restaurant.

"We think giving miniature plates with our custom design is a very good promotion. We also used this device at Nicolai's Roof in the Atlanta Hilton, and it was successful there, too," he added.

Probably no one summed up the case for custom design better than **Philip Recchia**, manager of Bear Stearns & Company's corporate dining room in Boston. "We wanted to offer the clients we entertain something special, something they might not get at a restaurant," he said. "We take pride in making clients feel as if we've invited them to our home. Custom china makes a statement. It's elegant, unique and personal at the same time. Just as important, it's got to be durable," Mr. Recchia said. He feels it adds up to a tough order: Prestige plus practicality.

"With custom china, we don't have to worry about something being out of stock a year or two down the road or that our pattern might be discontinued," he added. "Once Bear Stearns sets a standard of excellence - in anything we do - we like to maintain that standard." Custom design gives the company that option in its dining room.

"Our tableware must be versatile and complement several different decors. Our classic pattern - white with a black rim and gold bands, does the job very well," Mr. Recchia said.

"Our china reflects Bear Stearns' position as a major investment banking firm whose clients include large banks, mutual fund companies and important individual investors," he commented, referring to, "a certain image which our clients expect us to keep up.

"We bought Woodmere through a corporate tableware vendor and feel the follow-up service has been impeccable," he stated, pointing to another reason why many club managers select custom design: They get better follow-up service.

Woodmere will custom design china for you. Call us.

Courtesy of Dr. Patricia Tway

Comments on custom decorated commercial china from "Custom Design of China" article by Patricia Tway, Ph.D. Dr. Tway and her husband, Gene Tway, founded Woodmere China in 1975.

Hand Painting

Freehand painting is one of the most skilled jobs in the pottery industry and it takes years of training, artistic talent, and a steady hand to become an expert. Although advanced technological processes provide less labor intensive and therefore less expensive methods of decoration, there remains a small niche in the commercial china market today for hand-painted ware.

Genuine handwork, though sometimes quite apparent, is often difficult to ascertain. Look for brush stroke variations in pattern repeats, color overlap at edge of designs, and inconsistencies in line width and color depth. If possible compare pieces of a single pattern and check for irregularities.

Transfer-printed decoration with hand-painted fill.

Hand-painted plate well decoration. Close examination of this compartment plate reveals stroke irregularities.

Hand-painted "Natural Wood Design" by Buffalo China.

Though this cup and saucer are hand painted, the identical affect can be achieved with decals.

Hand-painted rim and detail.

Transfer-printed decoration with hand-painted fill; this process is sometimes called "print and tint."

Hand-painted embossed body

Overall swirl design applied with a sponge brush

Variegated banding surrounding and in center of hand-painted swirl design

Lining and Banding

Lines (⅛" wide and under) and bands (over ⅛" wide) are usually applied by a skilled "liner," although a number of manufacturers line round flatware with automated lining machines.

Ware revolving in the absolute center of a turntable (wheel) is touched by a color-loaded brush. Brush width, stroke angle, and pressure determine line and band width. Oval platters and non-circular hollow ware require a well-trained eye and extraordinary control. With the exception of very bright colors and precious metals, lines and bands are ordinarily applied to bisque. However, finished ware decorators and some manufacturers apply colored lines and bands to glaze-fired ware, then fire either in-glaze or on-glaze. *For line width and placement illustration, see Custom China Planner on page 340.*

Automated lining

Syracuse China and others began using a lining machine in the late 1940s. Color flowed from a container to a revolving disk. A rubber disk or roller passed over that disk, picking up color and depositing it on a plate. Line or band width varied according to the width of the rubber disk or roller.

Today many modern lining machines are capable of applying multiple lines and bands in varied colors simultaneously.

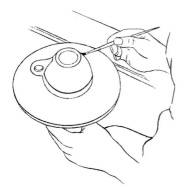

Courtesy of The Dudson Group

Dudson's "Artisan" line with overall multicolor banded design

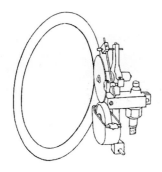

Early lining machine, circa late 1940s

Multicolored bands and lines

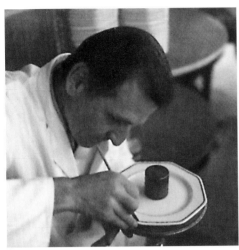

Courtesy of Bauscher

Non-circular shapes still require hand application

Variegated bands with single line

Courtesy of Bauscher

Modern mechanical lining and banding machine; with ware precisely positioned and line width and location set, color flows through tube to brush, applying lines and bands automatically.

Solid and variegated bands with lines

Stencil airbrushed designs: two-color on butter and two-tone on creamer

Airbrushing

Airbrushing has been a common method of underglaze decoration since the 1940s, particularly useful to band rims or as an accent.

As a compressor supplies air pressure to the spray gun, a fine spray of color is applied to greenware, bisque, and occasionally glaze-fired ware. Always a smooth application, ware is sprayed lightly with fine color graduations for a soft effect or heavily for solid coverage. In the late 1920s Syracuse China, then Onondaga Pottery, introduced a process they called "Syratone," spraying solid colored bands and overall solid decoration to the face of flatware and outer surfaces of hollow ware.

Stencil airbrushing
Syracuse China began stencil airbrushing, a technique they called "Shadowtone," in 1937. Other manufacturers followed, producing some of today's most highly prized commercial china. This decoration method was especially popular in the 1950s and 1960s. Color was sprayed through a stencil on to ware. Tepco China and presumably others made stencils from lead sheets, as lead is easy to cut, pliable, and holds its shape (i.e., the curved shape of cups and so forth). Most designs required several stencils and some were sprayed with a number of colors.

Stencil airbrushed design and airbrushed band and handle

Airbrushed handle on creamer and band on plate

Courtesy of Noritake

Ware is sprayed with airbrush as it rotates on a turntable.

Tri-color stencil airbrushed design

Airbrushed rims

Two-color stencil airbrushed design on plate and two-color airbrushed bands on cup and saucer

Airbrushed accent and stencil airbrushed design on plate; stencil airbrushed border on mug

Transfer Printing

This is an early form of mass-production decoration developed in Great Britain in the 1700s. Characteristically lines are uneven rather than solid and smooth in appearance and often show bleeding, particularly if cobalt blue. The process is still employed by manufacturers who decorate ware with detailed single color scenes, but is not likely to be used on today's commercial china.

Transfer-printed decorations are also used as hand painting outlines and filled or over-painted with colors, a process sometimes called "print and tint." *See examples on pages 342 and 343.*

The process
An image is engraved as a series of lines or dots on a copper plate. A mixture of color and oil is spread over the heated copper plate (usually mounted on a metal cylinder) and worked into the engraving. After removing excess color, the design is printed on strong tissue-like paper. Cut to the appropriate size, the transfer print is positioned on varnish brushed bisque and rubbed firmly. The tissue is soaked off in a bath of water, leaving a printed image on the ware. Manufacturer backstamps are frequently printed along with the decoration and placed on the bottom of ware as it is decorated.

Multicolor transfer prints
The process described above is used, but multicolor transfer prints require a copper plate for each color. The design is printed from the plates, one after the other, on the tissue-like paper; each must register (line up) perfectly.

Multicolor transfer print

Cobalt transfers tend to bleed.

Direct Printing

Simply put, this process is a very accurate automated form of rubber stamping. A design molded in soft silicone rubber is placed on a printing head. The printing head picks up color from a base plate. Then with extremely precise positioning the head presses on a piece of bisque, leaving a single color design and returns to the base plate.

While this technique can be used for multicolor designs, each color must be printed separately. Application is limited to plates where it is particularly suited to rim decoration. The accuracy and quality of this decoration makes it virtually indistinguishable from colored decals.

Courtesy of Villeroy and Boch

Printing head before and after direct printing

Courtesy of Villeroy and Boch

Only the plate rim is directly printed. Plate well and matching hollow ware are decorated with decals. The illustrated Villeroy and Boch pattern is ideally suited for this technique. Though generally thought of as a household pattern, "Basket" is used in many upscale dining concerns.

Decals

Decals are produced using a lithographic or silk-screen (screen stencil printing) process. They are applied by hand or machine to bisque (underglaze) or glaze-fired ware (overglaze). Overglaze decals are fired in-glaze or on-glaze. Unlike transfer prints, lines are usually smooth and even. Fills may be solid, graduated, or appear to be actual brush strokes.

"In 1908 the company (Onondaga Pottery, now Syracuse China) announced a major break though in decorated china, the development of underglaze decalcomania. With this new technique, multicolored china patterns were protected against heavy usage and wear beneath a hard glaze coat, providing an unprecedented quality and durability for decorated china. Equally exciting were the fresh opportunities for underglaze personalized crests and emblems on china, and customer lists soon grew to include railroads, steamship lines, private clubs, churches, schools, fraternal organizations, and other places where opportunities for personalized china existed." (Quoted from *The History of Syracuse China*)

Lithographic process and underglaze decal application

"Decals are normally used when the pattern is multicolor and of a complex nature that cannot be reproduced by transfer printing. A decal curve is determined for each item. The design is first drawn (engraved) on lithography stones, one for each color.

In a multi-printing operation the decals are reproduced on a special paper consisting of a heavy paper backing and a tissue top surface on which the design is printed.

To insure that the decal adheres firmly, it is necessary to apply varnish to the bisque. The tissue paper is peeled back and applied to the ware as the paper backing is removed. After application, the ware is run through the decorating kiln unglazed. This burns out any impurities in the decal or varnish and 'sets' the pattern in the ware. It is then glazed and the glost (glaze) firing seals the pattern underglaze and brings up the colors." (Excerpts quoted from article titled "Decal," published by *Sterling China*, circa 1950s)

Silk-screen process and underglaze decal application

"This process involves the photographic reproduction of prints for ceramic colors from an existing design. The printed sheets are made of special transfer paper to which the motif sticks, very much like a transfer. Shortly before its application, the motif is removed from the printed sheets by soaking the paper in water, and is then applied to the pieces which have been fired once (bisque). The relatively rough body is treated beforehand with a slip additive, so that the decals can be slid into position. There must be no creases or turned edges whatsoever; air bubbles and liquid residue are pushed to the side by rubbing with a squeeze and removed with a sponge. When the motifs are dry, they can be glazed and sharp fired. Some articles must undergo a mild firing at approximately 840°C (1545°F) beforehand, to burn off any residue matter before glazing." (Quoted from Villeroy and Boch's Product Information brochure)

Courtesy of Villeroy and Boch

Hand decal application on bisque (underglaze)

Silk-screen process and overglaze decal application

A plastic screen stencil made of light-sensitive material using a photographic positive is placed in a frame and lowered to fully contact water-soluble film-coated paper. Ceramic color is forced through the open areas in the screen as a rubber squeegee, the width of the screen, is drawn across it. Any number of colors can be used in a design, but each color requires a separate screen. The paper is dried between each color application and finally coated with lacquer. After soaking in water, the lacquer covered color slides off the paper and is placed on glaze-fired ware. Water and air bubbles beneath the decals are removed with a small squeegee. If not properly removed, bubbles break during firing, causing defects in the decal.

Hand decal application on glaze-fired ware (overglaze)

Computer-aided decal design in the 1990s

Decals are designed and printed to fit the shape and size of each item.

Automated decal application

"Decals are loosely applied to ware which is fed onto the heads of the continuously revolving circular press. As the ware passes under the pressure heads, the decal is rubbed down carefully and uniformly by a flexible weight. The ware then passes under water jets and is rinsed when the conveyor submerges near the end of the cycle. The washing operation removes the tissue from the decal and leaves the pattern itself intact, ready to be placed in the decorating kiln." (Quoted from article titled "New Decal Machine Installed," published by *Sterling China*, circa 1960s).

Firing decals

Underglaze: decals are applied to bisque, then glazed and glaze (gloss) fired at 2000°F+. Finished ware is glass-like in appearance. While heavily applied decal colors may cause slightly raised areas, the surface is glassy. Color stability at this temperature is somewhat limited; bright colors are out of range.

Underglaze fired decals

In-glaze: decals are applied to glaze-fired ware, then subjected to a decoration firing of 2000°F+, melting the glaze. This allows the color to fully sink beneath the glaze surface. Like underglaze decoration, finished ware has a glass-like appearance.

On-glaze: decals are applied to glaze-fired ware, then subjected to a decoration firing of 1440°F – 1620°F. The firing temperature is not sufficient to melt the glaze and allow the decal to sink beneath the surface, thus it remains on top of the glaze. Low-fire ceramic enamel decals have a somewhat glossy enamel (not glass-like) look, slightly raised and often pitted. Delicate multicolor on-glaze fired decals exhibit a somewhat rough dull, rather than smooth glass-like surface.

Precious metal decals and low-fire ceramic enamel decals (often used for very bright colors) are always fired on-glaze, as they would begin to disintegrate if fired to a higher temperature. Because commercial china is subject to tremendous wear from use and detergent abrasion, hotelware manufacturers generally use this method for precious metals only.

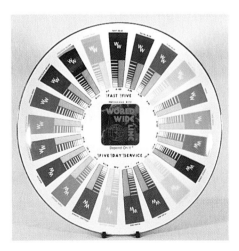

On-glaze fired decals

Burnished coin gold edges have satin finish

Bright gold bands and decal

Overall bright gold

Precious Metals

Ground gold or platinum mixed with flux and oils is applied by brush to produce lines, bands, or accents on ware. Precious metal decals are particularly well-suited for custom logo decorations. Burnished coin gold, while not as shiny as bright gold, is about four times more wear resistant. At least one manufacture, Homer Laughlin, now encapsulates gold, making it considerably more durable and microwave-safe. Though silver decoration has been used on occasion, what appears to be silver is nearly always platinum. They are easily distinguished, as silver tarnishes and platinum does not.

"In 1936 improved techniques for metallic decoration introduced longer wearing burnished gold applications, and for the first time custom decoration in platinum lines and bands were offered. Elegantly decorated service plate patterns appeared with full-rim coin gold bands and gold designs over solid color rims and surfaces." (Quoted from *The History of Syracuse China*)

After applying gold or platinum to glaze-fired ware, it is subjected to a decoration firing of 1440°F – 1620°F. The glaze does not melt sufficiently at this temperature to allow the metal to sink below the surface (i.e., in-glaze). If precious metals were fired to a higher temperature, they would begin to burn away.

Burnished gold

Though gold is sometimes polished by hand, slight variations of the following are more common: "When coin gold is fired in the decorating kiln, the result is gold in color but absolutely matte in finish. Each piece must be burnished with a fine burnishing sand to give it a satin hand rubbed finish. An electrical cotton buffer is touched to the gold as wet burnishing sand is fed to the buffer wheel. This is a rather delicate operation since the sand, pressure against the buffer, and texture of the buffer must be carefully watched." (Quoted from *Sterling China – How It's Made*, circa 1960s)

Acid-etched gold

A transfer print, printed with an acid-resistant compound rather than color, is used to transfer a design, usually a border, onto glaze-fired ware. In a hydrofluoric acid bath, the pattern is etched into areas that are not protected by the compound; i.e., the acid erodes the exposed glaze. Removal of acid and acid-resist reveals a relief design which is then covered with 22 to 24 karat gold and fired. Polishing leaves raised areas brighter and recessed areas matte.

Note: coin gold is an alloy consisting of 90% gold (.900 fine), 22 karat gold is 91.7% gold (.917 fine) and 24 karat gold is virtually pure gold.

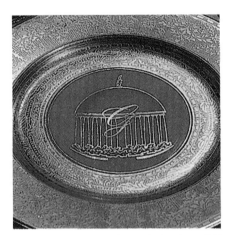

The Greenbrier brochure, 1996

Acid edtched gold on The Greenbrier service plate

"Platinum Pewter Scroll" pattern by Jackson China

Platinum band and logo

Courtesy of Öspag

Sponged gold: "Jewel" pattern by Lilien Porzellan

Dripped gold design

LUSTERS

The special decorating effects that can be achieved on china are limitless, but none bears a Homer Laughlin China signature more than lusters. Through years of design and manufacturing research, only Homer Laughlin mass produces luster designs cost-effectively in a wide variety of colors and applications.

The iridescent and opalescent colors create a rainbow that changes and plays with light. Each is custom designed and developed to specific requests. The luster effect can create new looks on traditional rim designs or be used in combination with additional decorating effects. They make an especially striking table setting when used on base or signature plates.

The decorating process is available in chromatic colors as well as metallics such as gold, platinum and silver, in both burnished and bright finishes. The patterns and textural effects include marble, fisheye and intricate veined patterns. Lusters are completely lead-free.

Melon Luster
3829

Courtesy of Homer Laughlin

Fiesta by Homer Laughlin decorated with solid colored glaze, shown with "Stripes" narrow rim banded pattern at 1994 trade show

Miscellaneous Decoration Techniques

Direct screening: ceramic color sprayed through fine mesh screen on bisque or glaze-fired ware.

Ground Laying: ware coated with a thin film of oil is "dusted" with powdered color. When fired it results in a solid color used as a background for additional decoration.

Sponged color: ceramic color applied to greenware or bisque or precious metals applied to glaze-fired ware with a sponge.

Rubber stamping: various manufacturers have made an attempt to decorate vitrified bisque with rubber stamped designs. However the non-porous surface does not absorb the color and decoration is distorted during glaze application. This technique has occasionally been used to apply gold decoration on glaze-fired ware.

Incised colored slip (sgraffito): after spraying colored slip (i.e., colored liquid clay) on greenware, a design is incised (i.e., carved) exposing the body color. *For a photographic example, see Illinois Central's "Coral" pattern on page 225.*

Jasperware: stoneware with contrasting hand-applied relief decoration; Dudson Brothers produced jasper hotelware until 1965.

Unglazed inclised slip: after greenware dipped in colored slip is dry, it is incised by hand, exposing the body color below. Rough edges are smoothed with a sponge. This unusual technique can be used only on the rims or exterior of food-service items, as hollow ware interior and plate well must be glazed.

Raised dot decoration

Pewter-like glaze

Raised enamel decoration by Jackson China

Pink body

Colored Body

Though technically part of the body composition, ware is colored for decorative purposes. Most American commercial china manufacturers produced tan and ivory bodied ware from the 1930s through the 1960s. The Buffalo, McNicol, Tepco, Sterling, and Jackson china companies, among others, made vitrified china in blue and pink bodies. Buffalo also produced a yellow body.

Various ingredients are used to achieve these colors. While each company presumably had its own "secret" formulas, the addition of the following elements or compounds will produce the color indicated:

   pink: manganese oxide and alumina

   tan: red iron oxide

   blue: cobalt carbonate

   yellow: rutile (titanium oxide with small amounts of iron and vanadium)

   green: chromium oxide

Laminated Body Colors

Commercial china has also been made in a combination of two body colors. Colored slip (i.e., colored liquid clay) was sprayed on greenware, creating a laminated effect. Buffalo China, who perfected the technique in 1931, called it "Lamelle": tan and white (Cafe au Lait Lamelle), blue and white (Lune Lamelle), pink and white (Rouge Lamelle), and yellow and white (Colorido Lamelle).

In the 1940s Sterling China began manufacturing "Sterling Inlay." While Buffalo's "Lamelle" is a registered tradename and is backstamped on ware, the term "Sterling Inlay" was simply used for in-house identification and perhaps advertising.

Tan body

Blue body

Buffalo Colorido Lamelle: yellow laminated on white body

Multicolored Body

Buffalo China also developed and produced the "Multifleure" body, an uneven blend of five colors (yellow, pink, tan, ivory, and blue) exhibiting a marbled effect.

Embossed Body

Body is molded in relief, that is, has a raised or recessed design.

Custom embossed design

With the introduction of their Econo-Rim shape in 1933, Syracuse China began using their "Artint" process. After ceramic color is applied to the embossed rim, it is wiped back with a sponge, leaving color only in the recessed design.

Custom embossed design

Courtesy of Homer Laughlin

Embossed design: "Royale" pattern by Homer Laughlin China

Embossed pattern: "Amano" pattern by Hall China

American Ceramic History

East Liverpool, Ohio

THE MUSEUM OF CERAMICS

A TRIBUTE TO

"AMERICA'S CROCKERY CITY"

OHIO HISTORICAL SOCIETY

SINCE 1885

*E*ast Liverpool's location on the Ohio River and near an abundance of clay—as well as the dynamic leadership of its pioneers and later entrepreneurs—molded a small frontier settlement into a thriving city of artisans. From the mid-eighteenth century until the 1930s, East Liverpool reigned as "America's Crockery City."

Located in a historic building, the Museum of Ceramics celebrates the region's pottery heritage, featuring a vast collection of ware from East Liverpool potteries and exhibits about the industry's impact on the town and its people.

The Museum of Ceramics
400 East Fifth Street
East Liverpool, Ohio 43920
(216) 386-6001

Hours:
March-Nov.: 9:30 a.m.-5 p.m. Wed.-Sat.; 12-5 p.m. Sun. & holidays; closed Thanksgiving.
School groups by appointment Dec.-Feb.

OTHER SITES TO VISIT IN THE AREA
After touring the Museum of Ceramics, visit **McCook House** in Carrollton and the **Youngstown Historical Center of Industry & Labor** in Youngstown. For information about events and other places of interest around the state, please call toll-free 1 800 BUCKEYE.

The Ohio Historical Society is waiting for you!
For information on society membership, ask the site attendant for an application or contact: Development Office, Ohio Historical Society, 1982 Velma Avenue, Columbus, Ohio 43211-2497; 1 800 686-1545 (toll-free in Ohio) or (614) 297-2332.

Printed on recycled paper

4/93

COVER PHOTO—The Museum of Ceramics is located in East Liverpool's former city post office, built in 1909.

Courtesy of Ohio Historical Society

East Liverpool's location on the Ohio River and the regional abundance of clay—as well as the dynamic leadership of its pioneers and later entrepreneurs—molded a small frontier settlement on the Ohio River into a thriving city of artisans.

For generations, East Liverpool was to the American ceramics industry what Pittsburgh was to steel and Detroit was to automobile manufacturing. From the mid-eighteenth century until the 1930s, East Liverpool reigned over the nation's ceramics production as "America's Crockery City." Although the ceramics industry declined steadily in the mid-twentieth century, the area's citizens remain proud of their role in molding this distinctive American industry.

SHAPING AN INDUSTRY

Early settlers of the East Liverpool area discovered an abundant supply of natural clays that were well-suited for a variety of products. Production was limited at first, as a few individuals made utilitarian crockery.

But by the late 1830s, entrepreneurs began to realize that the area's abundance of clay and coal could bring financial success to those who could use the Ohio River to ship large amounts of pottery to the growing markets for locally manufactured products.

Many potteries employed women and children, such as these women who are hand-painting designs on ceramic pieces circa 1900-10. Such handcrafted pieces are prized by modern collectors.

The first of these entrepreneurs was English-born James Bennet, who in 1839 established the town's first pottery with the help of his brother and other skilled craftsmen. Although the operation moved to Pittsburgh in 1844, other local entrepreneurs emulated Bennet's success. The skill and energy of potters such as Benjamin Harker, William Brunt, Jabez Vodrey, Thomas Croxall, William Bloor, and John Goodwin carried the industry through its infancy. The immigration of pottery workers from England's Staffordshire district provided skilled labor, as well as the expertise to open new works. Concentrating exclusively in the production of yellow ware and Rockingham pottery, for which the local materials were most suitable, East Liverpool potteries cemented their advantageous position in the emerging American crockery industry.

By the 1870s, the expansion of the national rail system allowed potteries to import the raw materials needed to produce whiteware, which became more popular with American consumers than the area's yellow ware and Rockingham pottery. Technological innovations—such as the automatic jigger that

COVER PHOTO—The Museum of Ceramics is located in the former East Liverpool Post Office, which was built in 1909 and is listed on the National Register of Historic Places.

Courtesy of Ohio Historical Society

East Liverpool, Ohio, is also known as "America's Crockery City." Dozens of factories, many of which produced commercial china, operated there at the turn of the century. The only commercial china manufacturers that remain today are Sterling China (offices only; factory in neighboring Wellsville) and Hall China, though Homer Laughlin China is located just across the Ohio River in Newell, West Virginia.

East Liverpool was a one-industry town: In 1900—about four years after this photograph was taken—more than 90 percent of the city's workers were employed in the manufacture of ceramics.

shaped ceramic pieces semimechanically, replacing skilled artisans with less-skilled laborers—spurred potteries into greater mass production.

As a result of these changes, the late nineteenth century was a time of tremendous prosperity in East Liverpool. By 1900, the town was known as "America's Crockery City," the center of U.S. pottery—a title it would hold for decades.

SHAPING A TOWN

The growth of the pottery industry drove the growth of the city of East Liverpool. As established potteries expanded and new potteries opened, demand for unskilled labor increased. Immigrants flocked to East Liverpool, swelling the city's population ten-fold between 1870, when it had a population of 2,000, and 1910, when it was a city of more than 20,000.

East Liverpool was a one-industry town. In 1900, more than 90 percent of East Liverpool's industrial wage earners were employed in the manufacture of ceramics.

The industry's impact, however, was not limited to population. Between 1870 and 1910, the city experienced tremendous physical growth. With prime locations along the Ohio River already claimed, new potteries were forced to locate in outlying areas, expanding the city's boundaries.

By 1910, though, the boom had reached its peak. Changes in tariff policy, which had sheltered domestic production, made foreign ceramics less expensive and easier to import. Many items that had been made from ceramics became available in

Among the most prominent of East Liverpool's products was Lotus Ware, produced by Knowles, Taylor, and Knowles between 1892 and 1896. The lustrous china is noted for its graceful shapes.

Courtesy of Ohio Historical Society

The museum's solid-oak trim and marble-and-terrazzo floor provide a beautiful setting for the extensive exhibits of ceramic ware and displays on the history of East Liverpool.

glass or tin, which were cheaper and less likely to break. The Great Depression of the 1930s delivered another blow, further decreasing East Liverpool's importance as a pottery center.

THE MUSEUM OF CERAMICS

The Museum of Ceramics occupies the former city post office, which was built in 1909 and is listed on the National Register of Historic Places. The state of Ohio bought the building from the federal government in 1970. Extensively renovated during the 1970s, the building opened as the Museum of Ceramics in 1980.

The renovated museum's solid-oak trim, ornately decorated domed ceilings, and beautiful marble-and-terrazzo floor provide a stunning backdrop for its exhibits. Displays include an extensive array of wares produced by East Liverpool potteries in their heyday, as well as dioramas showing how ceramics were created. Other exhibits depict the growth and development of the community and the lives of its people.

Among the museum's most prized pieces are examples of Lotus Ware, which was produced by Knowles, Taylor, and Knowles for only a few years during the 1890s. Noted for its pure-white lustrous finish, graceful shapes, and exquisite detailing, Lotus Ware is considered by some to be the finest bone china ever produced in the United States.

Life-size dioramas depict pottery workers at different stages in the ceramics process.

Courtesy of Ohio Historical Society

World Ceramic History

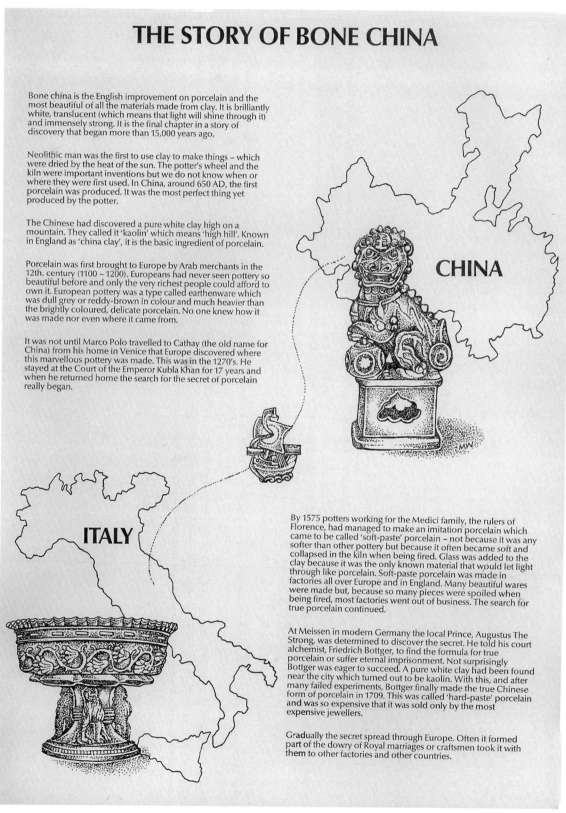

THE STORY OF BONE CHINA

Bone china is the English improvement on porcelain and the most beautiful of all the materials made from clay. It is brilliantly white, translucent (which means that light will shine through it) and immensely strong. It is the final chapter in a story of discovery that began more than 15,000 years ago.

Neolithic man was the first to use clay to make things – which were dried by the heat of the sun. The potter's wheel and the kiln were important inventions but we do not know when or where they were first used. In China, around 650 AD, the first porcelain was produced. It was the most perfect thing yet produced by the potter.

The Chinese had discovered a pure white clay high on a mountain. They called it 'kaolin' which means 'high hill'. Known in England as 'china clay', it is the basic ingredient of porcelain.

Porcelain was first brought to Europe by Arab merchants in the 12th. century (1100 – 1200). Europeans had never seen pottery so beautiful before and only the very richest people could afford to own it. European pottery was a type called earthenware which was dull grey or reddy-brown in colour and much heavier than the brightly coloured, delicate porcelain. No one knew how it was made nor even where it came from.

It was not until Marco Polo travelled to Cathay (the old name for China) from his home in Venice that Europe discovered where this marvellous pottery was made. This was in the 1270's. He stayed at the Court of the Emperor Kubla Khan for 17 years and when he returned home the search for the secret of porcelain really began.

CHINA

ITALY

By 1575 potters working for the Medici family, the rulers of Florence, had managed to make an imitation porcelain which came to be called 'soft-paste' porcelain – not because it was any softer than other pottery but because it often became soft and collapsed in the kiln when being fired. Glass was added to the clay because it was the only known material that would let light through like porcelain. Soft-paste porcelain was made in factories all over Europe and in England. Many beautiful wares were made but, because so many pieces were spoiled when being fired, most factories went out of business. The search for true porcelain continued.

At Meissen in modern Germany the local Prince, Augustus The Strong, was determined to discover the secret. He told his court alchemist, Friedrich Bottger, to find the formula for true porcelain or suffer eternal imprisonment. Not surprisingly Bottger was eager to succeed. A pure white clay had been found near the city which turned out to be kaolin. With this, and after many failed experiments, Bottger finally made the true Chinese form of porcelain in 1709. This was called 'hard-paste' porcelain and was so expensive that it was sold only by the most expensive jewellers.

Gradually the secret spread through Europe. Often it formed part of the dowry of Royal marriages or craftsmen took it with them to other factories and other countries.

Courtesy of Royal Doulton; designed and illustrated by Mary Wilson

While this article is titled "The Story of Bone China," it traces world ceramic history to the seventh century beginning with the original Chinese porcelain, then on through sixteenth century Italian soft-paste porcelain, followed by the discovery of hard-paste porcelain in Germany in 1709, and finally the development of English bone china.

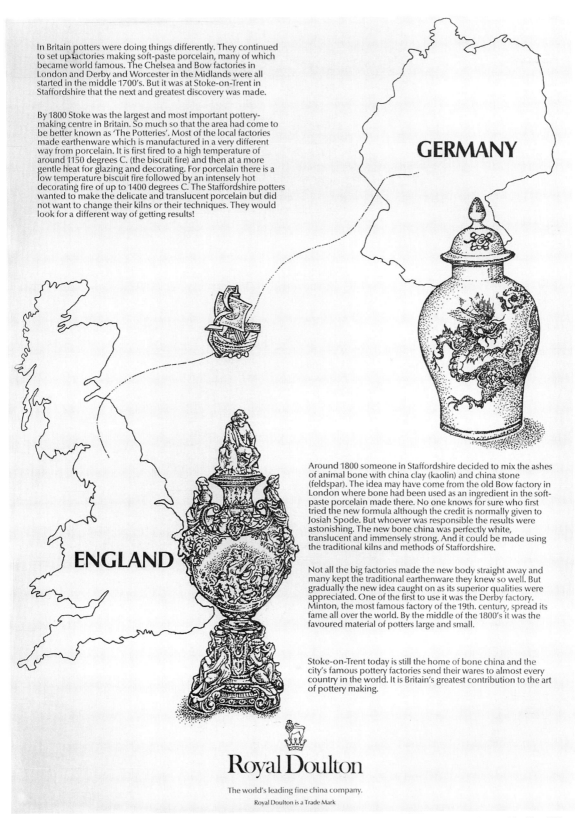

In Britain potters were doing things differently. They continued to set up factories making soft-paste porcelain, many of which became world famous. The Chelsea and Bow factories in London and Derby and Worcester in the Midlands were all started in the middle 1700's. But it was at Stoke-on-Trent in Staffordshire that the next and greatest discovery was made.

By 1800 Stoke was the largest and most important pottery-making centre in Britain. So much so that the area had come to be better known as 'The Potteries'. Most of the local factories made earthenware which is manufactured in a very different way from porcelain. It is first fired to a high temperature of around 1150 degrees C. (the biscuit fire) and then at a more gentle heat for glazing and decorating. For porcelain there is a low temperature biscuit fire followed by an intensely hot decorating fire of up to 1400 degrees C. The Staffordshire potters wanted to make the delicate and translucent porcelain but did not want to change their kilns or their techniques. They would look for a different way of getting results!

GERMANY

ENGLAND

Around 1800 someone in Staffordshire decided to mix the ashes of animal bone with china clay (kaolin) and china stone (feldspar). The idea may have come from the old Bow factory in London where bone had been used as an ingredient in the soft-paste porcelain made there. No one knows for sure who first tried the new formula although the credit is normally given to Josiah Spode. But whoever was responsible the results were astonishing. The new bone china was perfectly white, translucent and immensely strong. And it could be made using the traditional kilns and methods of Staffordshire.

Not all the big factories made the new body straight away and many kept the traditional earthenware they knew so well. But gradually the new idea caught on as its superior qualities were appreciated. One of the first to use it was the Derby factory. Minton, the most famous factory of the 19th. century, spread its fame all over the world. By the middle of the 1800's it was the favoured material of potters large and small.

Stoke-on-Trent today is still the home of bone china and the city's famous pottery factories send their wares to almost every country in the world. It is Britain's greatest contribution to the art of pottery making.

Royal Doulton

The world's leading fine china company.
Royal Doulton is a Trade Mark

Courtesy of Royal Doulton; designed and illustrated by Mary Wilson

Schroeder's ANTIQUES Price Guide

. . . is the #1 best-selling antiques & collectibles value guide on the market today, and here's why . . .

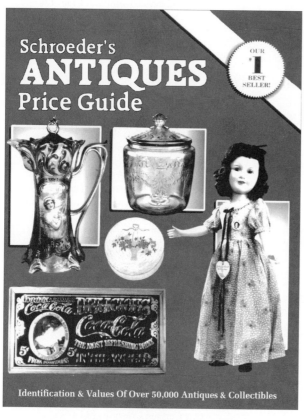

OUR #1 BEST SELLER!

Schroeder's ANTIQUES Price Guide

Identification & Values Of Over 50,000 Antiques & Collectibles

8½ x 11, 608 Pages, $12.95

• *More than 450 advisors, well-known dealers, and top-notch collectors work together with our editors to bring you accurate information regarding pricing and identification.*

• *More than 45,000 items in almost 550 categories are listed along with hundreds of sharp original photos that illustrate not only the rare and unusual, but the common, popular collectibles as well.*

• *Each large close-up shot shows important details clearly. Every subject is represented with histories and background information, a feature not found in any of our competitors' publications.*

• *Our editors keep abreast of newly developing trends, often adding several new categories a year as the need arises.*

If it merits the interest of today's collector, you'll find it in *Schroeder's*. And you can feel confident that the information we publish is up to date and accurate. Our advisors thoroughly check each category to spot inconsistencies, listings that may not be entirely reflective of market dealings, and lines too vague to be of merit. Only the best of the lot remains for publication.

Without doubt, you'll find
SCHROEDER'S ANTIQUES PRICE GUIDE
the only one to buy for
reliable information and values.

COLLECTOR BOOKS
A Division of Schroeder Publishing Co., Inc.